Facing the Challenge of Liability in Psychotherapy

Facing the Challenge of Liability in Psychotherapy

Practicing Defensively

Lawrence E. Hedges

With Specialty Contributions by Steven Frankel,
Ira R. Gorman, David G. Jensen,
and Pamela Ann Thatcher

JASON ARONSON
Lanham • Boulder • New York • Toronto • Plymouth, UK

Published in the United States of America
by Jason Aronson
An imprint of Rowman & Littlefield Publishers, Inc.

A wholly owned subsidiary of
The Rowman & Littlefield Publishing Group, Inc.
4501 Forbes Boulevard, Suite 200, Lanham, Maryland 20706
www.rowmanlittlefield.com

Estover Road
Plymouth PL6 7PY
United Kingdom

British Library Cataloguing in Publication Information Available

Library of Congress Cataloging-in-Publication Data

Hedges, Lawrence E.
  Facing the challenge of liability in psychotherapy : practicing defensively / Lawrence
E. Hedges.
    p. cm.
  Includes bibliographical references and index.
  ISBN-13: 978-0-7657-0386-6 (cloth : alk. paper)
  ISBN-10: 0-7657-0386-6 (cloth : alk. paper)
  1. Psychotherapists—Malpractice—United States. 2. Psychotherapy—United States.
  I. Title.

  KF2910.P753H43 2006
  344.7304'121—dc22   2006018089

Printed in the United States of America

∞™ The paper used in this publication meets the minimum requirements of American
National Standard for Information Sciences—Permanence of Paper for Printed Library
Materials, ANSI/NISO Z39.48-1992.

In Memoriam

This updated edition is dedicated to the memory of my longtime friends
and colleagues whose presence is felt throughout these pages.

Sean Stewart, Ph.D.
Marriage, Family, and Child Therapist
Seal Beach, California

and

Ira Gorman, Ph.D.
Psychologist and Court-Appointed
Child Custody Evaluator
Santa Ana, California

Contents

Physical Contact during Psychotherapy • Group Therapy
Informed Consent • Expert Witness Agreement

Section Two: Record-Keeping Forms
• Chart Progress Notes (Form I) • Chart Progress Notes
(Form II) • Chart Progress Notes (Form III) • Confidential
Psychotherapy Note • Periodic Clinical Reassessment/Review
Treatment Summary Information Guide • Special Release
of Confidential Psychotherapy Notes • Letter of Request for
Confidential Records • Release of Confidential Information
for Purposes of Consultation, Research, Teaching, and
Publication • Release of Protected Health Information (PHI)
• Termination Summary • Organizing Experience Worksheet

Section Three: Informed Consent Contracts for Supervision
and Ongoing Training for Therapists
• Informed Consent Regarding Supervision, Case Consultation,
Case Conference Seminars and Individual Tutorials
• Employment Agreement for Trainees • Personal References
for Employment as a Psychotherapy Trainee

Section Four: Special Information and Forms Regarding
HIPAA, Treating Children, Caregivers Authorization, and
Family Custody
• General Information on HIPAA • How HIPAA applies to
the Forms with this Updated Edition • Progress Note/Clinical
Record • Psychotherapy Note • Release of Information for
Outpatient Psychotherapy Records • Treatment Summary
• Account of Disclosures • Avery Labels: Notice: This Is the
Client Record • Avery Labels: This Folder Contains
Psychotherapy Notes • Avery Labels: Non-HIPAA Compliant
File • Treating Children in High Conflict Divorce/Custody
Situations • To the Child (and presented in language the child
can understand) • Caregiver's Authorization Affidavit
• Family Custody Evaluation Disclosure

Foreword to the Updated Edition

For more than two decades I have been teaching law and ethics to practicing mental health professionals from the standpoint of limiting liability by practicing defensively. This means knowing where the dangers are coming from and taking the necessary preventative steps to protect ourselves in the event of a licensing board action, an ethics committee complaint, or a malpractice suit.

Over the years my continuing education seminars and discussions with practicing therapists have gradually turned into this book that represents the contributions, wisdom, and experience of literally hundreds of mental health professionals throughout the United States. The overwhelmingly positive response to the courses and to this book has been extremely gratifying.

In 2002, *Facing the Challenge of Liability in Psychotherapy: Practicing Defensively* won the Gradiva Award for the best book of the year from the National Association for the Advancement of Psychoanalysis. Psychoanalysts were especially interested in the psychodynamics of the accusation and response processes which I outline in detail. Others have been more interested in the guidelines and forms for practice and record keeping, included in the text and on the accompanying CD-ROM. Yet others have valued suggestions on how to think about such standard of care issues as boundaries, dual relationships, recovered memories, and the current necessity for ongoing collaboration and consultation with colleagues. It is rewarding for me to watch colleagues everywhere wake up to the complaint-filled and dangerously litigious atmosphere in which we practice and begin taking the necessary steps to position themselves safely.

Four new areas of growing concern have warranted special attention in this updated edition: (1) issues in working with minors; (2) issues involved with child custody evaluations; (3) compliance with the new federal HIPAA laws; and (4) recent expansions of the therapist's duty to protect. Two experts, Dr. Steven Frankel and Dr. Ira R. Gorman have written chapters on liability issues with minors that all practitioners need to be aware of—whether or not they work directly with minors or deal directly with custody since these issues end up raising all kinds of questions even for general practice. Attorney David Jensen has contributed a chapter on the recent Ewing Cases and their implication for the duty to warn. In yet another chapter I cover the importance for all mental health professionals to comply with the new federal HIPAA laws regarding confidentiality, security of patient records, and electronic storage and transmission of protected health information.

In this updated edition the many different kinds of office forms necessary for running today's safe practice have been expanded, revised, and moved to the accompanying CD-ROM for easy access and modification on your computer. You might check my Web site, ListeningPerspectives.com, from time to time for other updates and relevant articles and information.

I hope you enjoy this book, feel deeply the dynamics of it and begin taking all of the necessary steps to practice your profession safely. I repeatedly tell therapists in the seminars I teach that we do not have to change how we practice in order to increase our safety. But we do have to be mindful of the kinds of dangers that potentially face us, and do things to position ourselves safely.

> Lawrence E. Hedges, Director
> The Listening Perspectives Study Center
> Orange, California

Acknowledgments

Many thanks to John Carter, Jolyn Davidson, Cheryl Graybill, Jane Jackson, Michael Kogutek, Jeanne Lichman, Roxie Persi, Sean Stewart, Marijane Ward, Cynthia Wygal, and the many other therapists studying at the Listening Perspectives Study Center who over the years have generously contributed to the development of these ideas and forms. Gerardo Arechiga has been responsible for the manuscript development and Ray Calabrese has coordinated the research project for twenty-five years.

Many thanks to the attorneys from whom I have learned the most regarding legal issues: O. Brandt Caudill, Steve Frankel, Richard Leslie, Michelle Licht, Pamela Thatcher, and Christopher Zopatti.

Jason Aronson, Judy Cohen, and David Kaplan have provided ongoing support and editorial expertise in getting this book sculpted and off to press. Thanks to Ross Miller, Art Pomponio, and Karolina Zarychta for managing the many changes in this updated edition and accompanying CD-ROM.

1

Facing the Challenge

Practicing Defensively

Consider for a moment the last time you attended a Saturday workshop or continuing education course. You got up in the morning anticipating with some pleasure meeting old colleagues and friends, but wondered if the course was really going to be worth your while. You pulled yourself together a little more casually than usual.

Hopping into your car, you snap on your seat belt. Moving into traffic, you slip a CD into play, and in short order you whiz up to the drive-thru window. Happily humming with your orange juice and coffee in the drink rack you peel away the waxed paper on your Egg McMuffin and hit the on-ramp. Egg McMuffin? You hardly ever get one of those anymore! Breezing through the light Saturday morning traffic, your spirits pick up as you come onto your caffeine and carbohydrate high. The eggs and sausage will get you safely through the morning.

You arrive at the parking lot, slide into a spot not too far from the entrance, gulp down the last swig of OJ, and release your seat belt. You have just wended your way through miles of a high-speed concrete and steel jungle—a treacherous pathway on which people get killed every day. But you arrived expectably safe and sound. You always fasten your seat belt. You drive safely, cautiously, and defensively. You are protected as much as possible by the safety features of your car. You have collision, medical, and liability insurance. Thus, you arrive refreshed and free from fear and stress.

I know that you immediately intuit my point. It is *because* we have tutored ourselves so well on the numerous hazards of the road, *because* we have unfailingly practiced caution and safety on a daily basis, and *because* we have taught ourselves to think of who might be in the other car that we are able to proceed so casually and carefree through incredible dangers that in an instant could leave us crippled for life or dead on the road.

This book provides the same sort of consciousness-raising about how we can wend our way safely and casually through our psychotherapy practice. There's no point fretting every day about the horrors of what can happen to us, cursing over how unfair things are, or blowing our cool when we hear about unreasonable actions being brought against unwitting and innocent therapists. If we are going to practice safely and defensively, let's simply get started learning the hazards and facing the challenge.

THE PSYCHOTHERAPIST'S LITANY FOR THE NEW MILLENNIUM

1. We can no longer practice alone!
2. We must have a *relationship* with an attorney!
3. We must have a *relationship* with a psychiatrist!
4. We must belong to a *peer consultation* group!
5. We must know and utilize *expert consultants*!
6. We must be prepared to reenter *psychotherapy for ourselves*.

FACING THE CHALLENGE OF OUR CHANGING TIMES

1. The *escalation of lawsuits* in our litigious society places us in an increasingly dangerous position.
2. *The demands of accountability* from the public put us in potential jeopardy with state licensing boards and ethics committees.
3. *Our malpractice "deep pocket"* makes us a ready target for clients and attorneys.
4. *The whereabouts of dangerous and potentially litigious people* has changed in modern society. Once locked away in insane asylums and mental hospitals, often tortured as evil or burned at the stake as witches, these badly damaged and often vengeful and dangerous people are now attracted to our psychotherapy consulting rooms.
5. *Tranquilizers and antipsychotic and antidepressant medications* often mask patients' deep relational traumas, giving us the illusion of meaningfully tapping into the developmental sources of their damage. We can be easily deluded by what can be called "archetypal content," "false-self" conformity, "mimical-self" imitation, and "cures" based on transference or resistance.
6. *The expansion of depth-therapy tools* over the past three decades gives us the illusion of omnipotence. Originally invented for the treatment of

neurosis in well-developed individuals, psychotherapy theory and practice have now been expanded to include narcissistic, borderline, and organizing (psychotic) levels of development—erroneously leading us to believe that all psychological states are treatable.

7. *Narcissistic, borderline, and organizing "pockets" exist in all people.* These pockets come in small, medium, and large! But the most likely to deceive us are the very small, hidden pockets of madness that are essentially universal, and the very large multisymptomatic pockets that are highly elusive and forever changing in their forms.

8. *We have absolutely no way of determining at the outset* who in our practice has experienced what kinds of infantile trauma or neglect, or of knowing how long-internalized patterns of deprivation, fear, rage, shame, hatred, and revenge are likely to be reexperienced in the transference-countertransference matrix, or in what ways the therapist may come to be fused and confused in transference with the original perpetrator of infantile trauma during moments of crisis or extreme stress, or what kinds of accidental or fluke events in or out of the therapeutic situation may trigger a dangerous or lethal transference reaction. Thus, thinking "This person would never sue me" or "It can't happen to me" is the kiss of death for psychotherapists. Never believe either slogan! Experience teaches us that the clients therapists like the best, are the most invested in, and have done the most for are the most likely to file complaints and bring lawsuits.

9. *Don't be a fool!* As a therapist you treat many deeply traumatized and damaged people. No matter how intelligent or emotionally intact the client seems or is, and no matter how much you like or respect the client who comes for help, deep and destructive pockets of psychotic terror and rage may later be unexpectedly opened and aimed at you. You invited the client into your consulting room and encouraged her or him to speak freely. It is then only a matter of time before long-frozen and unmetabolized deep pockets of trauma become activated for reexperiencing in the here-and-now memories of transference and resistance.

The study of long-term psychotherapy now makes clear that when primitive relational patterns are operative, normal ego and superego controls are temporarily suspended, ordinary reality testing is blocked, and the span of ego focus is significantly narrowed. If you are not prepared for the kinds of terrifying experiences you have invited into your consulting room, and if you have not created adequate safety nets for yourself and for your clients, you have only yourself to blame. No one was ever cured of anything in a court of law or in a licensing board hearing. Most complaints and lawsuits are triggered by unforeseen flukes or accidental mismanagement of an in-therapy, transference-based accusation against the therapist. You must protect yourself from accidental (and often unintentional) harm.

10. *Face the challenge: Practice defensively!* You drive your car defensively, you manage your finances defensively, you run your personal life defensively, you must also run your psychotherapy practice defensively! Don't put yourself, your clients, your colleagues, your family, or your personal estate in harm's way by being thoughtless or otherwise careless in your psychotherapy business!

2

Practicing Defensively

Basic Terms and Concepts

ETHICS COMPLAINTS

Associations of mental health professionals at the national, state, and county levels have ethics committees composed of professionals whose job it is to investigate complaints and to take disciplinary action against or rehabilitative action with members of the profession. Therapists practicing in California, for example, have the following national and state associations:

APA—the American Psychological Association and/or the American Psychiatric Association
AAMFT—the American Association of Marriage and Family Therapists
NASW—National Association of Social Workers
CPA—the California Psychological Association
CAMFT—the California Association of Marriage and Family Therapists
CSCSW—California Society for Clinical Social Workers

There are similar state and county professional associations in other states.

CIVIL LAW MALPRACTICE SUITS

Malpractice cases are heard by superior court judges and juries who make decisions based on the Constitution of the United States, federal and state laws, and a web of existing American "case law" decisions and precedents. The plaintiff bar—those attorneys who represent clients—is highly motivated to establish a national standard of care for the prosecution of mental health providers in order to make their jobs easier and more clear-cut.

STATE LICENSING BOARD ACCUSATIONS

Authorized by the state legislatures under business and professions codes, state licensing boards operate under the administrative branch of the government. State boards are generally composed mostly of lay people and some professionals—all usually political appointees of state governors. State licensing boards regulate and police the professions in the name of consumer protection. While we value such regulation, we must keep a wary eye out at all times for irresponsible policing activities. State laws, the rules of the licensing board, the ethics of the profession, and community standards of practice all have the effect of law, which the state boards are entrusted to enforce. Note here that community standard of practice is a broader and more appropriate term than state or national, in that it refers not so much to a geographical, political, or economic community, but to various communities of practicing professionals in which we as individuals have been personally trained and now work, and that may also be organized statewide, nationally, or internationally.

The names of boards vary from state to state but here are some examples:

BOP—the Board of Psychology (licenses and regulates psychologists)
BBS—the Board of Behavioral Sciences (licenses marriage and family therapists, social workers, and educational psychologists)
BRN—the Board of Registered Nurses
CMB—The California Medical Board (licenses doctors and regulates psychiatrists)

ADMINISTRATIVE LAW HEARINGS

The state administrative boards make decisions based on complaints from consumers. The process is generally as follows: After a client or plaintiff makes a complaint to a state licensing or consumer protection board, a state investigator (who knows nothing about psychotherapy) reviews the case and either dismisses it or writes up an accusation against the professional on behalf of the state board. Note that in administrative law it is ultimately the state (not the client) that accuses us of failing to fulfill the duties imposed upon us by licensure. Then an expert professional witness working for the state reviews the complaint, the investigator's report, and whatever other documents have been collected. The expert witness writes a report on the case and the accused professional or respondent is required to reply in a limited time period (such as thirty days). Based on the professional's response, the board makes a decision of guilty or innocent—without ever having seen or directly heard from either the client or the therapist. If guilty, the board prepares to sentence the professional. Disciplinary actions include loss, suspension, or probation of license; the requirement of remedial education, supervision, or therapy; and the payment of punitive fines as well as the payment of the entire cost of the investigation and the hearing (thus, in most states the boards are highly motivated to find the professional guilty). The professional has thirty days to appeal the decision of the board.

If an accused professional appeals the board decision, there is usually an administrative law hearing presided over by an administrative law judge (ALJ). The governor appoints ALJ's to rule on matters pertaining to governmental affairs. They are retired judges, probation officers, investigators, or other individuals favored by the governor and deemed to have some experience in the administrative branch of government. In an administrative law hearing, an attorney and one expert witness represent the accused professional. The complainant or the plaintiff is represented by a state deputy attorney general. The ALJ, who is employed by the state in the administrative branch of the government, makes recommendations to the licensing board regarding the complaint and the sentence. But the board generally has the power to reject the judge's decisions and recommendations so that its own decisions remain binding.

These standard operating procedures of state administration mean, in effect, that the licensing board has served as the accuser, the judge, the jury, the sentencer, and the collector of fees for the cost of the entire process—with no civil rights, little or no discovery process, no binding appeals process, and in most states no statute of limitations to protect the professional! I have seen professional licenses revoked and fees of from $20,000 to $70,000 imposed by boards on "guilty" therapists who have never even been interviewed by the board or had any sort of a fair trial. This has generally been an out-of-pocket expense. The cost of a defense lawyer, an expert witness, and the typical five years of remedial education, supervision, and psychotherapy can easily run into another $100,000 to $150,000. Until recently, psychotherapists have had no insurance coverage to defray these expenses. Procedures and costs vary according to locale and many states do not require the professional to pay the investigation costs.

POSSIBLE CHANGES IN ADMINISTRATIVE LAW

Because of widespread and unfair administrative procedures that are known to be politically and economically biased, the numerous publicly reported travesties of justice, and a recent series of successful civil lawsuits brought against state licensing boards by mistreated professionals, state legislatures from time to time attempt to limit licensing board power. But since legislative acts are subject to veto from the executive branch of the government, that is, the governor, most legislative attempts to change administrative procedures or to limit the power of licensing boards fail.

For example, both houses of the California legislature recently voted that in cases where the credibility of the plaintiff (the accusing client) is in question, the ALJ's decision would remain binding since the judge (the trier of fact), but not the board, has personally heard both sides of the case and therefore is in a better position to render a fair decision. All mental health associations supported the bill, as did the state organization of attorneys. But the bill was vetoed by the governor.

Another example is of a legislative act that recently passed in California, so that as of January 1, 2000, there is finally a statute of limitations on administrative actions of three years from the time the boards receive the complaint, and a statute of limitations of seven years from when the incident occurred for the boards to act—whichever comes first. Most states do not have statutes of limitations, so professionals can be and are prosecuted for complaints that are twenty or thirty years old. Perhaps the only reason the governor of California failed to veto this bill was because of some outrageous complaints that have been recently sustained by California boards in true *Les Miserables* fashion.

It is my belief that travesties of justice are a regular occurrence at the state board level. But because therapists and the public naively tend to believe that state boards rule in the best interest of the profession and the public, and because cases investigated are almost always shrouded in secrecy and confidentiality, no one ever hears about these travesties. I have been an expert witness to confidential board actions in twelve states—and have encountered numerous appalling travesties of justice.

There are few ways to open state boards to public scrutiny and accountability. The statistics they publish are inconsistent with outside data and perhaps even fraudulent because boards work in secrecy behind closed doors. A grassroots movement in Arizona gathered so many complaints against the state board that the state legislature refused to renew the board's authorization until it could demonstrate better accountability.

I recently was the expert witness in an investigation that in fact led to increased board accountability. But first some background. I have testified on behalf of numerous therapists who I have cause to believe have been the object of false transference-based accusations. In every instance in which I have had full access to the clinical record and have pointed to a given accusation as likely being transference-based and have stated the reason I believe it to be so, the ALJ has dismissed the complaint. But in each instance the licensing board in question has chosen to override the judge and to find the therapist guilty. The attorneys and therapists I have testified for have regularly assured me that in the final analysis my testimony has made a decisive difference in lowering the number of accusations actually prosecuted and/or in lightening the sentencing process. It seems, then, that I had at least succeeded in creating the shadow of a doubt in the judge's mind, which didn't finally get the therapist off the hook but apparently put the board enough on the hot seat that things went easier for the therapist.

But in this recent case, I wrote an extremely harsh report directed at the investigation and the expert witness report on a therapist whose work with a very damaged client I felt was fully responsible and ethical. Both the attorney and I were amazed when the board withdrew the official accusation in its entirety—something totally unheard of for this particular board according to the dozen attorneys I have since spoken with. Usually on the basis of a strong expert witness report a few accusations may be withdrawn, but the others are bandied about and bargained with. Thus, this total withdrawal of a set of complaints at the stage of an official accusation is a landmark event, because by the time a formal board accusation is made, considerable amounts of taxpayer money are involved and the board will not be able to recover its losses if the therapist is not found guilty. One attorney I spoke with cited the example of a therapist who was indicted on thirty-three counts by the same board. The defense attorney whittled the list down to only one count, which the expert witness addressed favorably and the ALJ moved to dismiss. But the board had spent a fortune going after this therapist and was determined he would pay the bill, so it cavalierly overrode the judge's decision and unfairly prosecuted him.

But in this case, in which the entire accusation was withdrawn, this particular board was by then well familiar with my false-accusation arguments, and the attorney general no doubt realized that in this circumstance the therapist would look good to the ALJ and the client would not appear at all credible. With my false-accusation argument properly aimed, the complaints were highly likely to be dismissed by the ALJ. Rather than risk the cost of losing an appeals hearing with the ALJ ruling against the board, thereby forcing the board to override the judge if it wished to recoup its money (so close on the heels of the governor's protective veto), it appears that the attorney general moved to cut the state's losses. If this theory is at all correct, it means that the vetoed legislative action did in fact work behind the scenes to restrain the board, and that the false-accusation argument is in fact hitting its mark silently in this most unexpected way. We can only hope so, but it is difficult to know what considerations go into creating a greater balance of justice. Perhaps, after all, some progress is slowly being made behind the scenes in the area of administrative law reform.

To deal effectively with unjust and faulty board actions, professionals must realize that the state entrusts the boards to police our actions and to prosecute us. Thus, as a body, we must stand against unfair enforcement and unwarranted intrusion by the state into our professional affairs. At the American Psychological Association convention in Boston, Division 31 (state and provincial psychological associations) hosted a symposium assembled by the psychologist Mark Peterson. A central emphasis of all the speakers was that state professional associations need to become more informed about all state board actions and need to remain in a constant watchdog and adversarial position. But against this position Ted Wendling, a journalist from *The Plain Dealer* in Cleveland, in a series of articles attempting to create a scandal about psychologists exploiting their clients and not being properly punished for their crimes, amassed data from a number of states (1999). His arguments are flawed on two counts. First, he makes the assumption that the psychological profession—not political and economic forces of states—is in control of the actions of state boards. Second, he assumes that if a board indicts a professional, the indictment is valid and analogous to a civil indictment, in which there is a discovery process, legal rights are extended to both parties, witnesses and testimony are allowed, and the justice system is not kangarooed. Based on what I have seen, the rule is not to believe anything state boards put out because it is all so highly subject to political and financial motivation. I am usually pathologically unparanoid and not very skeptical, but I have reached my limit based on what I have seen firsthand of the administrative justice system.

STATE BOARD INVESTIGATIONS

State boards estimate that, in general, approximately one-third of the consumer complaints they receive are dismissed immediately, one-third are investigated, and one-third become formal accusations. This indicates how many bogus complaints there really are! The best approach is to prevent an accusation from ever being filed. But once a formal accusation is made, it is almost never withdrawn, so psychotherapists must be quick in contacting an attorney and cooperative in responding to complaints. It is also important to contact your malpractice carrier *after* you call your attorney. The carrier may have its own incentive to provide legal coverage for you, and the insurance company's attorney may have the carrier's best interests in mind, not yours. In general, we are the recipients of the insurance company's managed care panel of attorney providers who sometimes operate under a potential conflict of interest! It is important that we be proactive consumers making certain that the attorney assigned to defend us has considerable experience in this area.

Do not rely on the goodwill of investigators, as they generally have a police mentality. You are accused of a crime and they are assigned to pursue an investigation. Admit nothing. Let your attorney guide you in making a safe response. A good fight at this stage is critical since even if the complaint is dropped by the investigator, it remains permanently on your record and, unless you are one of those operating under a recently enacted statute of limitations, the complaint remains in your file and can be revived twenty or thirty years later.

Never give up on fighting these complaints because they can come back to haunt you later in other ways. I advised one psychotherapist to fight her state board to the bitter end, but she declined because of the expense and because she was weary of dealing with the complaint, she was willing to let the board have its way. Subsequently she spent more than $50,000 in attorney's fees and two years fighting the same complaint with the American Psychological Association ethics committee and the licensing board of another state where she had applied for licensure. These agencies all communicate with one another. The only privacy they are supposed to respect is the complaining client's. Client complaint forms ask whether the client has also complained to the professional ethics committee and/or the state licensing board, and they have a box for the complainant to check (which complainants usually do) giving permission for the agency handling the complaint to send it to other investigating and enforcement agencies. We have no privacy in these matters.

Once a board decision has been made, it is difficult to get the matter heard in civil court because civil judges assume the matter is about government administrative matters that they know little about. However, if you have fought it, and the ALJ rules in your favor as the "trier of fact" who has heard face-to-face testimony by both sides of the question, then your chances are increased of getting a fair civil review later if you need it. Fighting complaints at all levels is worth your trouble and expense because the interlocking system is so complex, dangerous, and powerful. There are the additional complications that arise from being excluded from malpractice coverage, managed care panels, professional organizations, national registers, and hospital privileges if there are complaints on your record. So do your best to eliminate them completely.

RESPONDING TO SUBPOENAS

Don't play hard to get when it comes to subpoenas, because servers enjoy chasing people. Call immediately to tell the attorney who issued the subpoena that you cannot even say whether or not the complainant is or was your client without a bona fide signed release. Then follow up the phone discussions with a letter, sent by certified mail, verifying your position. When the release arrives, carefully check the client's signature against the one you have on file, and if you have any misgivings insist on a notarized signature. Release nothing until you have talked personally with your client about the implications of releasing private material and/or you are sure that you have a bona fide signature on a release. With couples or family therapy, of course, *all* members must sign a release. I always try getting subpoenas for records immediately quashed for any reason I can think of because I never feel right about releasing confidential material.

Call your client's attorney or your own, explain the situation and that you want the subpoena quashed (voided), and have him or her handle it directly with the requesting attorney rather than attempting to do it yourself. Explain that your records contain private and confidential material that could be damaging to your client and/or to others. Explain that even though the client has signed a release, the circumstances are coercive to your client, and you are ethically obligated to fight for the protection of the privacy of therapy against coercive situations that could be harmful. State your concerns in a letter to the client's attorney and send it by certified mail, with a copy to your client.

If necessary, cite the Jaffee Supreme Court Case (*Carrie Jaffee v. Mary Lou Redmond*, case number 518US1, June 13, 1996) in which a policewoman shot and killed a man in the line of duty. She entered psychotherapy with a social worker who refused to release the records when subpoenaed. The lower court judge interpreted the refusal as an indication of the policewoman's guilt and so ruled. The Supreme Court was assisted in its opinion by all of the national mental health organizations. It ruled that maintaining the private sanctuary of psychotherapy was in the public weal and that until and unless an equally compelling public interest superseded, that confidentiality shall be maintained. Murder charges were not seen as a sufficiently compelling public interest, and psychotherapeutic confidentiality was maintained. No one yet knows how far-reaching this landmark decision may become. HIPAA Standards (to be discussed later) underline the importance of confidentiality.

You can copy the files yourself and charge $0.25 per page. If you put your records in the hands of a copy service, you are within your rights to charge for your time spent monitoring your records while they are being copied. You are the owner of your records, so never let them leave your sight for any reason. If the stakes are high, don't leave crucial records in your office where they can be stolen! Group records or records that contain other people's confidential information must never be released. Your oath to "tell the whole truth" fortunately does not extend to revealing other people's privileged and confidential information.

If a client is mentally incompetent or dead, you need certification that the person signing the release is the guardian or executor of the estate. Always check documents and signatures, insisting on a notarized signature when in doubt. Refusing to release your records for good reasons is defensible, whereas careless releasing is not! It is always best to discuss options directly with your client and to document this discussion. Consult an attorney when in doubt.

PROFESSIONAL MALPRACTICE AND ADMINISTRATIVE HEARING INSURANCE

Professional malpractice insurance covers you for civil lawsuit claims made in superior court. A few years ago, when premiums were skyrocketing due to increasing litigation, insurance carriers developed a less expensive "claims made" type of coverage, which essentially ends when you terminate the policy or retire from practice, unless you (and after you are dead, your estate) keep purchasing annual "tails." The more expensive "occurrence" type of coverage protects you for all time against liability while the policy was in effect and is clearly the preferred coverage. Buy the maximum insurance available.

Administrative law insurance, which is sold under several different names, is a new supplemental coverage option that has been added to most malpractice policies. It covers the escalating costs of administrative law complaints and board hearings. Some companies offer only $5,000, but the better policies offer $25,000 and $50,000 options. Again, take the maximum, since it is not expensive and it is not uncommon for administrative hearings to cost $30,000 or more. A good defense may well run $50,000, which would otherwise come out of your pocket.

The plaintiff bar has, as expected, reorganized its prosecution strategies now that most malpractice insurance carriers have limited coverage for sexual offenses to $25,000 or no coverage at all. As a result, administrative complaints and their costs are escalating. Not only can attorneys easily tap into this type of coverage for their fees, but also if they win at the board level on a miscellaneous set of nonsexual complaints, they then have paved the way for a lucrative civil malpractice suit. So although sexual misconduct charges may be rapidly becoming a thing of the past, anger over violations lives on in new and more disguised and dangerous forms.

Malpractice insurance is run like managed care, in that the attorney assigned to you is on a panel working for the insurance company and despite a fiduciary responsibility to you may have mixed motivations in the case. It is best to keep your own personal attorney for a second opinion from time to time, regardless of what it costs—it's part of the price of doing business these days. This issue should make you think twice about the clients you choose to work with in your practice and to be attentive to how you work and how you document your work.

An administrative action has the full power of the state and can entail almost anything, including confiscating all of your client records, interviewing all of your present and past clients, and closing down your practice immediately—confidentiality notwithstanding. Essentially, you are in the hands of the police. So if you receive a board complaint, it is in your best interest to be as cooperative as possible and initiate a discussion immediately with a reliable attorney who will guide you every step of the way—requesting extensions, gathering arguments, and working effectively for you.

3

Practicing Defensively

Psychotherapy Practice Issues

STANDARD OF CARE

The following factors are included in the concept of standard of care:

Statutes, such as child and elder abuse reporting laws;

Regulations of the licensing boards, such as record keeping and informed consent requirements;

Standards of professional associations, such as the APA's "Ethical Principles of Psychologists and Code of Conduct" (2002) and "General Guidelines for Providers of Psychological Services" (1987);

Specialty guidelines, such as forensic and child custody practice guidelines;

Court decisions, such as the obligations of Tarasoff, in which there is a duty to warn third parties who are in imminent danger; and

Concerns of professionals, such as those cited in peer-reviewed journal articles and convention presentations and panels.

The standard of care in the end boils down to a set of conflicting opinions regarding what the average expectable practitioner in your community of practitioners might do given the same basic situation. The accuser will attempt to hold you to unrealistic and idealistic standards and will use your ethics codes and other publications in your profession to demonstrate how off-base your judgments and actions were.

The plaintiffs attorney will be able to locate a professional colleague to serve as an expert witness against you and to clearly state that what you did or failed to do constitutes unprofessional conduct or gross negligence under the law, citing title and code number as to where you went deplorably wrong. Your attorney and expert witness must present a strong and plausible counter-argument. Expert witnesses are obligated under law to be unbiased and ethical in their opinions. But there is a wide range of variability and diversity in opinions, which is why expert witnesses who are charged with the duty to render unbiased scientific opinion are widely referred to by attorneys as "whores of the court"!

There is no national standard of care—that mythical beast that an aggressive plaintiff bar is doing its best to create to make prosecution of therapists easier. Instead, in psychotherapy we have a set of relationship issues to which standard of care advocates attempt to attach imaginary ideals, mythical boundaries, and binding moralities. In civil courts, where there is a discovery process and issues are impartially weighed, we have a fighting chance when questioned. But under administrative law, we are assumed guilty of a client's complaint until we are proven innocent. In this moralizing climate, "You shouldn't have done that" reigns supreme until and unless you can muster a massive and convincing counterargument. Even though there is no national standard of care, and even though community standards are highly variable, we must be ever watchful and cautious at every juncture because a client who is hopelessly confused and concrete or an attorney who is dangerously idealistic and moralizing may well be pointing the accusatory finger at us. Third parties who are angry at us or aggrieved for any reason can file board complaints and lawsuits that we are obligated to respond to. Or they can agitate clients to do so.

Thus, I believe that practicing defensively means generally operating in the most cautious and conservative manner possible. But every time I try to make this point I am nearly shouted down by a room full of angry therapists: "I'm not going to let *them* tell *me* how to run my practice!" "I started this work because I wanted to help people in need." "Help means being real, human, and emotionally available." "If I can't be spontaneous and caring in this work, I quit." "I didn't get into this work to have crooks and charlatans in the capital or in lawyer's garb tell me what to do." "People have a right to be alive and this means us." "I'm not going to change how I run my practice to make those jerks happy." We can be warm, human, and emotionally available helpers and yet still be aware of the anxiety, the unreasonableness, the threat, and the rage that exist in our clients and in the community. Naive moralizing masquerading under fancy titles such as "standard of care," "boundary violations," and "dual relationships" is dangerous and shortsighted. We live in too dangerous a world to trust people to act fairly and in our best interests or to run our psychotherapy practice with only humane concerns.

It is a collective fantasy we have nourished for years that psychodynamics are not dangerous. It is wishful thinking that our clients have not been traumatized and damaged early in life, leaving them with bitter, cruel, cold fantasies of someday, somehow, getting revenge. It is misguided for us to think that we can open our consulting room to people trying to overcome life's traumas without being at risk for stirring up their worst transferences—and our own as well. I'm not saying that we have to change how we work. But I am saying that we now need to be ever mindful of the treacheries of deep transference terror and widespread fantasies of righting unspeakable wrongs. As helping people in psychotherapeutic, trusting relationships, we set ourselves up to have this deeply buried transference rage aimed squarely at us. Why then are we shocked when, from time to time, it becomes blindly acted out against us?

If the accusation finally arrives, are our safety nets securely in place? Can we demonstrate that everything we did was as well thought out and as carefully planned as possible? Can we show beyond a doubt that anyone in our position would have made the same choices for the same basic reasons? Have we been documenting the case consultations we have been getting from colleagues, the conversations we have been having with our client about our concerns, and the ways we have followed up on difficult moments? Accidents occur, and when a judge is called upon to decide liability, can we unequivocally demonstrate that we have erred in the direction of thoughtfulness, care, and caution?

The concept of standard of care means to me that abstract idealizing standards that have nothing to do with the highly personal relationships that develop in psychotherapy may well be applied to our work if any element of deep transference or countertransference ever goes awry. Practicing defensively means educating ourselves about what attorneys and licensing boards are considering as standards of care and being sure that we can plausibly defend our practices and techniques against these arbitrary and idealized standards. It means learning to step outside ourselves and to view our work with the eyes of others who do not think or practice as we do. It means thinking through each step of our work, consulting with colleagues about it, considering alternatives, processing options with our clients, and carefully documenting the entire process and follow-up. This is what we must do to practice defensively.

INFORMED CONSENT

Informed consent is a risk/benefit analysis of psychotherapy services. It must include more than statements regarding fees, procedures, and confidentiality. All foreseeable risks must be disclosed, including the risk that therapy may not work for clients in the ways they expect or hope. Informed consent must include documentation that the client has the capacity to understand the information provided and has freely and without undue influence expressed consent. It must provide the client with sufficient information so that risks and benefits can truly be understood and weighed and alternatives can be chosen.

Informed consent includes clear statements about your theoretical orientation, the projected course of therapy, other options available to the client, the client's right to seek outside consultation and to terminate at any time, and the foreseeable risks, such as that therapy might make the client feel worse before feeling better and the possibility that the client might not improve or become happier. You need to document how informed consent was presented to the client, and your assessment of whether or not the client understood it. You might need to repeat it on successive days or put it into writing. You may need to note a global assessment of functioning (GAF) score, or some other objective assessment in the client's chart.

Informed consent is an ongoing process, not a one-time event, and it must be addressed at regular intervals. Whenever new features are added to the therapy situation or to the person's life situation, the risks and benefits need to be reconsidered. On the CD-ROM accompanying this book there are a series of sample informed consents that address a variety of issues. In the Periodic Clinical Reassessment/Review form, there is a section in which to regularly note updates in informed consent. Documentation of periodic risk/benefit discussions needs to be in the client's record in order to create a "trail of responsibility." With this book and access to a computer you have the forms you need to get started maintaining better trails of responsibility.

Informed consent also entails affirming clearly the professional and business (contractual) side of the therapeutic relationship at each stage. We tell the client that reasonable practice in our profession requires that we maintain certain kinds of paperwork, agreements, and records. Our colleagues expect it of us, and the state that licenses us expects it. But even so, our records remain basically confidential. Few clients have difficulty understanding this business side of psychotherapy. They have sought out responsible professional help. They respect us for taking our business with them seriously. The few exceptions are clients who refuse to sign forms, who do not want the therapist to take notes or keep records, who refuse to have previous therapy records released, who object to the therapist seeking consultation, and who refuse to go along with recommendations that particular circumstances require. In such cases we must be prepared to terminate therapy in the client's best interest as well as in our own if the client cannot cooperate in the business requirements of our trade.

Many therapists continue to feel that they must keep on working with a client no matter how the client reacts to these business requirements. But it simply doesn't make sense to allow our lives and livelihoods to be at risk because a damaged client refuses to cooperate with our usual and customary treatment requirements. These therapists continue to struggle with this aspect of practice. Perhaps our collective fantasy that we have at last arrived on the scene as the warm, protective, and loving parent or healing force to rescue the client from a life of exploitative relationships and crippling symptoms causes us to lose track of the simple fact that we practice psychotherapy in a state-licensed business environment and that, like all shopkeepers, we need to be minding our business well. Informed consents are simply ways of being certain that the business-contractual side, the mutual understanding and agreement side of our work, is clear to both parties.

DIAGNOSTIC ASSESSMENT

Business and professional people regularly conduct diagnostic assessments at the outset of a business relationship and periodically during the course of the relationship to determine what their clients' needs are and how to go about addressing these needs. Similarly, a psychotherapy assessment needs to be a vital part of the ongoing relationship with the client. If the confidential seal of your records is broken and third parties come to view this ongoing diagnostic assessment, will you have documented your thinking well enough and often enough to appear in the most favorable and credible light possible? Have your assessments been carefully thought through and documented at periodic intervals? Is there evidence that you have weighed a series of possibilities, discussed them with your client, and then made choices that seem optimal or at least plausible given the information you were working with at the time?

There is no clear-cut or widespread community standard of care for diagnostic assessments since we have so many diverse schools of thought and practice in psychotherapy. But if you want your own work to stand up to critical scrutiny, there are a few factors you need to consider. You must (1) make a diagnosis, (2) note it in the case file, (3) use it in your formulations and communications to third parties, (4) share it with the client, and (5) update it periodically. In reviewing the results of your assessment with your client, present your impressions honestly and record the results of the discussion. If you don't wish to confuse the client with *Diagnostic and Statistical Manual of Mental Disorders* (*DSM*) terminology, simply document how you presented your assessment findings. For example, you might choose to review a series of *DSM* descriptions with the client. Then document the client's reactions, the discussion that ensued, and your follow-up of any concerns or issues. If you are beginning long-term relational therapy, your assessment statement would center around what kinds of relationships have failed for the client and what kinds of relationships have worked. What have been the results of relationship problems in the client's daily life and what do the two of you plan to address? I frequently jot down possible transference themes as they appear and the implications of those themes for life and for therapy.

Lawyers recommend that we use the *DSM* format as much as possible in our files and case notes because even though the *DSM* was developed and revised in an atmosphere of economic, political, and academic psychiatry, it has, over time, earned national and multidisciplinary prestige. As such, it represents a homogeneous, even if mythical, standard that your work is likely to be judged by in court. It would be a mistake to state when questioned that you don't believe in diagnosis, because then you would have to explain how you otherwise assess client needs, and in your professional capacity, respond to them. If you choose to use other concepts and terms in your practice, be sure they are in the file and are readily translatable into *DSM* terms in a deposition.

The preference for the *DSM* rests on the public nature of its categories and definitions. The possible advantage of less specific but clear diagnostic statements is that your meanings can later be clarified and/or elaborated to anyone who asks. For example, therapists who practice bioenergetic psychotherapy may assess a client as having a schizoid or masochistic body type, which, within the language of their common practice, carries a host of implications for what the nature of the client's problems are and what kinds of therapeutic interventions are warranted. If bioenergetic therapists are further able to state the diagnostic assessment in ego terms and *DSM* terms, they have a range of possibilities. But these possibilities must all be stated or at least briefly alluded to in the case file in order for them to be plausible later. What too many unfortunate therapists have discovered is that when ideas and concepts about the assessment and treatment processes are not at least noted in the record, their after-the-fact attempts on the hot seat to account for how they were thinking and what they were doing are implausible to a trier of fact. And it is even worse if the client has notes or journal entries for such discussions that summarize what she or he heard in therapy sessions. Those notes are more plausible than your non-notes, regardless of how distorted or misconstrued they may be.

Lawyers tell us that we must use the same diagnosis for treatment that we use for insurance or other documents and forms. This has not in fact been the practice of most psychotherapists in the past nor do I believe it is in the present. Most of us have been taught to pay minimal attention to *DSM* formulations, which are often useless to us except to enable the client to receive insurance coverage. Further, we have learned that some diagnoses, such as of severe pathology, perversions, or addictions, can jeopardize the client's present or future insurance coverage or employment opportunities. Although such information is supposedly confidential, *DSM* codes are quickly computerized and thus become accessible to many people. A divorced parent with a diagnosis of sociopathy, perversion, or psychosis, for example, might not be allowed to have custody or full visitation rights if attorneys pry open the case file. (See the later chapter on HIPAA for my comments on the DSM versus the ICDM diagnostic codes.)

Thus, we are in a bind in trying to put honest assessments into the record that will not unfairly bias third parties against the client should the seal of confidentiality ever be broken. I have generally addressed this problem by using an appropriate broad-based *DSM* category, and then writing a series of relevant descriptions in my own terms that I could elaborate on if asked.

You might take it upon yourself to become familiar with how to use multiple diagnoses or add "rule out" clauses to indicate what possibilities you are considering and why. Comment on your assessment of the client's ego strengths such as memory, reality testing, judgment, and mental capacity. Otherwise you might later be accused, as was one therapist I recently represented, of undertaking regressive, uncovering therapy with a client who has insufficient ego strength to undergo regressive therapy. At the least your diagnostic formulations should in some way reflect your assessment in your own terms and your reasons for choosing to proceed as you did.

Defense attorneys tell us that it is important that we be able to demonstrate consistency between our diagnosis and the treatment plan we set up at the beginning of treatment and periodically revise along the way. The diagnostic impression can and often ought to change with changing information, but we need to document why the change is made and how that change is reflected in our ongoing treatment plan. There is a place in the Periodic Reassessment and Review form (on the CD-ROM) to update and elaborate ongoing assessments and the treatment plan.

Deciding on a firm *DSM* diagnosis may take several sessions. I recommend an extended assessment period (six or more sessions) to allow for a good formulation, to get a clear picture of what kinds of treatment will be required, and to determine whether or not you want to take on this client or to refer him or her elsewhere. By "good formulation" I don't mean a refined *DSM*, but rather a series of clearly documented concerns that would demonstrate to anyone nosing through your file that you had considered this person carefully and had not missed any possibilities. Until then, you might in your notes use such phrases such as, "The diagnostic dilemma is between A and B," or "The tentative impression is C," or "Rule out D."

The California Board of Psychology has ludicrously mandated in recent newsletters that informed consent and fee setting occur at the first session. But often at the first session we don't really know whether or not we want to take on the client, what the client needs to consent to, or what might be an appropriate treatment and fee. Further, it is countertherapeutic to present long, legalistic documents requiring signatures before we have formed any kind of relationship with the client. I have addressed this problem by developing a streamlined two-page Informed Consent for Psychotherapy Assessment Consultation (on the CD-ROM) that generally covers the basics and commits me only to a few assessment sessions, a recommendation, and a fee for assessment sessions. Without some such device clearly limiting your commitment and liability, case law can be interpreted as holding that the minute you see a client he or she is "in treatment" with you. Therefore, without an instrument to limit your obligations and liability you may have difficulty later referring or terminating the client.

Also don't agree to actually see anybody else's clients for weekend or emergency coverage without limiting your liability by having your own informed consent document in place! Consider using my Informed Consent for Psychotherapy Assessment Consultation to cover you when the charge comes that you accepted the client and failed to provide proper treatment. With the consent for assessment consultation in place, your function is limited, especially when the reason for seeking consultation states, "Seeking weekend or emergency contact while primary therapist is unavailable."

Diagnostic assessment and treatment planning has no national standard of care since there are many ways that professionals do an ongoing assessment of needs and consider how the psychotherapeutic work can address those needs. While *DSM* concepts have the value of using an established common terminology, they are derived from conflicts and compromises in the field of psychiatry and therefore are based on a series of somatic and medication considerations and political, economic, and academic compromises that do not concern most practicing psychotherapists. But from the standpoint of a trier of fact, it makes sense that a psychotherapist would conduct an assessment of the situation, discuss it with the client, document the client's response, revise the assessment periodically, and tailor the therapy to address the client's needs. Your case files should reflect these considerations. Practicing defensively includes creating trails of responsibility through your work, and one of these trails is an ongoing assessment of needs and clear statements about how your treatment process is addressing these needs.

LIMITING YOUR LIABILITY IN WORKING
WITH CHILDREN AND ADOLESCENTS

Testifying in child custody hearings is always risky. Do not agree to evaluate or to testify if you are the therapist of the child or of anyone in the family, for you may immediately be caught up in an unethical dual relationship. If you are ordered by the court to testify (not merely subpoenaed by one of the attorneys), explain your position of not wanting to be in an untenable dual role, but then provide whatever information the judge demands.

If you are a court-appointed evaluator, you can reduce your risk by clarifying your role in advance and in writing with both attorneys, including how you will proceed, your fee structure, and how your report will be prepared and presented. Personally solicit their cooperation and agreement, and have them explain your working procedures to their clients. Then proceed in a similar manner with the parents, clarifying in writing your position, procedures, and fees, that you are being asked as an expert to render an opinion, and that it is, after all, only one professional's opinion. Have all parties sign indicating their understanding and agreement before you begin. Personal contacts with all concerned are always a good idea. Follow up with attorneys and clients in as personal and thorough a manner as possible to avoid later misunderstandings. Take careful notes and document all meetings and phone calls. As an expert witness your job is to render an objective and document-supported opinion, so be careful to remain neutral and to present as clearly as possible the pros and cons of both sides. I prefer to avoid making a direct recommendation unless circumstances make it necessary. By carefully delineating the strengths and weaknesses of each parenting resource, I can then step back and allow the judge to do the actual deciding. Since the largest source of complaints has recently become complaints against therapists and court evaluators in relation to custody issues, Dr. Ira Gorman has contributed a special chapter in this book and special forms are on the Web site. Also, since complaints regarding therapists' work with children and adults have sharply risen in recent years, Dr. Steven Frankel has contributed a chapter and special forms on the CD-ROM that address considerations for practice.

In filing mandated suspicion of child and elder abuse reports, you are on solid ground if you have explained in your initial informed consent the limitations of confidentiality in this regard. You should further explain that it is not your job to determine if child or elder abuse exists, but to report the mere suspicion of it. In your treatment notes avoid unexplained quotations that could later be taken out of context such as, "I could have just beaten him to death for that." Be sure that a retrospective examination of your notes will not reveal that you had grounds for suspicion and failed to report them. Certainly do not note that you considered reporting and did not, unless your consultant agreed or the Child Protective Services, (CPS) worker (whose name and date you have documented) also says there are no grounds for reporting. Making an anonymous call to a CPS worker asking for advice and documenting that person's opinions is often a wise idea before actually reporting.

An adolescent usually requires complete confidentiality for therapy to work, and this can be explained to parents. Be sure to get their consent in writing so you cannot later be held liable by them for knowing about the adolescent's dangerous activities and failing to report them to the parents. See the Informed Consent for Work with Children and Adolescents on the CD-ROM.

Before agreeing to assess or treat a minor whose parents are legally separated or divorced, you should insist on having a copy of the court order for custody, or, if no order is in place, a written agreement that is signed by both parents. Do not rely on the parents' word, because they may not understand whether or not they have the right to authorize diagnosis and treatment. Consult an attorney if you have questions. See my Informed Consents for Working with Children and Adolescents and for Infant Communication Work for further guidelines.

RECORD KEEPING

Law and ethics require that we exercise due diligence in keeping confidential and secure the records of all of our professional contacts. Licensing boards, attorneys, and judges expect us to comply with case law, professional ethics, and administrative regulations. Our confidential notes are a public record that must exist (1) for the purpose of aiding the treatment by refreshing our memories on important material, (2) for informing other professionals who may subsequently be involved with the client, (3) for protecting ourselves and our profession against accusations, and (4) for giving ourselves credibility in the event our case records are ever opened for any reason. There are many reasons why our records might be opened and we need to be prepared by having kept adequate notes.

Ethical codes and laws are uniform in requiring that notes be made that are appropriate to the nature of our practice and that reflect the nature of each professional contact. As of January 1, 2000, the California legislature has acted to define as unprofessional conduct the failure to keep records that are consistent with sound clinical judgment, the standards of the profession, and the nature of the services rendered. But, fortunately, there are few other fixed standards regarding records because psychotherapy practice is so diverse in nature.

Use your professional discretion when determining what kinds of notations are to be made. For example, a psychoanalytic practitioner seeing an intact client four times a week may routinely note only a few themes or dreams, whereas a forensic examiner doing interviewing and testing with highly unstable clients in controversial court cases will need detailed and accurate notes at every point. Here are a few general guidelines.

1. Make some kind of written note in your files regarding each and every client contact.
2. Maintain your record keeping system in chronological order so there can never be a question of the record having been rearranged or altered in any way. Don't fudge on this or think you can get away with anything! Altering records is a serious criminal offense. Handwriting experts can testify whether or not notes were made at the same time and computer experts have ways of ascertaining if there have been deletions or additions on your disks—so play it safe. You may cross things out with a line, alter statements, or make insertions freely, as long as you initial and date the changes and as long as the original is left intact and readable for later legal review.
3. Consider using a spiral notebook with one page for each client, with your notes flowing continuously on both sides. The page can then be removed and filed, and another page begun. If you carry the notebook around with you, use only first names or code names until the pages are filed.
4. The best system I have found is the Cross electronic notepad, which keeps dated notes in your hand that can be downloaded onto your computer and then cut and pasted into the client's security-coded file and/or printed out for hardcopy filing. Then you have your ongoing handwritten original that an officer of the court could inspect to verify the chronology if questioned as well as a computer-generated set of notes on each client. I then delete the notes on my hard disk and record over them, thus making it more difficult for the disk to be decoded in case of theft of the computer. (Computers are attractive to thieves.) Also, regularly print out and delete password files to avoid easy access by hackers. When you dispose of your computer or hard disk, you must actively delete and record over confidential files; deleting and reformatting your disk are not enough. New Federal HIPAA regulations regarding technological security is reviewed in a later chapters.

    I began regular note taking in 1996 and struggled through a series of systems until psychologist John Carter came up with the spiral notebook idea above. Ray Calabrese gave me the Crosspad with IBM

Ink Manager software for Christmas in 1998. My note taking now has become as natural as putting on a seat belt when I get in the car. I don't feel right about going home at night if I didn't make notes during, between, or after hours! Microsoft has recently released Notepad software worth looking into.

5. Accurate voice recognition systems are just being perfected and point toward another potential way of note keeping. I fantasize talking into my computer quickly after each hour or at the end of the day.

6. If you are using a word processor and/or a voice recognition program, make certain that you exercise due diligence in protecting files with passwords and keeping all electronically stored materials under lock and key. Be aware that computer experts can easily break codes and can detect alterations on hard drives.

7. Audio- and videocassettes are not only cumbersome to store but are also at risk of being lost or stolen until they are destroyed. If you record sessions to review or for supervision, consider using only one 100-minute cassette or a rewrite disc for each client, continually overrecording it.

8. When you go over documents that the client has signed, such as informed consents and client information forms, mark the important items and make notes in the margin of your questions and discussion with the client. Initial and date the notes.

9. Never take identifiable confidential material from your office unless it is enclosed in a large self-addressed and generously stamped envelope marked "Confidential medical records: Drop into any mailbox or call (your number)." You could be mugged or in an accident, and your case files could go astray. The wife of one of my colleagues tells of the time she went rushing to the emergency room after her husband had been in a serious accident that totaled his car. When she arrived he was laid out on a gurney barely hanging on to consciousness but clinging desperately to his briefcase that contained testing files he had taken home to work on. "God forbid the client folders had ended up lost in a wreckage garage or junkyard somewhere," she says.

10. Most of the time we can keep our note taking to a minimum as long as we briefly reference all important issues that come up. On the one hand, we wish to protect our client's and our own privacy by not extensively noting the details. But on the other hand, many clients keep journals and write notes about what they believe you did or said (or didn't do or say). If their record is examined and you have no notes on the matter, your testimony from memory is highly suspect compared to journal notes supposedly written at the time by clients. Your notes should contain at least a brief clarifying statement. I recently had oc-

casion to disqualify completely the computer journal of a client based upon presumed falsification since the notes the therapist had reliably kept and had a secretary file and initial were grossly discrepant from the journal presented by the client as evidence for the accusation.

11. Authorities differ on how to best handle documentation of discussions and events that could be construed as dangerous or incriminating to the therapist. For example, the standard of care that attorneys attempt to hold us to is that with suicidal clients we do a written suicidality assessment before allowing the client to leave our office. But having documented such an assessment in the record just before a serious or successful suicide attempt, we are in a position to be held liable for a faulty assessment or for a failure to act to prevent the attempt. In such situations we are in a bind, and our best professional judgment is required.

12. Do not keep multiple sets of notes. All of your notes will be subpoenaed and you will be asked under oath to testify that you have no other records. Falsifying or withholding parts of the record is a criminal offense.

13. Therapists sometimes keep a personal journal or make notes for other personal purposes (such as publishing) in which (de-identified) client material may be referenced. If you keep this kind of personal journal, be certain the material you put in it could never be construed as a client record or an attempt to evade the case record. If you mention the existence of such personal notes to your attorney or in court you will be required to produce them.

14. At all important documentation junctures (such as a change of an aspect of informed consent, a release of information, a letter structuring expectations or limitations, or a letter stating why you are terminating the client), explain to clients that the state requires certain kinds of paperwork be kept in your files and that you need their signature or initials acknowledging that they have received (and discussed with you) the document in question. You may wish to use the metaphor of signing for a traffic ticket—their signature simply indicates for the record that they have received it.

15. If your client refuses to abide by any one of your treatment requirements such as going for a medical/psychiatric consult, attending a 12-step group or signing for receipt of a document, you must consider terminating therapy for non-compliance rather than putting yourself at risk. Most clients are aware of the liability conditions that we all live under and are willing to cooperate with you. Those who are not aware of liability factors or who wish to put you in a dangerous liability position constitute a high-risk population.

16. Document carefully all unusual events, interventions, and contacts, all irregular contacts such as cards, letters, e-mails, phone calls, gifts, physical contact, unscheduled meetings, and any locations in which you see the client other than in your regular consultation room. Be sure to include *how the event* or request came up, what your *therapeutic intent* was in the way you handled it, *how the interaction was processed* at the time (possibly giving a GAF score), your *follow-up discussions* and understanding with the client, your understanding of *the transference and resistance memories involved, your countertransference reactions* (simple, brief, and labeled as such), and *the results of any consultations* you may have sought on the matter.

    The plaintiff bar and state boards are regularly demanding documentation of professional consultation and peer consultation as a part of their mythical national standard of care. Viewed across the board, outside consultation is not a very common practice among psychotherapists and it certainly does not represent any usual or expectable standard of care. Therapists who seek out consultation on a regular basis or even on an as-needed basis are still the exception to the rule. Even therapists who seek consultation on a few troubling cases may have twenty or thirty other cases in progress on which they have never sought consultation and never will. Yet one of these cases could present legal problems just as easily as one of the more troublesome ones. When trying to present a picture of yourself as a thoughtful and responsible therapist to a trier of fact, the notation from time to time that you raised a question with one of your colleagues, spoke with your case consultant, did a case presentation to your peer consultation group, or consulted an expert increases your credibility.

    Therapists cannot be expected to be consistently objective, and seeking an outside opinion is a good thing. Give yourself a break. Consult in different ways as often as you can and document the results. I was interested to hear that all members of the ethics committee of Section One (psychoanalytic practitioners) of Division 39 (psychoanalysis) of the American Psychological Association agreed to set an example by seeking out three peer case consultations each year in the spirit of updating their professional knowledge and safeguarding their objectivity.

17. In your notes predict possible transference developments that could turn sour and get aimed at you. That you saw the danger developing ahead of time and even attempted to discuss the problem with your client demonstrates thoughtfulness, care, and responsibility. When serving as an expert witness I cull through the case notes, carefully looking for all unusual events that might be telling in terms of how the

deep dynamics that unfolded in the treatment have become mirrored in the accusation. I am ecstatic when I find an occasional note that a particular conversation seemed to point toward a transference distortion and no doubt reflects the kinds of misunderstanding, trauma, or abuse the client experienced in his or her family of origin.

18. There are conflicting opinions about how personal or countertransference disclosures are best handled and documented. Be judicious in what you say, both to your client as well as in your notes, as disclosures can easily be misunderstood or distorted and used against you. If we believed our clients would be cured of anything by our disclosing personal information, we would hand out our life story at the first session! But we don't believe that. And there is wide variation among therapists regarding self-disclosures and how they may or may not be seen as helpful in the therapeutic process. If you choose to make disclosures then in your notes simply state that certain feelings naturally came up on your part as a result of the interaction with the client and that they were discussed with the client with a therapeutic purpose in mind. State the obvious in your notes, but leave out any details or complexities that could be easily misconstrued. Record simply and in your own terms how you experienced and processed the matter at the time. Avoid overly vague statements such as, "Transference and countertransference feelings were discussed," because such comments are useless later and could get you into trouble. At the minimum, state what feelings came up and how they were discussed. Document, as usual, your therapeutic intent, the process of the discussion, the outcome, and your follow-up with the client. Obviously gratuitous disclosures that have no therapeutic purpose should be avoided.

19. Using countertransference as a working tool, which many therapists have good reasons to do, requires that you make some clear statement early in the record of how and why you do so. Thereafter, be explicit in stating the therapeutic intent, process, outcome, and follow-up of the countertransference disclosure, but be professional and to the point. Then when you are accused of violating the clients' boundaries by sharing all of your personal problems with them on a certain date, at least you have a responsible note that you can use as the basis of your explanations.

20. When contemplating doing something unusual in therapy or when making notes about something you don't ordinarily do, always ask yourself four questions:
    a. What is the *therapeutic intent*?
    b. How would *peers* view this?

   c. How would *I* view this if another therapist were doing it?

   d. How would *lay people* view or be able to understand this?

RELEASING CONFIDENTIAL INFORMATION AND SIGNATURES

You know not to release any information without a signed consent. But do you always think to check the signatures against the ones you have on file? Do you think to have the signature on a release notarized if identity is in question? Especially watch child custody releases and other government and agency releases. Bogus requests are not uncommon and you don't want to be sued for breach of confidentiality.

Attorneys recommend that before we release any information we should discuss it with the client and document the discussion regarding the purpose of the release and the implications of signing away privileged confidentiality. Document your discussion of what other options may exist to avoid unnecessary disclosure of personal information and your judgment as to whether or not the release situation is coercive. Always vigorously protest releasing any confidential information on the basis of a coercively signed release. In the later HIPAA chapter are guidelines regarding the new legal classification "Psychotherapy Notes" and a new carefully worded release is on the CD-ROM. Here are a few tricks you may wish to try:

- Give out only a summary of already public and verifiable information when reporting to agencies such as probation or civil custody. Include only the general reasons for therapy and the client's attendance record. State that the client is using the time in therapy well and is progressing satisfactorily. If you must be more specific, state a few general comments about working on feelings and behaviors related to the reasons the client is being seen. Be brief and non-specific. It is not your job as a psychotherapist to satisfy such external demands, and it puts you in an unethical dual relationship which you can explain to your client as well as the outside source.

- When I am working with a therapist who is on probation with a licensing board, I have been asked by the board to go one step further and provide a full report. I respond that if I did so I would be in an unethical dual relationship with my client by serving the board in this way on my client's behalf. The point is that reporting more than what is minimally required to the board is a breach of professional ethics. I tell the board that if I come to believe that my client may possibly be an active danger to the public, I will communicate that fact immediately. I have the client review the letter and countersign my file copy (before I send the letter) with a statement that he or she agrees to the provisions of the letter. I explain to the client that should I ever feel obligated to report a mandated concern to the board, I would never give any specific information, but simply state that the board should conduct an evaluation—much as I am required to do when reporting a suspicion of child abuse. This approach reassures the client that I will fight to preserve confidentiality at all costs so that the therapy can proceed without the client's having to manipulate me or censor the content of the therapy.

- Rather than reveal substantive information, including diagnosis and mental status, refer either the agency requesting the information or the client to a reliable diagnostician. Explain that you would be engaging in an unethical dual relationship as the therapist if you provided a report to a third party. Further, a diagnostician is likely to be more objective.

- When your records are subpoenaed, try to have the subpoena quashed, and then insist on taking the sealed records directly to the judge yourself. The seal on the records should read, "WARNING! THIS ENVELOPE CONTAINS THE CONFIDENTIAL PSYCHOTHERAPY RECORDS OF _____. SEVERE DAMAGE MAY BE DONE TO THIS PERSON OR TO OTHERS IF THESE RECORDS ARE MADE PUBLIC. ANYONE DARING TO BREAK THIS SEAL VIOLATES 2000 YEARS OF ROMAN AND ANGLO-SAXON LAW WHICH GUARANTEES SANCTUARY AND PRIVACY TO ALL CITIZENS." Whenever I have done this no judge has ever broken the seal and my records have always been returned promptly to me. Judges have to demonstrate accountability too. Retain a copy of the records that you can personally certify to be complete if later asked. Ask to be released of the demand for records on the basis of privilege and confidentiality (whether the client has signed a release or not), and on the basis of the reasoning of the 1996 Jaffee Supreme Court decision. Further, Federal HIPAA Laws protect Psychotherapy Notes. [See the HIPAA chapter for explanation.]

- The principle that matters is that confidentiality be guaranteed and that we fight to maintain it. Agencies and attorneys have a job to do, and asking for records or demanding a report is the easiest and quickest way for them to get the information they need. We must make their job difficult in order to protect our client and the privilege—even when the client signs a release. It can too easily be demonstrated later that the client was coerced into signing the release against her or his will, that we knew that the client objected, and that we were aware the record contained potentially damaging material. Judges are generally willing to support our cause if we state it strongly.

- Explain to the client that you are fighting for her or his privacy, and why.
- When the agency requesting information states, "We need a report on the therapy, Doctor," or "All the other therapists we work with release therapy notes and reports," or "The client has signed a release," respond as follows:
  1. Sympathize with the agency's situation.
  2. Explain the problem regarding the unethical dual relationship.
  3. Suggest alternate ways of obtaining the information, such as an independent evaluation.
- Regarding confidentiality, err in the direction of caution, with one exception. When there is mandated reporting, a potential Tarasoff situation (discussed at the beginning of this chapter), or a Ewing situation (discussed in chapter 12), consult an attorney immediately, document your response, and proceed with caution. Defense attorneys generally agree that it is easier to defend a breach of confidentiality where the innocent third party was protected from harm than it is to have to justify asserting confidentiality in a way that ultimately led to suicide, murder, or serious injury to an innocent third party. Also, the specifics of the reporting laws regarding the circumstances of minors having sex with minors are usually so complex that you can't possibly be sure you have calculated the minors' exact ages correctly, so seek legal advice.
- You can show your notes and records to the client and supply him or her with a copy or a summary, if you feel it is appropriate. But the physical notes are your property and you may later need them to protect yourself, so never let them out of your possession. Providing a summary is always the best solution.
- Clients do not have the right to determine what should be in your records, how the records are maintained or copied, or whether or not sessions are recorded. If they object, explain that the state gives you and them no choice in the matter and that they must cooperate in record keeping if they wish to remain in therapy with you.
- You may at some point be held accountable for your record keeping by a third party. It is essential that your psychotherapy work be documented in a plausible way for your own and your client's protection, so you must use your own best judgment about what goes into the notes. A colleague of mine, back in the days before note taking became important and before the advent of phenothiazines, was accused of heinous crimes by a deeply damaged and distraught female client. The state immediately swooped down on his office, confiscated all of his files, and then raided everything else in his office and home that might conceivably contain incriminating evidence. Clients past and present were contacted by a team

of state investigators with lies that the good doctor had confessed to such and such crimes, and were asked to state their experience. Seemingly incriminating comments were used out of context against him. State investigators have no professional codes of ethics to live up to and few limits to their roles as policing agents. In the end, the therapist, who was of retirement age, chose to surrender his license rather than to have the unstable client go into a full-blown psychotic break in the courtroom, from which, he was convinced, she would never recover.

- Make a copy for your record, with or without the client's permission, of anything a client shows you, gives you, or allows you to borrow. This is not the client's choice or yours; the state and the profession mandate such records. Your license, livelihood, peace of mind, and personal security can be at stake!

- If you leave an agency or clinic, be sure you take full copies of all of your client records or at least any that might later be a problem. In the event of a later suit by a client, the agency or your former supervisor may be in an adversarial role against you, and you need to have your own copy of the complete record. It is your right to retain a copy of your notes.

- Never send copies of your therapy notes or raw test data to anyone unless you are absolutely sure the notes will not be misused or unless you are absolutely forced to do so by a judge. Discuss the dangers with the client and document the discussion. Limit what you release to summaries that have few specifics and little confidential information. You might want to be cooperative and helpful, but the risks are too great that your notes and data will be misused. The stakes are too high.

- Be especially careful with records and information that are not your own (i.e., that are generated by someone else) and that you have no right to release. Anyone wanting that information must go to the primary source.

- Create "trails of responsibility" wherever you can. Create letters to clients (countersigned in receipt), chart review forms for yourself and your assistants, performance reviews for employees and students, client evaluation forms, and anything else that might demonstrate to a chart reviewer that you are on top of things at all times! The forms on the CD-ROM should help you manage most of these problems.

It's often not what you do that counts, but how you do it. Show thought, consultation, responsibility, and an attitude of keeping the client informed at all times. None of the following record-keeping procedures exist as a standard of care, as they are not done routinely by most therapists, but they are important and for your own protection.

- Keep notes virtually forever! Despite ten-year statutes and case law guidelines (ten years past majority for minors), there is no firm and final statute of limitations on many things in administrative law and ethics committees. Even your estate can be sued after your death. If at some point you shred your notes, retain a summary.
- Make a professional will stipulating the person responsible for the custody of your records. Each file should have a termination summary readily available in case someone later decides to purge your files (guidelines are on the CD-ROM). Your will should stipulate that only closing summaries can be released to properly identified clients or with properly documented releases, and that other materials will only be released by a qualified mental health professional appointed by your custodian and then only with a judge's order—not with an ordinary subpoena.
- The custodian of your records should be alerted to notify all present and past clients of your death and how their files can be accessed. Specifying a $0.25 per page cost to be paid in advance will limit the requests. The custodian is ideally someone licensed in mental health and/or sworn to absolute confidentiality. You must ensure that person's appropriate status. Stipulate that if more than a summary is to be sent, then a mental health professional opinion and legal opinion must be sought.
- Practicing defensively entails having an imaginary third eye that scrutinizes what you are doing. Once this imaginary eye is in place—the same eye that keeps you safe on the road—you will be better able to face the challenge of liability in your practice. Always proceed as if your records are going to be reviewed by a judge and jury or by a state investigator for the licensing board.

4

Practicing Defensively

Complex Treatment Issues

Psychotherapy is conceptualized and practiced in different ways by different schools of psychotherapy as well as by different individuals within schools. For example, psychoanalysts generally refrain from physical contact with clients, while humanistic groups generally recognize the importance of holding and hugs, and body psychotherapists see physical contact as an essential component of their work. Practicing defensively, then, cannot refer to any specific ways of conducting therapy, and standard of care cannot refer to any specific therapeutic technique. Ethics codes state lofty principles that guide members of the profession in their work, and licensing boards have set up regulations by which improper conduct can be judged. But, unfortunately, ethics principles and regulations of licensing boards have all too often been interpreted as narrow and concrete moral guidelines regarding what therapists should and should not be doing. For example, while the American Psychological Association (APA) Code of Ethics allows bartering for services under certain responsible circumstances, when instances of bartering come before the California Board of Psychology, a charge of unprofessional conduct is routinely made. In this discussion the two enduring criteria that are used in civil court to define malpractice—exploitation *and* damage—will be our guide.

REFERRING FOR OUTSIDE ASSESSMENT

If psychotherapy clients ask you to sign authorizations for disability, for the Department of Motor Vehicles, or for other benefits, refer them to third parties for assessment and certification. Stay in the single role of therapist; do not enter into the dual relationship of assessor and therapist.

IRREGULAR TIMES, CIRCUMSTANCES, AND PLACES

Seeing clients on an irregular or occasional basis or in locations other than your professional offices usually does not violate any standard of care per se, but it may present a difficulty for you if you ever have to explain yourself. What follows are a few commonsense guidelines.

In general, the community standard of care under most circumstances is that therapy sessions should be held at least once a week. The disadvantages of a less frequent schedule of sessions should be discussed with the client, and the reason for choosing such a schedule should be documented in the notes. Also document how the schedule affects the treatment plan. Put the therapy agreement in writing, and both you and the client should sign it, as a guard against later distortions or misunderstandings. Therapists often cringe at the thought of putting things in writing and having the client sign or initial in agreement. They fear the client will object, be hurt, quit therapy, or fly out of the room in a rage. However, I find in practice that this almost never happens, and when it does it may be best that the client stop therapy. I find, instead, that clients are usually very reassured that the therapist is concerned about how an irregular schedule might adversely affect the therapy but is willing to try it on a temporary basis, if necessary. The therapist thus presents himself or herself as respectful of the professional, contractual, and mutual-respect aspects of the therapeutic relationship. We can have unusual schedules, but our reasoning and procedures with the client need to be thoroughly documented and consulted on. If later we are called to account, we have documented evidence that we were facing a therapeutic dilemma that we approached with thought, consultation, and an attitude of professional responsibility.

If the client resists the idea of eventually having regularly scheduled once-a-week sessions, give the client notice in writing that you cannot continue the less frequent schedule past a certain date. If necessary, terminate, close the file, and end your liability with a letter that explains that you do not believe it is in the client's best interests to be seen less frequently than once a week. Discuss the termination with the client, and make the proper referrals. If the client does not attend the termination session, send a certified letter. You can leave the door open to therapy in the future, if you choose. (Further considerations about terminating a client for noncompliance are discussed below.)

LIMIT SETTING

When struggling with resistances, set limits and dates, and put into writing why you believe regular sessions, medical consultation, recovery group, or third-party case monitoring is essential to treatment. For example, insisting on recovery group participation for clients with addictions and eating disorders is now often considered to be within the acceptable standard of care by many third parties, though many therapists would consider insisting on such a referral as making an inappropriate demand on their clients. Put your concerns and your requirements into a letter that you personally hand to and discuss with your client. Then have the client countersign your letter, indicating that it was received and understood. Send the letter by certified mail if the client misses the session. But it is best to go over the letter in person and explain the need to work within certain professional parameters. Document reactions, consultation, and follow-up. Proceeding carefully is not a widespread standard of care, but in the interest of practicing defensively you are attempting to cover all bases in the most responsible way and you are creating trails of responsibility for yourself.

GUARDING AGAINST VIOLATIONS OF YOUR E-BOUNDARIES

Clients with borderline and organizing transferences may request extra telephone contact between sessions. In *Listening Perspectives in Psychotherapy* (1983) (see the chapters on borderline personality organization) and in *Working the Organizing Experience* (1994c) (see the chapters on case management of psychotic states), I detail a set of considerations for volunteering extra telephone contact when it is needed, which may make your job easier in the long run. But with changing technology, some new concerns have come up. Some clients may e-mail or fax frequent and long messages, letters, pages from their journal, or notes on their dreams. The therapist should be sure that each of these communications is discussed in session. Have the client read the messages in session so that personal attention and dialogue can be devoted to the concerns raised.

When e-mail messages become too frequent, too lengthy, or too personal, so that the client does not want to go over them in session, go immediately on the alert. Where are these messages coming from? Why are they not important enough to devote time to? What are you expected to do with them—especially if they are confused, confusing, or disturbing to you? Clients often want to gloss over these questions with rationalizations: "I just need to talk to you at certain moments and voice mail or e-mail lets me do it when I'm thinking about it." Or, "If I didn't call or e-mail, then I would forget it." The many implications of the client's self-minimization, not caring if the messages get through, or not being concerned about how they are impacting the therapist need to be taken up directly and forcefully. Clients who relate this way usually show little interest or concern in exploring these or related issues, but the organizing or psychotic transference elements must be addressed. The therapist is not being responded to or related to as a real person with whom to share communication, but more as a mythical fantasized object who is being attached to meaninglessly. To allow this to continue without regularly addressing it and pressuring for real communication in sessions is to collude with the delusion that serves as resistance to exploring the terror and pain frequently at the heart of the organizing (psychotic) transference.

Do not allow clients to put your e-mail address on their buddy list or to show up on each other's IM (instant message) screens, as this runs the risk of colluding with the delusion. You do not need to know when the client is on-line, and you do not want to have to read and respond to extraneous messages from clients when you are on-line. In addition, sending e-mail messages back and forth maintains the delusion that you are constantly available in thought and deed. This is especially troublesome when free-association messages arrive, such as "I just feel like killing myself" or "I could just murder my son." What are you supposed to do then? Since all such messages must be noted and/or printed out for the record, you must also show timely and professional responsiveness. Do you call the client immediately? Do you do a suicide or abuse danger assessment? What other cues and comments can an attorney hurl at you that were sent in an e-mail that you should have been immediately attentive to or careful to systematically follow up?

This technology has crept up on us, and suddenly our personal and private time and space are being invaded by clients wanting to maintain fantasized communication with us that is antitherapeutic and that we cannot ignore. It is best to retain the old posture of taking up all outside communications directly with the client in session and actively discouraging voice mail or e-mail communication that cannot be dealt with directly and that in fact places burdens on you. No long letters or journal entries should be sent to you unless the client intends to read them in session. No voice mail or e-mail should be sent that isn't urgent, and you should not be on clients' buddy lists.

You can explain to the client in a straightforward manner, "I value each and every thing you have to say to me and I want to be in a frame of mind to take you in seriously and to consider thoughtfully and deeply what all the messages you give me may mean to you. Off-the-cuff messages sent and received are fine among friends, but I am your therapist and I want no thought or word you give me to go unnoticed, unattended to, or unheeded. I realize that my taking you so seriously may be a bit burdensome to you at times when you might simply enjoy sharing your thoughts freely with me, but I value every minute, every detail, and every thought and image you directly share with me, and I do not feel comfortable engaging in casual or careless conversation or communication with you. Our mission together is too important." If there is a need for the client to experience timeless reverie with you, then let it be in the session, where you are prepared to deal with it and contextualize it. However, as with all general guidelines about the psychotherapeutic process, the above comments have to be tailored to each case. Some of this "reverie" electronic communication may be important, especially early in therapy during the safety-establishment phase.

The transference behind lengthy and/or heavy impersonal messages is almost invariably of an organizing or psychotic type. The client is terrified of deep and intimate interpersonal engagement because intimate connection was perceived as the agent of trauma in infancy. A replication of the trauma, which in the client's mind is linked with intimate "I-thou" contact, is dreaded and therefore avoided. For the therapist to go along with casual communication not in real time and space is to collude in the resistance memories and to avoid the painful and often terrifying and disruptive process of transference remembering.

Some therapists say, "I listen to the voice mails or read the e-mails because that's the only time the true feelings come out and I learn what's really going on. I hate to stop that flow by restricting it." But don't fool yourself. Almost invariably, these juicy tidbits, as with endless recovered memories of child abuse, endless reciting of paranoid delusions or hallucinations, or endless switching of personalities, are not relevant and usable communications. They are merely the resistance to approaching for, reaching out for, achieving, and sustaining valuable interpersonal connections.

SUICIDE CONTRACTS AND PRECAUTIONS
AGAINST SELF-ABUSIVE ACTIVITIES

Suicide and self-abuse contracts alone are an insufficient standard of care. Common sense requires that you do a risk assessment and take emergency measures if the risk is high. If the risk is moderate, you must mobilize social and family support. If the risk is low, you can continue with careful follow-up. While most attorneys want us to document all suicidal and self-abusive gestures and risks carefully in our notes, some experts point out that a documented risk assessment immediately before a seriously damaging or successful suicide attempt could put us in potential jeopardy. But we want to err on the side of safety. It is always best to document carefully and to seek peer and specialty consultation to cover yourself. You can more easily be defended for a well-reasoned, good-faith breach of confidentiality in a clearly dangerous circumstance than for suicide, homicide, or for serious self or other injury.

All therapists need ongoing continuing education in the area of suicide risk management since research findings continue to expand this critical area of practice. Psychologist/attorney Bryant L. Welch lists eight areas of ongoing concern (Welch 2000).

SUICIDE LIABILITY RISK MANAGEMENT: A SUMMARY

1. Do an initial comprehensive suicide risk assessment of the patient and make assessment an ongoing part of treatment. Be mindful of the suicide risk factors, tapping the latest available literature on the subject.
2. Don't allow yourself to deny a suicide risk.
3. Spend adequate time with the patient.
4. If necessary, make it clear to the managed care company that a lack of treatment could be seen as negligence and result in a lawsuit.
5. Practice full disclosure with the family of the suicidal patient.
6. Educate the patient's family about the signs of potential suicide.
7. Employ good follow-up practices with patients.
8. Always follow good documentation procedures.

Pope and Vasquez (1991) list the following areas to evaluate in determining the risk of a suicide.

1. A direct verbal warning is the single most useful predictor.
2. The presence of a plan increases the risk.
3. Eighty percent of completed suicide attempts have been preceded by previous attempts.
4. People give away their plans by indirect references.
5. Depression is a significant predictor; 15 percent of clinically depressed people kill themselves.
6. Hopelessness is highly associated with suicide intent.
7. One-fourth to one-third of successful suicides are associated with drug or alcohol intoxication.
8. Suicide rates are higher in diagnosable clinical syndromes such as depression, alcoholism, primary mood disorders, and schizophrenia— and with clients who have relatives who have committed suicide.
9. The suicide rate for men is three times greater than for women, and five times higher for young men.
10. Suicide risk increases with age and the life cycle, peaking between the mid-50s to the mid-60s.
11. In the United States, Caucasians have the highest rate.

12. Suicide rates are higher among Protestants than among Jews and Catholics.
13. The risk is highest for those living alone, less if living with a spouse, and less if there are children.
14. Bereavement over lost loved ones in recent years increases the risk.
15. Unemployment increases the suicide risk.
16. Illness and somatic complaints, just like sleep and eating disturbances, increase the risk.
17. Those with high impulsivity are at increased risk for taking their own lives.
18. Rigid thinking increases the risk; for example, a person who says such things as, "If I don't find work in the next week the only real alternative is to kill myself."
19. Any stressful event is likely to destabilize a person, putting her or him at higher risk for suicide.
20. The risk is greater after weekend hospital leaves and after being discharged from a hospital.

Clients who engage in chronic and intractable suicidal gestures, self-mutilating activities, or other potentially self-abusive or harmful behaviors may need to be terminated and referred out of individual psychotherapy on the basis of unmanageability. The resources we have at our disposal often do not meet the client's needs. This must be explained to the client early in therapy, and limits must be set and put into writing with consequences that are effectively followed through on. I have seen many therapists struggle compassionately for long periods of time with clients, making clear in a no-fault, nonpunitive fashion that they are not equipped to deal with such intense and dangerous expressions, so that these forms of communication have to be renounced in order for therapy to continue. It is usually the therapist's resistance to limit-setting and systematic follow-through that slows down the process. But the bottom line is that no therapist is in a personal or professional position to receive endlessly, or to respond effectively to, chronic life-threatening or safety-endangering communications.

If it is not possible to contain the therapy work in manageable limits, the client must be referred to a more appropriate intensive therapeutic resource or to a setting where different liability parameters exist. (See my later suggestions on terminating a noncompliant client and for considerations on how to do limit-setting work, systematic terminations, responsible referrals, and precautionary follow-ups.)

Almost all clients confronted in this seemingly harsh way about how important their therapy work is, how crucial safe and manageable nonthreatening communications are for the sanity and well-being of the therapist, and how the client must find alternative forms of experiencing and communicating her or his concerns, in fact, do find different, creative, and contained ways of continuing their therapy work with the therapist safely. But the therapist has to believe that alternate forms of communication are essential for mutual safety and that they are achievable within the creative potential of the client for the limit setting to work effectively. If the client truly cannot comply in this way your liability is simply too great to continue with her or him.

I had a strange experience a few years ago in which a man whom I had consulted with on a series of other high-risk clients wanted to run by me the first few months of his work with a new client. He had her sign the Informed Consent for Assessment Consultation and told her he would consider making a therapy commitment to her on the condition that during an extended trial phase she could and would conform to certain parameters for treatment that he deemed necessary. Seeing her at the first session as highly unstable and risky, this skillful therapist launched into a series of carefully calculated contracts for psychiatric consultation, an active third party case manager, certified recovery group participation, emergency hospitalization procedures, and interviews with family members to set up support plans. These are strong preventative measures but he correctly sensed what the noncompliance problems were likely to be. He is an extremely warm and compassionate man but he showed her he meant business with the result that she was "cooperating like a lamb."

I say he correctly sensed her deep vulnerability and acting out potential because at some point in the consultation I felt I knew this client and asked him who her previous therapist had been. As chance would have it, I had consulted with her very warm and empathic previous therapist off and on for six months through a long and trying period of limit setting around irresponsible and dangerous self-destructive behaviors and noncompliance with the therapeutic requirements set forth by the beleaguered and frightened therapist. There were pleadings, phone calls by the therapist to various support clinics and psychiatrists that the client failed to follow up on, and letters written to the client stating the therapist's limitations, until finally the therapist, feeling very defeated, was forced to termination and referred the client to several nonprofit clinic settings. The client had begged to continue but the therapist by that time was firm in her determination not to collude in life-threatening and endangering communications.

When the client located her new therapist through friends she had learned her lesson by being painfully thrown out—and now she was being most cooperative. Several years later the treatment goes well and I am convinced that it is because finally one of her long line of therapists knew enough in advance and cared enough to firmly insist on nonthreatening, safe forms of communication from the outset that both client and therapist could work with comfortably and effectively.

I have, needless to say, witnessed some other particularly bitter instances that did not work out so well. But the therapists' sufferings taught them what their own limits of tolerance were and what kind of clients they would never agree to take on again. I strongly believe that we can engage in transformational therapy regardless of the kind or depth of pathology per se. But we must have the client's basic cooperation and a level of available resource appropriate for the work. Sometimes it is the client's cooperation we lack. Most of the time it is the resource to contain the therapy on an outpatient basis satisfactorily and safely that is not available. But sometimes the training, experience, and skill of the therapist do not permit a sufficient understanding of the nature of deep organizing transferences and how to respond to the profound regressions, physical agonies, and mental terrors inevitably encountered in long-term, relationally oriented, dynamic psychotherapy.

In another malpractice case I consulted on not long ago, the self-injuring client had ended up in the emergency room requiring stitches an average of three times a month for more than four years, despite heroic efforts on everyone's part to contain and limit the acting out of the reexperiencing of early and damaging abuse. I discovered the following pattern: some event in the real world or some memory of trauma would precipitate a crisis, setting off a severe depression and panic attack for which the client would go to the therapist's office on an emergency basis seeking containment and physical calming. Frequent sessions, phone contacts, and emergency procedures were set up, including a backup emergency room team. However, the client's financial resources and the community's available support resources did not include hospitalization, day treatment, or ongoing therapeutic support. The limit was six sessions of crisis work. The therapist felt stuck with no place to refer her client and did her best to be available to keep her contained and alive. There were only a few signs of progress.

The local psychiatrist experimented with a wide variety of antidepressants, antianxiety agents, and sleeping pills, finally settling on mild doses of Thorazine to treat extreme panic attacks and dissociative episodes. The client was diagnosed primarily as posttraumatic stress disorder in the context of a severe borderline personality disorder, but, unfortunately, not as dissociative identity disorder or ambulatory psychosis, because of her high intelligence and verbal skills. During her panic attacks the client could, with a little time and talking down, be calmed by the therapist and sent safely home. But at home she would then dissociate, cut herself, fall asleep, and be awakened later in a pool of blood by her roommate, a friend, or the therapist stopping by to check on her when she failed to answer her phone. The situation was grim and frightening to the therapist, and the emotional pattern from the abuse of the family of origin had been formulated many ways with a host of terrifying and seemingly believable memories continuing to emerge.

Friends counseled the client to seek out another therapist, who, in turn, began alternate ways of containing her and calming the panic. Over time, the second therapist became similarly bogged down in unsuccessful containment tactics so that the therapeutic dialogue came to revolve around not only the neglect and abuse from her family of origin and from several previous boyfriends, but also from her former therapist—resulting in the not-so-veiled suggestion by the second therapist that the client sue her.

The pattern that I felt was being missed by all concerned was that the apparently successful intimate interpersonal, and usually physical, containment and calming provided by caring others including the therapists regularly stimulated the reexperiencing of the internalized experience of infantile abuse in a dissociated state. What was not being systematically attended to was the client's persistent and predictable agony associated with intimate connection and the terror that nurturing containment invariably set off in her.

When therapists mistakenly believe that attunement, connection, containment, and holding are experienced as desirable, good, and safe by such a client, what is being systematically overlooked is the terrifying transference that is immediately set off by the connection or threatened connection—that the organizing-level transference is dynamically associated with trauma and abuse that are actively reexperienced by the client as an abortive attempt at mastery. Mastery of primitive trauma cannot possibly succeed without systematic attention being paid to the physical agonies and mental terrors being regularly stimulated by caring connections, similar to those experienced in infancy as traumatic. In *Terrifying Transferences: Aftershocks of Childhood Trauma* (Hedges 2000b), eleven psychotherapists with different orientations join with me to portray the in-depth experiences of this kind of therapy. There is a similar set of illuminating in-depth case studies presented by eight therapists and discussed by peer review teams of therapists in *In Search of the Lost Mother of Infancy* (Hedges 1994a). There are also numerous poignant vignettes that illustrate the full statement of theory for this deep transference work in *Working the Organizing Experience. Transformation of Psychotic, Schizoid, and Autistic States* (Hedges 1994c). These books are replete with references to research in treatment with primitive mental states, and, in his foreword to the latter book, James Grotstein brilliantly reviews the literature leading up to our present state of understanding of how psychotic states emerge in psychotherapy.

ACCUSATIONS AND PROFESSIONAL APOLOGIES

Massachusetts has enacted a professional apology statute barring the use of an apology by a professional as evidence against the professional in court. Harvard studies have shown that an empathic "I'm sorry" increases the chances of healing a wound, thereby enabling the therapist to stay more connected. All of our professional organizations should endorse similar legislation soon. California now has a similar provision in the Business and Professions code.

Virginia Wink Hilton (1993), in her article "When We Are Accused," points out that a three-part response to accusation arises almost instinctively from most of us: (1) denial—"I didn't do it," (2) defense—"I did the best I could," and (3) blame—"She knows better than this; this accusation is pathological." The real problem, says Hilton, is that an accusation often is aimed, somewhat successfully, at a core emotional wound of the accused, at a blind spot or Achilles' heel. Until the accused is able to work through the core wound as it is active in the present relationship, it is unlikely that he will be able to give a satisfying response to the accuser who "knows" she is right.

Hilton charts a course for us: (1) Avoid denial, defensiveness, and blame; (2) use consultation to work through the core wound the accusation touches in oneself; (3) show the client that you know how deeply he or she has been wounded by you or by the position you have taken; and (4) provide some reassurance that this particular kind of injury can somehow be averted or softened in the future—that is, "This won't happen again to you or anyone else."

Hilton also believes that the most sensitive moment in the accusatory process is when the client first broaches the accusation with the therapist. First, she says, it takes a lot of courage to confront someone you believe is, or has been, abusing you. Second, given that transference distortions are likely to be in operation and the high probability that the accusation will be successfully aimed at a core wound of the accused, it is important for the therapist to make every effort to grasp what the client is saying, to show an understanding of how the client feels you have hurt him or her, and to acknowledge how determined the client is to see to it that you do not do so again.

Understanding the client correctly and extending deep empathy can save professionals a lot of time, expense, and grief. You can easily acknowledge that you now see that what you did (or didn't do) caused hurt to the client, and to make matters worse, it was *you* of all people, someone who "should have known better." Acknowledge that despite your best intentions, you failed to show a full understanding of the client. "No wonder this hurt so much." The Informed Consent for Long-Term Psychotherapy (see the CD-ROM) provides further guidelines for handling difficult accusatory situations in therapy.

Acting out of transference-based false accusations against therapists in complaints and lawsuits will not stop until therapists become knowledgeable and skilled in working with traumatized, abused, and terrified primitive layers of the human mind. Unjust prosecutions will not stop until licensing boards, administrative law judges, and ethics committees come to appreciate how transference from infantile trauma operates.

WHEN THIRD PARTIES ARE IN POTENTIAL DANGER

When you have information that your client or some other identifiable person may be in danger or endangering others (such as a pilot or bus driver using drugs), consult an attorney regarding your responsibility—unless your Tarasoff duty clearly requires immediate action. As a preventative measure, you can give an up-front disclosure before things reach a crisis point when you have a duty to report imminent and foreseeable dangers. The general rule here, as elsewhere, is to inform clients. Talk with them about everything that might come up well in advance and get consultation yourself so you are clear on your course of action. Explain what factors might force you out of the role of therapist, such as child or elder abuse. When it comes to other Tarasoff or Ewing situations, such as HIV contagion or sexually transmitted diseases, check immediately with an attorney if you have questions about your legal duty regarding a client's endangering others or giving you information about endangered others. Under certain circumstances you may be able to take action without breaching confidentiality. But HIV and other sexually transmitted disease information is now usually protected by law, so be careful not to disclose it to anyone, including the managed care provider.

The duty to warn is a complex issue that is still being reviewed and litigated, so our professional obligations continue to shift. For example, a Texas court decision went against the well-established Tarasoff decision and the California Ramona ruling regarding duties to third parties—even though those decisions have by now been codified into law in many states. The recent Ewing cases have set new duty to warn precedents which are reviewed later in this book. This is another example of why we cannot practice defensively without an ongoing relationship with a *therapy-knowledgeable* attorney whom we can call upon at any time for quick advice when complex and detailed matters come up.

TELEHELP AND TECHNOLOGY

The theory of Telehelp is to make better services available to rural areas. But speaking to someone in a carefully monitored rural medical program directly on the telephone or videophone is not the same as faxes, e-mails, or Internet communications. The APA ethics committee has stated that therapy is primarily a face-to-face personal encounter that relies on nonverbal cues and body language, so that real presence in real time is important on an ongoing basis. Interim and/or emergency or support telephone contacts are permitted if you document the need, the appropriateness, the discussion, the process, your consultation on the matter, and if there is some regular or periodic face-to-face contact as well.

Electronic communication always compromises confidentiality and thus poses many dangers for us. As the technological future unfolds, the closer to video and real time electronic contacts are made, the better. Health care delivery is not yet litigated to the extent that contract law is. But lawyers are looking for new kinds of cases so they can make new laws for us!

Refrain from giving Internet or media advice without consulting your malpractice insurance carrier and your attorney. For additional considerations, see the Informed Consent for Phone, Mail, and Electronic Communication (on the CD-ROM).

If you engage in client contact over the telephone or Internet, be aware that you are not licensed to practice in other states and there are many ethical considerations and contradictory laws to consider. Electronic communication remains a fuzzy legal area, so be very cautious, document thoughtfully, and seek expert consultation. Portable cell phones are highly susceptible to breaches in confidentiality, but a voice-scrambler feature helps by randomly switching the signal around among ten channels. In one recent suit for breach of confidentiality, a neighbor, who happened to know the client, listened into a cell phone conversation and reported what she heard to another concerned party.

Teaching and academic work done over the Internet are left alone for the time being, but litigation in our field is increasingly holding supervisors, trainers, and training institutions liable. Since the plaintiff bar can no longer make money on sexual misconduct allegations, attorneys are looking for other deep pockets and other practices to hold us accountable for.

CONSIDERING THE POTENTIAL PITFALLS OF ADULATION OF PSYCHOTHERAPISTS

When clients tell you that they have a sexual or other personal or special interest in you, be sure to document what they said, how you responded, your consultation with a peer, and how you systematically followed it up. Similarly, when clients tell you a dream in which you are a sexualized or idealized participant (in either a clear or a disguised way), document and consult.

Document excessive interest in your personal life or indications that the client wants to be very special to you. Document feelings of envy or jealousy shown toward your friends, colleagues, and/or family. Deal with stalking in any form promptly and effectively, and document it.

Be careful about the client's gifts, seductive attire, cards and letters. Avoid giving or receiving gifts unless they can clearly be seen as tokens that are special or meaningful to what you are working on in therapy. Note: $25 is the maximum IRS allowable gift, and $50 is the maximum allowed for congressional representatives on Capitol Hill, so stay within those limits. Document thoroughly. Limit client contact outside of the office as well as physical touching.

When a client appears in your fantasies or dreams, document it outside of the record first, then consult with a colleague and consider including it in the record. If you should choose to share your dreams, feelings, or fantasies with clients, document them along with all countertransference disclosures, as previously discussed.

Seek consultation whenever you find you are reluctant to consider a client in clinical terms or find yourself interpreting client material in terms of symbols or experiences that come from your own life. Especially watch countertransference disclosures that relate to your own troubled past or present, as they are easily misconstrued by clients, lawyers, state investigators, and judges.

Good therapists can easily be taken in or confused by the power of lifelong transferences of clients. When you find yourself feeling special toward or doing special things for clients, such as making special accommodations, dressing special, or watching what you say to clients for personal reasons, you are on the path to being seduced! Don't be ashamed, you are only doing your job of empathetically connecting. But seek consultation immediately to recover your grounding. Document in general terms the issues and the consultation, but omit particulars that could be used against you.

SEX AND OTHER RELATIONSHIPS WITH CLIENTS AND FORMER CLIENTS

The 2002 APA Code of Ethics forbids sexual relationships with clients forever, even after therapy ends. It further limits all relationships that run the risk of being exploitative or damaging by virtue of the power differential that exists between a psychologist and his or her clients, supervisees, trainees, students, and other employees. This new prohibition includes all relationships with supervisees, students, and other subordinates over whom you have ever had a power-differential relationship in the past. Start now by limiting personal and/or intimate relationships that could ever conceivably be potentially damaging or exploitative or could be construed as such by outside third parties.

Here we learn another subtle lesson in the way licensing boards and plaintiff attorneys attempt to set up arbitrary and false standards of care. Only psychologists are now under the "No sex forever" rule, though research on transference lasting forever has been available for years. But it will quickly be applied to all psychotherapists and then by implication to all others who function like psychologists. Thus, even before the other professions deliberate on the issues, their members will be silently expected to be operating under this standard. This is the way case laws you never heard of are seemingly made to apply to you and to what you do every day. Somewhere a case is tried and a precedent is set. The principles enunciated by the judge in the decision now become implicit standards by which you can be judged under similar circumstances. This is why, to practice safely, we need an attorney available to guide our decisions. There are numerous liabilities, and the number continues to grow.

TERMINATION OF THE PROFESSIONAL RELATIONSHIP

Terminating a psychotherapeutic relationship is more complex than terminating other kinds of personal and professional relationships. The only widely recognized standard of care issue here, however, is that ending may precipitate a flood of emotional issues that need to be carefully handled. Wrongful termination and/or abandonment charges usually revolve around insufficient time, consideration, discussion, referral, or follow-up. There are a few basic considerations that can guide your thinking.

Be sure to explain clearly in your initial and ongoing informed consents the clients' right to terminate at any time and that you will from time to time be evaluating with them their progress and the possibility that other forms of treatment might be more effective. The APA Code of Ethics requires that you terminate a person who is not improving. This means in long-term work the burden of proof is on the therapist to document in regular notes, periodic reviews, and peer consultations that, despite expectable regressions, definite progress is being made and what that progress looks like. Document all patient responses that indicate progress is being perceived and all discussions about what is improving and why. Patients can later complain that they were making no progress and that you wouldn't let them terminate, but when your notes reflect frequent reviews with the client as well as cards and letters with messages to the contrary, you are on firm ground to defend yourself.

You can terminate a person for noncompliance with any aspect of the treatment plan, for example, for irregular attendance, frequent absences, failure to pay the fee, and failure to follow prescriptions such as seeing consultants, taking medications, signing documents, or attending support groups. You must give warning in writing and allow the client the time and opportunity to talk things over. You need to obtain a signature indicating that the client has received the warning and has been advised of the conditions for continuing treatment and that she or he will be terminated unless these conditions are met. If the client misses the termination session, send a certified letter. Include three referrals to places that may be better able to serve the client's needs. Taking your time and documenting each move carefully is more important than getting paid, so don't foolishly refuse to see the person (gratis) to review termination, referral, and follow-up matters.

The client's unwillingness or inability to comply with the treatment plan is reason to terminate. But to be safe, run the situation by a psychotherapy consultant and possibly by an attorney to be sure you give proper notice, plenty of time for discussion, and a systematic closeout, referral, and follow-up. You can terminate and refer clients because you believe you do not possess the requisite training and expertise to treat them further. You have gotten consultation and concluded that their present needs are no longer appropriate for your particular forms of treatment and expertise. You can terminate and refer clients for their refusal or inability to pay your fees. But be sure that you have given sufficient warning, have processed the termination thoroughly, and provided adequate referral and follow-up services that are accessible and affordable.

Fee collection processes after the professional contact has terminated are never a good idea. If you haven't collected your money ahead of time (as in testing or forensics) or if you haven't collected it at the time of service or regularly as you go along, you can be accused of a dual relationship (i.e., serving as a banker), or much worse bogus charges of negligence and unprofessional conduct can be trumped up to block or delay the collection process. So consider the lost dollars your lesson in poor judgment, poor business practices, or bad luck. Send a few bills and if no response arrives, write off the balance. This is the cost of doing business with some clients. Learn whom not to take on.

Liability being what it is today, we are no longer safe seeing clients occasionally or when they are in the mood to come in. Regular once-a-week sessions indicate that clients are under your care or in treatment with you. This is especially true for unstable, high-risk, or dangerous clients. If they refuse or are unable to maintain an ongoing and reliable treatment relationship, terminate them and refer them to a nonprofit or public crisis clinic where they can be seen less frequently or as needed.

Allow time for discussion of termination plans, whether or not you get paid for your time. Never abandon clients in a crisis—or at least not until they are securely under other appropriate professional care. Be sure to follow through until the client is safely connected elsewhere. For clients who are dangerous to themselves or others, follow-ups for a 90-day period are recommended.

When you are terminating a client for noncompliance, it is best to refer to nonprofit clinics or government agencies that have sliding fees, psychiatric access, and a team approach. These settings generally have better resources and liability coverage than we do. You can be held liable for any and all your referrals but a licensed public clinic is nearly always a safe bet.

If you are choosing to refer or terminate clients, put into writing the reasons why, what aspects of the treatment plan they have failed to follow, what kinds of services they need, and where they may obtain those services. Present the letter in person during a session (if possible) and ask for a signature of receipt and/or send the termination letter by certified mail. You can offer to receive cards and letters if you wish, but be clear that you are not providing interim services and the door is not open until and unless clients enter another treatment contract with you. Explain why after termination you cannot be available for them to check in with unless they go through another assessment and contract process. The situation and your after-therapy policies would be somewhat different with clients who are terminating after a successful course of psychotherapy. But still, do you want the responsibility, and liability, of seeing a client on an occasional or as-needed basis? Probably not.

You can be faulted for failing to follow up on a referral or termination by not making contact with the client or with the therapist to whom you referred the client to be sure that the client has made the connection or is otherwise doing okay. The client's failure to connect to a subsequent therapist or treatment facility still leaves you with a potential liability as the most recent therapist who might have done something more than you did.

The APA 2002 Code of Ethics has finally added another critical cause for termination—abuse of the therapist. This has been a known problem in certain cases for years but now constitutes a cause to terminate. Since abusive clients are highly likely to complain or sue, therapists are advised to work closely with professional and legal consultation while terminating such clients. However, under no circumstances should therapists allow themselves to be in dangerous situations without personal security measures firmly in place

5

Minding the Mind Business

Practicing defensively involves not only how we practice psychotherapy but also how we address a number of administrative issues. We may need outside consultants who can guide us in these matters, although issues such as consultation with therapists and hiring interns and psychological assistants are more straightforward.

MANAGING MANAGED CARE

Managed care generally supports only short-term psychotherapy, not the long-term intensive psychotherapy that this book focuses on. But when you do work for managed care companies, remember that *the professional contract is always between the client and you* and that you are professionally liable to the client, but you are otherwise contractually liable to the managed care company. So read your contract carefully to be sure it does not put you into conflict with your professional role responsibilities. You should explain to managed care clients at the first session the distinctions between long-term and short-term therapy, and that their insurance only covers short-term therapy. Make clear to clients (1) the nature of their coverage, (2) their responsibilities to you, (3) how this kind of therapy terminates, (4) how you would or would not be able to continue working with them privately, and (5) what their options are for pursuing or continuing therapy elsewhere.

You must also explain the nature of your contract with their managed care company, the dual role you are in, and the potential implications of that role in the therapy. Document your discussion and clarifications after the first session. Some therapists who work for managed care companies have a special managed care informed consent form that covers all these issues, and they have clients sign it as a disclosure statement at the first session. You also need to consider carefully at the first session whether you want to continue seeing clients or refer them back to the case manager. Referral and termination may present difficulties at a later time in the therapy. There is no point in agreeing to work with untreatable, uncooperative, or unmanageable clients who may pose a problem later.

Study all managed care contracts carefully so you are not caught in professionally compromising situations. Do not criticize managed care coverage in the sessions, but rather discuss the client's benefits in a neutral way and describe how therapy will need to proceed. When clients have problems with the coverage, suggest that they contact the benefits manager, who is really in charge. Never compromise your professional judgment or your duty to your client because of decisions managed care companies make.

Be especially careful when releasing or terminating unstable, disturbed, or potentially suicidal or dangerous clients under managed care. It can be maintained under law that if you keep appealing administrative decisions that limit the duration or type of therapy, the managed care company has to pay for client services in the meantime. Managed care companies are increasingly being forced to show accountability for treatment decisions, so they are generally more cooperative with providers now than they have been in the past. By appealing decisions indefinitely you force the carrier to share liability for dangerous or unstable clients. If you follow the case manager's treatment plan without appeal, the liability is all yours. Read your contract carefully and use whatever appeals processes are possible. It is better to incur the managed care company's anger than risk a lawsuit. You can explain the position you are ethically obligated to take, and why you realistically have no option but to continue seeing the client as your appeals for more treatment are pending. Thus, on the one hand, you inform clients of the conflict of interest that you necessarily work under when contracting with their carrier and the short-term nature of their benefits, and, on the other hand, you insist with managed care on the integrity of your professional judgment, and don't back off until both you and the client are safe.

The first assessment session may be your only opportunity to refer elsewhere a client who might turn out to be trying and traumatic for you in the long run. Use this opportunity to reject cases on the grounds of the special expertise, medical or otherwise, that you believe may be required to provide appropriate treatment.

CONSIDERING INCORPORATING

Therapists incorporate their practices for a variety of reasons. If you are considering doing so, your accountant can help you decide what is important for your circumstances. However, corporate "shields" will not give you additional malpractice or administrative complaint protection.

On the other hand, the nonprofit corporate shield does work to limit your potential liability somewhat and may also protect you somewhat from negative board actions. The legislatures and courts have an interest in nonprofit organizations created "by the people, for the people, to serve the people," and more protection is built in when nonprofit organizations are functioning properly. This is why high-risk clients are often best referred to such nonprofit agencies. Additionally, high-risk clients can usually be legally treated by non-licensed staff therapists who work in nonprofit agencies, further limiting the potential civil liability of the therapist as well as the danger of administrative complaints. Despite how limited we may think agency or unlicensed therapy is, beginning therapists with more heart than training and who are supervised often do surprisingly well with very difficult cases! Referrals to responsible nonprofit settings with sliding scale fees, the possibility of additional weekly sessions, and reasonable medical and emergency coverage are appropriate for these types of clients.

VICARIOUS LIABILITY AND MAKING REFERRALS

The important principle here is that several professionals working together as a group, with a group name and group advertisements, are jointly held responsible for one another's professional conduct. So if you are merely sharing office space, use written disclaimers such as the one found on the Informed Consent for Psychotherapy Assessment Consultation (see the CD-ROM). Post a sign in your waiting room that states, "All clinicians in this office conduct independent practices."

With in-house referrals, be sure to specify the independence of the other professional. Kickbacks of any kind are, of course, illegal. The question that can be raised regarding in-house referrals is what did you have to gain. Be sure the professionals you refer to are ethical and competent, because as the referring person you will be named in any subsequent lawsuit against them. This is another liability-limiting reason for referring to responsible nonprofit, public, or community agencies and medical treatment resources.

Be wary about making referrals to managed care panel members. Don't recommend someone just because you have heard of that person and he happens to be on a panel of providers. You can be held liable for any referral you make, even to an attorney, a chiropractor, a beauty salon, a psychic, or your favorite deli!

ADVERTISING YOUR WARES

The cardinal rule is, be professional and promise nothing, especially if you are advertising a specialty treatment program such as for eating disorders, addictions, or pain control. Also, when identifying yourself to the public as "Christian," "gay," "New Age," and so forth, be aware that you are setting yourself up to collude in defenses that revolve around group identity. When the transference later thickens, you can be seen as colluding with poor, limiting, narrow, or self-destructive lifestyle decisions. If you're a Christian, then how can a client have unchristian thoughts while he's with you, much less express them to you? If you're gay, the client can suppose that you agree with whatever gay thing he is doing, no matter how dangerous. Use specialties and special identities for marketing if they help, but promise nothing and be aware of and document potential problems. Therapists setting up practices that mingle religion and psychotherapy need to be mindful about the hazards of mixing the two, such as complaints that you are a licensed therapist but are teaching that "prayer alone heals."

PROFESSIONAL AND PEER CONSULTATION

Frequent consultation on cases is rapidly becoming touted by the plaintiff s bar and by licensing boards as the national standard of care. But in fact few cases ever get consulted on. If you do not belong to a peer consultation group, consider forming one that meets regularly to review cases. Keep a group log of cases discussed for documentation purposes. If you hear of a breach of law or ethics in the group, you are obligated to get your colleagues to address the problem, but not obligated to report it unless reporting is mandated.

The purpose of case consultation or peer consultation groups may be primarily educational and consultative. But since these processes are confidential and entail discussing personal (i.e., countertransference) as well as professional issues, a therapist can usually claim privilege based on business and profession codes regarding "peer counseling." California has such a provision. Therapists must check their own state or province.

Liability issues are involved in supervision, case consultation, and educational consultation. I developed the Informed Consent for Case Conference

Seminars and Individual Tutorials (on the CD-ROM) because clients who had been brought up in consultation groups years before later named consultants on the case in a complaint against the therapist. By distinguishing clearly among (1) statutory supervision, such as is required for licensure and in which the supervisor is co-responsible to the client; (2) case consultation, in which the consultant actually sees the client in one form or another such as in psychological testing and thus shares in the liability; and (3) individual tutorials and case conference seminars, which are primarily educational and personal in nature and in which the educational consultant cannot be held liable because the information is partial, anecdotal, and disguised and the goals primarily educational and/or personal rather than clinical, I found I could appropriately limit my liability as a consultant on cases.

SUPERVISION AND EMPLOYMENT OF STUDENTS AND INTERNS

Supervisors, agencies, and training institutions are now regularly being named in legal actions and board complaints against therapists and therapists-in-training. Supervision is usually done via verbal reports of the therapist to the supervisor. The crucial question is: Have you done everything possible to supervise in an effective and reasonable manner? Be sure you have, and that you have documented it! For example, in specific circumstances are a verbal report and a verbal response sufficient in supervision? Research indicates that what is often most important in psychotherapy happens nonverbally. Since supervisors are usually seen as having authority and control and a duty to the client, what else did you as a supervisor do to be sure you were getting accurate information? Consider some form of audio or video taping, client satisfaction inventories, conjoint sessions with the therapist and client, and/or occasional sessions alone with the client. How creative can you become in your particular setting? What follows are some questions and suggestions that may help guide your thinking.

Do you begin your supervisory relationship with a written contract stating what you do and do not expect of a trainee? Do you spell out in advance what infractions you may report to the school or licensing board, what constitutes adequate functioning, and what will be done to monitor and report less-than-satisfactory performance? Have you put into writing what behaviors might result in immediate termination, such as criminal or fraudulent behavior or sexual contact with a client? The Employment Agreement for Trainees (on the CD-ROM) can be used as a model.

Document carefully all that you do and all materials that you review. Consider dating and initialing all forms and notes you have gone over. Then if some documents escape your attention and are later brought up in connection with a lawsuit, you are in a position to say that you were never privy to this information. Create as many "trails of responsibility" as you can. Consider setting up a system of random file checks. The charges for your time and work can be included in your overhead just like the fees for accounting, clerical time, and your supervisory time. Have trainees keep one 100-minute cassette going on each client at all times, constantly re-recording it so that only the two most recent sessions are available for you to monitor. Document your impressions. Material from critical sessions can be extracted and filed when desired. Consider using for each supervised session a one-page form for progress notes that has critical item checklists and a place for the trainee to initial and for you to make supervisory comments (sample forms are on the CD-ROM).

When you are supervising unlicensed therapists, most schools and boards require that a letter be given to all clients that is signed by you and countersigned and dated by clients regarding the unlicensed status of the therapist and stating how to contact you directly for questions and complaints. Informed consents of supervisees need to be essentially the same as or similar to your own.

You cannot be held responsible for everything your supervisees do, but you must do everything possible to ensure the safety and well-being of the client and to ensure against foreseeable dangers, such as boundary violations, dual relationships, and therapists having sex with clients. If any client or trainee refuses for any reason the note taking or recording that you deem essential, then she or he must be terminated in order to limit your liability. Your right to do this needs to be clearly spelled out in the contract you have the person sign at the beginning of the relationship.

Since there is a recent upsurge of complaints against supervisors and administration of training clinics, I would suggest all clinics carefully review their polices, procedures and forms and revise or carefully write manuals and training documents that tighten the reins on students and provide better student contact and less liability for supervisors. What has passed for adequate supervision in the past is no longer viable!

CONSULTATION AND TRAINING
WITH PROFESSIONAL COLLEAGUES

To the degree that you do not have firsthand knowledge of the client, you may not be held responsible for your consultation work with licensed colleagues. But you do need to have an informed consent for the therapist to sign at the beginning of your relationship specifying that: (1) the consultation is educational and/or personal in nature; (2) for ethical reasons all client material must be carefully disguised; (3) information provided the consultant is necessarily confidential, though incomplete and anecdotal; and (4) therefore nothing you may do or say is to be construed as fully informed or responsible advice on how to treat the client. In other words, their license, not yours, is on the line in the work with the client. (See the Informed Consent for Case Conference Seminars and Individual Tutorials on the CD-ROM.) I long ago stopped using the terms group and individual supervision in all training and consultative situations in which I could not reasonably maintain case responsibility and liability. "Supervisor" conveys a sense of responsibility that "consultant" and "tutor" do not.

Therapists may opt to call individual and group consultation "peer consultation," and thus claim privilege (in most states) since personal material is involved and all such sessions are confidential in nature. With an informed consent in place and client privilege specifically ensured, as a case consultant or tutor you can save yourself a lot of time and court expense later.

LEGAL FEES AND EXPERT WITNESS ISSUES

Your informed consents should contain (as the sample forms on the CD-ROM do) a clause specifying that the client is responsible for any and all legal costs arising out of your contact with her or him. Otherwise, if you go to court, you may go as an unpaid percipient witness to facts. Only if you are designated and sworn in as an expert witness can you be certain of charging a forensic fee and freely give your opinion, unless you have a clause in every informed consent holding the client responsible for all legal fees that may come up and then you can charge your regular fee. The Legal Fees and Expert Witness Availability form (on the CD-ROM) should be signed by responsible parties before you agree to do expert witness work for people who are not your regular psychotherapy clients.

VOLUNTEER WORK AND SPEAKING CONTRACTS

When you do pro bono work or when you do public speaking or teaching for a fee, you should always set up a contract or letter of agreement (signed by all parties) specifying the nature and extent of the services, who is professionally liable, what the fees and expectations are, and what other conditions and penalties (including legal fees) there may be.

CONSIDERING A PROFESSIONAL WILL

When a therapist becomes incapacitated or dies it is important for everyone involved to have adequate instructions available to manage the client's feelings of loss and abandonment and to ensure confidentiality and proper disposition of records. All therapists should have professional wills.

In your will, designate a licensed therapist or a committee of therapists who can be available to step in and carry out instructions on your behalf. The will authorizes the emergency team to have access to your professional and financial records and appoints someone as custodian of records. It further specifies how your patients, present and past, are to be contacted and perhaps even contains a letter from you to clients explaining whom they can contact for further help and how they can access their records. Are you willing to have their files transferred to another therapist or do you only wish to have copies sent, and if so, copies of what? If you only want summaries sent, specify so or specify under what conditions a full record can be sent. Be sure to specify to the custodian of records not to send records in your file that belong to someone else, such as a previous therapist's report or other consultations that you do not have the right to release. Specify how long records are to be kept, how and when files can be purged to a summary-only status, and what records should be kept indefinitely. Are there records that should not be released to clients or should not be released without a court order? Under what conditions, if any, are your HIPAA protected Psychotherapy Notes to be released?

Your professional will should include instructions to the emergency team as to where to locate present and past appointment books, ledgers, computer and voice mail security codes, special abbreviations or notations you use routinely, and any other information required to follow your instructions. Those who follow up should conduct face-to-face interviews with all current clients, provide three referral sources, and call for follow-up to be sure your clients have connected elsewhere. Instructions should be left for client contact with the family, funeral attendance, and so forth.

Interns and assistants practicing under your license must also be provided for. Check the laws on whether they can see clients under interim supervision or whether an interim therapist must be appointed until they are re-registered under someone else's license. Where are their contracts and how can agreements be terminated effectively.

ARBITRATION AND LIMITATION OF LIABILITY AGREEMENTS

In an effort to limit exposure to litigation many hospitals, doctors, and HMO contracts now include mandatory arbitration clauses. For such a provision to be fully effective, it must be executed at the beginning of treatment to ensure arm's length negotiation before the trust relationship has developed. Arbitration offers a significant cost savings over lawsuits in superior court and is a process that is likely to be much less stressful and time-consuming to both parties. The California statutes on arbitration require a specific statement to be a part of the service contract, that is, the informed consent. The statement must be in 12-point red-ink caps followed by a citation of Article 1 from the code in order to be legally binding. I have printed this arbitration agreement exactly as specified by California code at the end of the Informed Consent for Psychotherapy Assessment Consultation (on the CD-ROM). (See attorney O. Brandt Caudill's discussion of arbitration and limitation of liability clauses in Hedges et al. 1997.)

Another way of limiting liability that is being considered by psychotherapists is to put a ceiling on the dollar amount ahead of time. A California appellate court case, *Markbourough California Inc. v. Superior Court* (1991), successfully upheld a $50,000 limitation of liability clause in a contract against a million dollar claim.

I do not yet use either of these provisions, but I am asking myself why not! If I were attempting to devise a limitation of liability statement, I would use the arbitration agreement as a model—the 12-point red-ink caps. I would further specify a $29,000 limitation for less than twenty hours or six months of contact with the client and a $69,000 limitation for more hours or calendar time. This is because $30,000 and $70,000 settlements are reportable to the California and federal memory banks, respectively, which keep track of medical professionals. We hope our non-medical professional organizations will soon move to parity with medical providers because at present their limits for data bank reportability are considerably higher. I would also double-check my statement, procedures, and numbers with an attorney. Such limitations would, of course, not hold up in court if intentional malfeasance were to be established.

6

Therapeutic Hot Spots

Boundaries, Dual Relationships, and Recovered Memories

THE SENSE AND NONSENSE OF BOUNDARIES

People with a prosecuting mentality who sit on licensing boards and ethics committees have long been seduced by the plaintiff bar into naive and nonsensical moralizing with regard to the concept of boundaries as applied to the practice of psychotherapy. Clearly a spatial metaphor derived from ethological concerns of territoriality, the concept of boundary refers to an imaginary line that I claim demarks what is mine from what I am willing to acknowledge as yours. Ethologists such as Robert Audrey in *The Territorial Imperative* (1966) and Konrad Lorenz in *King Solomon's Ring* (1952) have studied extensively how members of various species work to establish and maintain these ever-shifting imaginary lines and how the power to establish and maintain functional boundaries both within and between the species operates in rich complexity.

The clearest referent in human life to the concept of psychological boundaries is real estate, where lines of possession can be arbitrarily concretized by geographical landmarks such as rivers, mountains, and lakes or by reference to magnetic compass points. Ethologists are fond of demonstrating, however, that even in sophisticated human life it is still primarily aggression and the capacity and willingness to subdue and dominate others that in the final analysis determines the placement of these arbitrary lines—lines that nonetheless remain in perpetual question according to prevailing social concords and discords. Contemporary psychobiologists such as Humberto Maturana and Francisco Varela (1987) have revised evolutionary theory considerably by utilizing communication theory and the concept of an environmental niche that each group of creatures learns over time to exploit by autopoetic (self-creative) means. The confines or the fixed and flexible functional boundaries of such niches effectively define the species and the various members of the species—male, female, young, dominant buck, ruling hen, and so forth—and cannot simply be defined by concrete references to genetics, anatomy, or geography.

The further study of life space and boundaries inevitably takes us into the area of the signs and signals that are used to demarcate and to defend territorial claims. For example, a duck displaying a dark spot on the back of its head communicates fear and a willingness to retreat that marks the cessation of invasive-competitive aggression. An aggressive display on the part of a hen warns would-be predators that she will stop at nothing to protect her nest and brood. The possessor of a territory by virtue of his marks communicates to would-be invaders that he has the competitive edge with his aggressive intent to defend at all cost what belongs to him. At the level of human interactions, boundary signs enter the realm of the symbolic-cultural, linguistic, subcultural, and familial. And, *in the final analysis, the personal sense of boundaries rests on a lifetime of private and internalized experiences and the way each person symbolizes those experiences.*

If the life and livelihood of a practicing psychotherapist means so little to people sitting on a licensing board or ethics committee, naively and thoughtlessly moralizing about boundary violations when in fact boundaries are so personal, then we are all in danger, but that is our situation today. In my work consulting with and defending psychotherapists against transference-based false accusations, I have repeatedly seen concepts such as "unethical dual relationships," "unprofessional conduct," "standards of care," and "boundary violations" carelessly bandied about—much to our detriment.

The California Association of Marriage and Family Therapists (CAMFT) is an alert, proactive, and aggressive professional organization standing against abuses of power by the state, represented chiefly by the California Board of Behavioral Sciences (BBS) that regulates, polices, and prosecutes marriage and family therapists in the name of consumer protection. CAMFT has sponsored many profession-protective bills, one establishing statutes of limitation for licensing board prosecutions—three years from when the complaint comes to the attention of the board and seven years from the date of the alleged unprofessional incident. The governor of California deplorably vetoed the CAMFT-sponsored bill designed to ensure a fair hearing for accused therapists by holding the administrative law judge's opinion binding when the credibility of the accuser is in question. This bill was a measure to prevent in certain cases the politically appointed, economically biased, and mostly nonprofessional state board, whose members have not interviewed the accuser or accused, from cavalierly overriding the judge's opinion and prosecuting therapists solely on the basis of a single client's complaints, which it regularly does.

The appalling situation thus remains that licensing boards simultaneously act as the accuser of the therapist and as the prosecutor, the jury, the judge, the sentencer, the probation officer, and the collector of all fees including payment of the complete expenses for its investigation—all without hearing a single direct word from either the complainant or the defendant. Further, the accuser remains anonymous, protected by board secrecy and client confidentially—violating another constitutional provision that guarantees that the accused has a right to be publicly faced by the accuser. It is doubtful that so many false accusations would be filed if clients knew that their names would be in local newspapers along with the bogus charges they were pursuing against their therapists. The boards' policies of control and secrecy over the client complaint process encourage false accusations and ensure that therapists will be prosecuted. This same basic form of administrative law exists throughout the United States and Canada.

Psychotherapists must remain alert against encroachments into our professional life by state boards attempting to regulate us individually and collectively with a police and prosecution mentality. CAMFT is forever pounding its fist on the door of the BBS and has successfully pressured for many changes in the agency's policies and procedures, including the replacement of its former executive director. By way of contrast, the California Psychological Association (CPA) has entered into a lucrative and blatant conflict-of-interest contract colluding with the Board of Psychology in policing the state-mandated continuing education programs for psychologists in the name of consumer protection. Through this move, the state board has successfully taken unto itself the power to homogenize psychological practice and to define the effective standards of care for psychologists through directly supervising CPA's accreditation of continuing education programs, thus threatening to destroy specialization training and to limit the diversity of practice in psychology in California while simplifying further its task of prosecution. Fortunately, Continuing Education Providers have been somewhat successful in braking the hold the BOP had over CPA by forcing the BOP to recognize Accreditation by the American Psychological Association over which it has no control. CAMFT wisely rejected a similar conflict-of-interest contract offered it by the BBS and has stood firmly against all regulation of mandated continuing education by the state as well as any other kind of boundary violations of professional therapists and of the profession by the BBS.

The worst part about the irresponsible cry of "boundary violation" by state boards is that it is done in the name of an unenlightened and naively moralistic and dogmatic set of skewed prosecution concepts regarding dual relationships, professional boundaries, and standards of care. After a century of professional research and advancement, we have finally arrived at the knowledge that human minds evolve out of early human relationships, and that the only deeply transformative experiences we can offer as helping professionals require our personally engaging our clients in intimate emotional relationships that have the power to bring into sharp view how previously internalized destructive relationships persist to color the client's experience of current significant relationships.

The central concept of the contemporary relational approach to transformational psychotherapy remains that of transference. We learned in childhood certain emotional patterns of perception and response to relationship dilemmas that we encountered at various stages of our development, and we tend to repeat unwittingly those emotional patterns in later relationships. It is this tendency to repeat familiar perceptions and approaches to relationships that intelligently fuels the psychotherapy process by showing therapists how people have become caught in various symptom-producing dynamics and activities, and by pointing to fresh ways of transforming clients and creating new relationship possibilities.

The information about deeply ingrained patterns of clients' very early emotional relationships that is required for successful psychotherapeutic work is only available through the revival of transference memories as they are actively relived in the here-and-now trust relationship of the present with the therapist. Thus, clients who have been abused or otherwise traumatized in early childhood can only be freed from crippling symptoms and limitations to the extent that they can be encouraged to reexperience in some form or another the therapist as the perpetrator of subjective pain and injustice, and then enabled through the central tool of psychotherapy—transference interpretation—to realize that it is not the actual therapist or therapeutic situation as it exists today that actively persecutes, but the sense of the internalized perpetrator from the primordial past living on in their relational and bodily memories. This is the essential meaning of transformational cure in dynamic psychotherapy that people with prosecuting minds fail to grasp out of ignorance, blindness, or maliciousness.

Clients desperately resist the revival of traumatic transference experience. Thus, at all points of transference elaboration in the therapeutic relationship they are highly motivated to externalize blame onto the therapist and the therapeutic process for the agony and misery they are currently experiencing, rather than to continue to allow an escalation of the pain and terror in the transference feelings until the sense of the internal persecutor can be successfully ferreted out, defined, and worked through. Experience with the ubiquitous false accusations that characterize the long-term, in-depth psychotherapy process reveals that complaints that go awry and end up in an investigation or litigational process are most often triggered by out-of-therapy fluke incidents that tip the delicate balance of desire and fear operative in on-going transference development in the direction of a negative therapeutic re-action that effectively functions to put an end to the confusing and agonizing process of transference and resistance remembering (Hedges 2000b).

In a later chapter I provide a brief sketch of four developmental levels of early relationship experience that are distinctly different and that require different therapeutic understanding and approaches as they appear in the course of transference remembering:

1. Relational memories from the triangular family life of the four- to six-year-old are generally revived by means of words, stories, symbols, and impulses that were painfully repressed at the time.

2. The self-consolidation and self-fragmentation relationship memories from the three-year-old relationship era are later remembered in the ways that people seek out, demand, and utilize or fail to utilize self-confirming interpersonal resonances in the present.

3. The four- to twenty-four-month-old relational bonding memories become available in the therapeutic interaction through the affective ways in which the client experiences the therapist and interactions with the therapist as good, ideal, and enhancing, or as bad, abandoning, and damaging.

4. Relational traumas from the last trimester of intrauterine development and the first four months after birth are somatopsychically recalled later in life by people coming to experience intimate trust relationships as being characterized by cruel neglect, terrifying rejection, and life-threatening, body-shaking, and mind-shattering confusion and hatred that become systematically projected into the therapeutic situation and onto the person of the therapist.

Because of their desperate resistance to the here-and-now emotional re-vival of relational and bodily traumas, clients are tremendously motivated to abort the therapeutic process and to externalize the blame for experienced pain, terror, and damage onto the therapist and others with whom they have or have had trust relationships.

This was what the recovered memory fiasco of the early to mid-1990s was all about. We had a nation of therapists trained to help people focus on the symptomatic physical and mental manifestations of anguish, terror, pain, be-trayal, and damage that their clients had experienced as children. But thera-pists who had not schooled themselves in the subtleties of remembering by means of transference and resistance experience naively colluded with their clients' wish to externalize the blame by helping them point the finger at past perpetrators and to act out the resistance to here-and-now transference remembering by confronting the remembered perpetrators—usually parents, relatives, neighbors, or others involved in early trust relationships.

A decade of successful prosecution against such irresponsible therapists and tactics of recovered-memory therapy has now established that it is possible for the human mind to construct vivid and terrifying memories of events that never happened in the ways that people recall them, that people who have been abused and traumatized in childhood have generally always retained memory for some or all of the abuse, and that taking literally memories recovered in psychotherapy, hypnosis, or truth serum interviews is to fail to take seriously the person who has been traumatized and/or abused in childhood.

The recovered memory movement of the 1990s clearly paralleled a social movement to lift the cultural veil of denial from our growing awareness of the widespread abuse of children, women, and other marginalized people through the ages, and how destructive this abuse is to both the individuals and to the social order that has been willing to sustain it. As a civilization we are slowly coming to acknowledge the ravages of destruction inherent in the maxim "might makes right." We are bringing into public awareness how people can and often do use whatever power differentials they have at their disposal to exploit and damage others by violating their human rights and personal boundaries. But the most subtle and elusive issue involved in understanding interpersonal boundaries and their violations is how extraordinary, idiosyncratic, and diverse the personal structures and vulnerabilities of each person's sense of boundaries truly are. To do justice to this diversity, given the infinite boundary-building experiences available to developing human beings and how easily individually structured personal boundaries can be unwittingly violated, would require a detailed theory of internalized interpersonal relationships and extensive case illustrations showing what in various instances might conceivably constitute violations of personally established boundaries.

It is absurd for licensing boards to pontificate moralistically on this complex realm of private human experience or to imply that they understand what a client's personal boundaries are and what constitutes a boundary violation for that client. Naive and irresponsible moralizing such as we see today in the name of prosecuting psychotherapists and policing consumer complaints can only lead to endless travesties of justice.

I can suggest for further mediation and investigation several illustrative situations that may challenge the moralizing about boundaries that now characterizes the prosecuting mind. Consider how an infant who was damaged by never being held might, in adulthood, demand and legitimately need various kinds of holding in a transformative therapeutic experience. For that client,

physical or mental holding by a therapist would not be a violation of boundaries. But the therapist's failure, due to doctrinal restrictions, to reach out for
meaningful moments of interpersonal contact might well constitute a violation of the client's need to develop fresh forms of interpersonal trust with
newly formed boundaries.

Or consider a client who was so traumatized in infancy that personal relationships have been impossible for a lifetime until safety and trust were developed with a therapist who could attune to the ways in which neglect and
hatred had been experienced in her early milieu and have been repeatedly experienced in all subsequent relationships, including the therapeutic one. As a
result of her therapeutic experience, the client is at last able to negotiate a loving relationship that leads to a wedding. The therapist is the only person who
knows what this strenuous adventure has been for her, and thus should be
present to celebrate this supreme and victorious moment of a lifetime. The
therapist wants to attend the wedding and feels it vitally important to give a
meaningful gift signifying her recognition of the crucial importance of this
life passage. But because the state licensing board naively moralizes and re-
moves therapists' licenses for engaging in these kinds of "unethical dual relationships," she feels prohibited from either attending the wedding or giving
a gift. The massive violation of trust and replication of infant abuse that the
bride-to-be now reexperiences destroys five years of therapeutic relationship-
building along with valuable parts of the minds of both client and therapist.
Because it is only possible for this woman who was so badly damaged in infancy to experience certain kinds of events in very concrete ways, she relives
in a most agonizing and destructive way the cruel hatred she once knew at the
hands of her infant caregivers. Thus a massive violation of delicately formed
boundaries is thoughtlessly perpetrated by members of the board in their absurd and blanket policies adopted in the name of policing therapists and protecting consumers.

Or consider a therapist treating over a period of several years a deeply vulnerable person damaged by early birth trauma and repeated hospitalizations
and surgeries in early childhood. As the relationship builds over time, panic attacks and deep dissociative reactions with self-destructive gestures escalate,
frightening both the client and therapist. The therapist has been well schooled
in the pervasive forms of holding and containing treatment for borderline
clients widely practiced today, and has regularly sought expert consultation
and psychiatric backup, but the panic attacks, posttraumatic stress disorder
(PTSD) symptoms, and suicidal gestures become more frantic. Friends tell the
client that she isn't improving and that she should seek a new therapist. Members of her eating disorder group feel she doesn't need therapy at all and that
the seemingly heroic holding measures of her therapist violate her boundaries,

are unethical, and should be reported. Seeking relief, she accepts weekend hospitalization where the emergency room psychiatrist, who has a cognitive-behavioral orientation, tells her that she has been in therapy too long with no signs of progress. He questions the ethics and practices of such a therapist, prescribes a new medication, and takes her into his own practice. Deliverance from the pain and agony of remembering infant trauma is now at hand, as the rage left from infancy surfaces and takes a vengeful turn against the therapist. Therapy abruptly ends and a board complaint is filed.

Where did the holding and containing therapy so widely practiced go wrong? From a cutting-edge perspective we are able to discern that because of the massive trauma the client had experienced in infancy and early childhood, at each stage of intimacy development with the therapist a fear of connection was gradually building. The holding and containing techniques employed, which are well within community standards of practice, have only served to escalate the terrifying transference left by therapeutic replications of the unspeakable pain, the debilitating fragmentations, and the unbearable rages once experienced in infancy. Frantic attempts on the part of the therapist to hold, to calm, and to contain, which invariably work well with borderline clients, fail miserably when the yet lower levels of organizing transference formation are activated. The therapist is then fused, and confused, in transference with the perpetrator experience of infancy—the parent who failed to protect the child from the unspeakable agonies and experienced abandonments of her infantile hospitalizations, surgeries, and recuperation periods. The therapist will undoubtedly and inappropriately lose her license or have it suspended for her many heroic efforts that can be easily interpreted by outsiders as boundary issues, dual relations, failures to uphold community standards of care, unprofessional conduct, misdiagnosis, and faulty technique—all pointing in the board's naïve opinion to gross negligence on the part of the therapist.

Thus we can see that in virtually every aspect of relationship development of the psychotherapeutic process, any event that can be seen as a boundary violation can equally well be seen as a potentially healthy and crucial boundary development in delicate and nascent form. Only other experts with extensive experience in the practice of long-term transformational therapy should stand in judgment of what any particular activity or event may or may not have represented in the moment of the therapeutic engagement!

Civil courts have long insisted that a heavy burden of proof be required of the prosecution when charges of professional malpractice are made, since the life and practice-sustaining stakes for the defendant are so great. Courts regularly insist that both exploitation and damage be in clear evidence in order to establish malpractice, and that there is a clear, impelling, and unambiguous causal link between damage sustained by the accuser and the actions or inactions of the accused. When licensing boards prosecute only because a particular activity is interpreted by their often uninformed and unprofessional opinion as indicative of an unethical dual relationship or a boundary violation, and therefore a failure to uphold the community standard of care, they are failing to seek clear evidence of damage and exploitation. Specific questionable actions and activities that may or may not have occurred in the course of the therapy do not constitute clear evidence. When untrained boards sentence a therapist harshly on the basis of a client complaint without a fair trial and without regard to upholding an appropriately rigorous burden of proof, they operate on the absurd and un-American principle that the therapist is guilty until proven innocent.

The careless prosecutions currently being pursued by licensing boards and to a lesser extent by ethics committees are all the more alarming because of the re-strategizing by the plaintiff bar after the malpractice insurance carriers' recent refusal to fund any longer the investigation and litigation of sexual complaints. The result is that false accusations of sexual contact are carefully avoided in favor of a potpourri of ill-sounding nonsexual complaints that are bandied about under such headings as dual relationships, boundary violations, failure to uphold community standards of practice, unprofessional conduct, and professional negligence. The prosecution strategy is to win a licensing board conviction, which isn't difficult because the routine operations of licensing boards are heavily biased in favor of conviction. Then the judge and jury in the anticipated upcoming civil malpractice trial can be informed that the state licensing board, which is vested with the task of consumer protection, has already found the therapist guilty in the administrative law court and voted unanimously to convict him of unprofessional conduct and gross negligence. The judge and jury are told that the reasons for the state's prosecution have to do with unethical dual relationships and illegal boundary violations—whatever the hell those are! And what do ordinary citizens sitting on a jury know about such things? Thus, they accept the government's word that the public must be protected from unscrupulous practices and fraudulent professional perpetrators. This process easily slides from commonsense understandings of boundaries into nonsensical moralizing about boundary violations that can then be used to justify mindless prosecution of psychotherapists. It is ironic that those most loudly crying "Boundary violation!" are doing so by accusing therapists in a most unfair manner that appallingly violates the boundaries of all of us as individuals and as a profession.

IN PRAISE OF THE DUAL RELATIONSHIP[1]

In 1973 the American Psychological Association (APA), in an effort to curb sexual exploitation in the psychotherapeutic relationship, opened a Pandora's box when it coined the term dual relationship in its Code of Ethics. Since then, every aspect of the psychotherapeutic relationship has been colored with continual concern, frustration, and doubt. The faulty shift of ethical focus from damaging exploitation to dual relationships has led to widespread misunderstanding and incessant naive moralizing that has undermined the spontaneous, creative, and unique aspects of the personal relationship that is essential to the psychotherapeutic process. Dynamic and systems-oriented psychotherapies cannot be practiced without various forms of dual relating. But we have wrongly been told that dual relating is unethical.

The good news is that the pendulum has started swinging back. The APA Insurance Trust maintains that not all multiple roles are dual relationships. But the implication is still that duality may be unethical. The code of ethics for the California Association of Marriage and Family Therapists categorically states that "not all dual relationships are unethical." The 1992 APA Code of Ethics returns us to sanity:

> In many communities and situations, it may not be feasible or reasonable for psychologists to avoid social or other nonprofessional contacts with persons such as patients, clients, students, supervisees, or research participants. Psychologists must always be sensitive to the potential harmful effects of other contacts on their work and on those persons with whom they deal. . . . Psychologists do not exploit persons over whom they have supervisory, evaluative, or other authority such as students, supervisees, employees, research participants and clients or patients. . . . Psychologists do not engage in sexual relationships with students or supervisees in training over whom the psychologist has evaluative or direct authority, because such relationships are so likely to impair judgment or be exploitative. . . . Psychologists do not engage in sexual intimacies with current patients or clients. . . . Psychologists do not accept as therapy patients or clients persons with whom they have engaged in sexual intimacies [and] do not engage in sexual intimacies with a former therapy patient or client for at least two years after cessation or termination of professional services. . . . The psychologist who engages in such activities after the two years following cessation or termination of treatment bears the burden of demonstrating that there has been no exploitation, in light of all relevant factors. [¶ 1.17]

Thus, after twenty years of grief, the term *dual relationship* as an ethical definition was entirely eliminated from the revised APA code. The current ethical focus becomes one of remaining mindful of the ever-present possibility of damaging exploitation. But the malignant concept of dual relationship that the APA introduced and has now eliminated has infected ethics committees, licensing boards, and malpractice litigation everywhere. We still have a major battle ahead to undo the severe damage done to the psychotherapeutic relationship by the pejorative use of the term *dual relationship*.

As the pendulum has swung back, such writers as Kitchener (1988) and Tomm (1991) argue that dual relationships need to be considered more carefully. Here are the main points that have emerged:

1. Dual relating is inevitable and offers many constructive possibilities.
2. Dual relationships are only one way an exploitative therapist or an exploitative client may take advantage of the other.
3. Metaphors are mixed when duality is treated as a toxic substance that impairs judgment.
4. A priority of emphasis on the professional role serves to diminish personal connectedness, thereby fostering human alienation and endorsing a privileged role hierarchy.
5. Exploitation in relationships is always exploitation and unethical regardless of whether it occurs in a dual context.
6. Multiple connections that cross boundaries between therapy, teaching, supervision, collegiality, and friendship can be celebrated as part of the inevitable and potentially beneficial complexities of human life.
7. The power differential in any relationship can be used to empower the personal and/or professional development of both parties as well as to exploit them.
8. A frequent therapeutic goal involves helping students, supervisees, and clients understand and negotiate the multiple and shifting layers of human relatedness and human relational systems.
9. It is preferable to humanize and to democratize the therapeutic relationship rather than to encumber it with unnecessary trappings of professional expertise and higher authority.
10. The therapeutic role can be misused by cloaking it in paternalistic, patronizing attitudes of emotional distance and myths regarding the superior mental health of practitioners.
11. Incompetent and exploitative therapists are the problem, not dual relating.
12. What is needed by therapists is classification and discussion of the subtle kinds of exploitation that can and do occur in professional relationships, not a naive injunction against dual relating.
13. To categorically prohibit dual relationships reductionistically implies that there is no continuity or overlap in roles in relationships and that therapy can be separated from the person of the therapist.

14. Dual relationships are inevitable, and clinicians can conduct them thoughtfully and ethically, making whatever happens grist for the mill.
15. Dual relationships represent an opportunity for personal growth and enriched human connection that benefits both parties.
16. Human connections evolve spontaneously and change over the course of time naturally and unpredictably, and therapy need not block this natural process.
17. Duality provides an important pathway for corrective feedback, potentially offering improved understanding and increased consensuality.
18. Duality opens space for increased connectedness, more sharing, greater honesty, more personal integrity, greater responsibility, increased social integration, and more egalitarian interaction.
19. Dual relating reduces space for manipulation, deception, and special privilege, gives more opportunity to recognize each other as ordinary human beings, and reduces the likelihood of persistent transferential and countertransferential distortions.
20. Interpersonal boundaries are rarely rigid and fixed, but rather fluctuate and undergo continuous redefinition in all relationships, including the therapeutic relationship, which deliberately focuses on developing, consciousness of boundary fluctuations and discussing such changes.
21. Dual relationships represent the exact kinds of complex interpersonal situations that our professional skills were developed to study and enhance, so as to increase the beneficial possibilities of human interactions and transformation.

The very heart and soul of psychotherapy—transference and transference interpretation—by definition always constitute some form of dual relationship. Freud's (1912, 1915) initial definitions of psychoanalytic technique revolve around the "love" relationship that begins to form between physician and client in the course of psychoanalytic free association. Freud suggests the image of an opaque mirror to describe the neutral stance that the psychotherapist seeks to achieve vis-à-vis the patient's neurotic conflict. Freud's images make clear the ultimate impossibility of ever attaining perfect mirroring or perfect neutrality. Despite the psychotherapist's attempt to form a real relationship based on mirroring and neutrality, relationship expectations brought from the client's past inevitably begin to make their presence felt as a duality.

The decisive moment in psychoanalysis and in all dynamic psychotherapies is when the duality is at last recognized and successfully interpreted by the psychotherapist. There exists at this moment the real relationship that has evolved over time between two people. But another reality is suddenly recognized and defined by the transference interpretation. In the former reality the psychotherapist has a caregiving, curative role, and the client has an obligation to relate to real needs of the psychotherapist including fees, attendance, and respect for the setting that supports and protects the personal and professional life of the psychotherapist as well as the client. But when transference reality can be discerned and discussed by two, the therapist functions in a completely different relationship to the client—one of professional interpreter of the emotional life of the client—that is brought to the real relationship set up by the psychotherapeutic situation. At the moment of interpretation, the therapist steps into the role of a third party viewing the realistic, interaction of the two and comments on a heretofore hidden reality-the transference, the resistance, or the countertransference.

Greenson (1965), in acknowledging the real developing relationship, speaks of the "working alliance" to acknowledge the realistic collaboration and mutual respect of two. Greenson's formulations stand as a correction to the faulty belief that the client's attitudes and fantasies are mostly transference distortions, when in fact a significant real relationship develops (dualistically) quite apart from the professional task of transference interpretation.

Bollas (1979) further clarifies the nature of the real relationship by pointing out that Freud (unwittingly and forgivably) designed the psychoanalytic listening situation in order to "act out" with his patients the earliest caregiving roles of parenting, so as to promote the transformational aspect of psychotherapy. The transformational role of the psychotherapist is a realistic role distinctly different from that of transference interpreter. Psychoanalytic transformation occurs by means of this dual transforming/interpreting relationship.

Schwaber's (1979, 1983) clarifying work arises from an orientation emphasizing the subjective aspects of self. Her ideas focus on the role that the reality of the psychotherapist and the psychotherapeutic relationship play in evoking transference. Following Kohut (1971, 1977), she emphasizes the reality of the ongoing nature of the relationship that evolves in the psychoanalytic listening situation. Transference from past experience is to be discerned on the basis of something the psychotherapist actually did or did not do and the emotional reaction that the psychotherapist's actual activities elicited. Schwaber highlights the real relationship based on the psychotherapist's effort to listen and to respond as empathically as humanly possible. Transference is then thought to be perceivable against the backdrop of failures in the psychotherapist's empathic understanding. That is, the psychotherapist actually engages or fails to engage in real interpersonal activity, the disruptive results of which the psychotherapist could not have possibly foretold. According to this view, the working through of the "selfobject" or narcissistic transference constitutes a new edition, a novel interpersonal reality that the psychotherapist and client now have to address with new and different understanding and interpretation. Thus, not only is transference discernible by virtue of aspects of the real relationship coming up for discussion, but the working through is seen as an entirely new and evolving (dualistic) form of personal relationship.

Strachey (1934) quotes Melanie Klein as saying that psychotherapists are generally reluctant to give mutative interpretations (those that promote change) because full instinctual energy would thereby be directed realistically at the person of the psychotherapist. This situation is feared and avoided by psychotherapists who fail to interpret so that the full power of transference can come into focus in the here-and-now dualistic relationship. Thus, the two key curative agents in psychoanalysis—the establishment of the transference neurosis and the mutative interpretation—both function to bring past emotional experience to bear on and to intensify the reality of the present interpersonal relationship. These two realities will never become completely sorted out. One's past emotional life forever colors present relationships. Thus, even the most classic of psychoanalytic doctrines holds that the duality between the realistic present and the transferential past can never, in principle, be eliminated from human relationships.

Another line of psychoanalytic thought revolves around the notion of "corrective emotional experience" (Alexander 1961). Various realistic and active procedures may be introduced into the relationship for the purposes of promoting or maintaining the analysis (Eissler 1953; Ferenczi 1952, 1955, 1962). But the need for such reassurance, suggestion, or gratification will later have to be analyzed as transference. According to this view, the client's emotional past was flawed and the therapist is (realistically) going to be able to provide a better (corrective) emotional experience. The psychotherapist by this view may actually step out of his or her usual role as psychotherapist and "do things," intervene in active ways to help the client relate to the therapist and to stay in therapy. Psychotherapists who advocate the need for active intervention under certain circumstances implicitly recognize that the therapeutic action of psychoanalysis requires various forms of duality to become effective. Dual relationships can thus be seen to form the backbone of dynamically oriented psychotherapy.

In general, there is a greater subjective sense of reality in the psychotherapeutic relationship the farther down the developmental ladder the issue is that is being attended to. Winnicott (1949) points out that the earlier in development the impingement on the infant's sense of "going on being" is, the shorter the span of the ego—meaning the less that can be considered at any one moment in time. Thus, when early developmental issues arise in therapy, less reality testing is available, and only a greatly narrowed picture of the world and the analytic relationship is possible. Many early developmental issues are activated in psychotherapy. Consequently, a narrow, concrete, subjective experience may well take on a fully formed reality sense, when in fact only a small segment of the overall reality context is being considered.

Thus, at the psychotic or primary organizing level of human personality there is the risk of a complete breakdown of the sense of complex shared realities when the "transference psychosis" emerges in the therapeutic relationship for study (Little 1981, 1990). All people have deep layers of psychotic anxiety that may need to be activated at some point in therapy. This means that in any analysis a psychotic core may emerge for brief or extended periods of time during which the client's usual capacities to test reality and to abstract from broad experience may be functionally impaired such that the psychotherapist may become part of a delusional transference experience—possibly a dualistic one that can threaten the therapist emotionally and realistically.

At the level of symbiotic (borderline, four- to twenty-four-month-old) issues it requires considerable time and relating to establish interpersonal symbiotic scenarios as visible in transferences that become emotionally replicated in the therapeutic relationship. I have written extensively about the complicated interactional sequences and dilemmas that therapists encounter when responding to replicated symbiotic (borderline) transferences (Hedges 1983, 1992). Interpreting the countertransference becomes a critical aspect of responding to the many projective identifications, especially those encountered in this work.

The theoretician exciting great interest today in clinical circles is Winnicott (1958, 1965, 1971), who, in his studies of the early mother-child relationship, demonstrates clearly the way the boundaries between mother and child and later between therapist and client continuously mix and mingle, and how this ongoing process of merging, separating, and re-merging must be replicated when studying early developmental issues in the transference-countertransference relationship. Infant research (Stern 1985) further underlines this mixing of boundaries at early developmental levels. Little's (1990) deeply moving account of her own analytic work, which led to a complete psychotic breakdown in her analysis with Winnicott, demonstrates this aptly. No one makes clearer than Winnicott the importance of the actual reality of the therapist and the setting. His work demonstrates that the therapist must be realistically available to the client for long periods while restricted areas of the personality have an opportunity to expand. In his focus on early developmental issues Winnicott demonstrates that interpretation can only follow actual involvement and improvement. This kind of duality is essential to the transformation of all primitive mental states.

Unfortunately, the organizing or psychotic transference that therapists seek to mobilize was born out of trauma and life-threatening terrorizing experiences of infancy. So when the transference begins to be reactivated in the safety and intimacy of the therapeutic relationship, there is a delicate balance between the client's desire for cure through reexperiencing the transference feelings and the client's resistance to the cure, which produces a negative therapeutic reaction. Clinical experience shows how easily a fluke outside occurrence can tip this balance in the direction of disaster.

At the moment of a severe negative therapeutic reaction, symbolic speech and discourse are replaced by destructive concretization. Rage or lust is mobilized and with it a clarity of understanding about reality that is subjectively experienced as right, good, monolithic, absolute, and beyond dispute or discussion. A moral crusade characterized by vengeance and righteous indignation is on. The therapist is the enemy, the perpetrator of crimes, the exploiter. Evidence is gathered, much as a person gathers evidence to support a paranoid pseudo-community, in order to support and bolster his or her views against the alleged misbehavior of the therapist.

When aspects of the organizing (psychotic, schizoid) level become activated, the client often develops the conviction of a special, privileged understanding regarding the reality of the therapeutic exchange. Reality no longer is a matter for mutual discussion, or for consideration by various standards of social consensus, or for contradictory or varying viewpoints. "This is real. Don't give me any bullshit. You are shooting secret cosmic rays from behind your chair at me." "This is incest. You have damaged me irreparably by allowing me to feel close to you." "Because you have stepped out of your neutral role and given me advice, opinion, suggestion, or help, you are in an unethical relationship with me. I cannot seek consultation with a third party as you have asked because I would be ashamed at how I seduced you into actually helping me grow. You are the guilty party because you have the power and should have known that revealing personal aspects of yourself and reaching out to me in realistic and 'helpful' ways would be experienced by me (in transference) as incestual and abusive. Your 'good nature' and 'willingness to help me grow' are devious things you do for self-aggrandizement, to make your own ego swell with pride. You have exploited me for the sake of your own ego, your narcissism. You have damaged me by overinvolving yourself in my therapeutic growth. I demand recompense for the violations you have indulged yourself in and the damage you have done. You seduced me (or let me seduce you). Now you will pay." No amount of objective feedback, attempts at rational discussion, or weighing of considerations is possible at such a shocking moment and there may not be another moment in which these psychotic transference convictions can be discussed before an ethical or board complaint is filed. If no moderation or mediation softens the position before accident intervenes, we see suicides, destructive mutilation, and homicides, as well as legal and ethical claims facing the therapist as a result of good therapeutic mobilization of unconscious organizing affects. The therapeutic activation has succeeded. But the cure has failed and the therapist is in realistic danger. Our focus for the future must be on how to better understand and prevent such dangers.

As our experience with the emergence of psychotic transference (even in better-developed personalities) expands, the need becomes increasingly clear for the presence of a case monitor to follow the course of treatment so that when reality controls are lost by the client in psychotic transference, a third party who is knowledgeable about the course of the treatment and who has some relationship with the client is able to intervene to prevent such a dangerous and destructive negative therapeutic reaction (Hedges 1994c). The Informed Consent for Long-Term Psychotherapy (on the CD-ROM) offers a few guidelines for a case monitor.

All people have experienced an early developmental (organizing or psychotic) period with constricting limits and constraints, and are therefore subject to psychotic anxieties and transferences—meaning that the therapist is, in principle, never safe from the possibility of a destructive emergence of an abusive psychotic transference that is experienced as very real by the client and aimed at the therapist's person. No amount of good judgment ahead of time is fail-safe protection against such potential disaster. Viewed from this angle it is always an error to trust the goodwill, good nature, and truth-searching qualities of the client since they can suddenly be reversed in a psychotic episode. The subjective experience is so real it cannot be interpreted successfully and the therapist becomes the victim.

Therapists facing misconduct charges regularly report that they "never would have dreamed therapy could have produced such a miscarriage. She [the client] seemed like such a trusting person of good will, and of upstanding moral character. She was so involved in her therapy, so respectful of her therapeutic partner. How could such vengeance and hatred be directed at me, the very person who has probably done more for her in terms of opening herself up than anyone she has ever known?"

As our therapeutic tools for bringing out early traumas improve, practicing psychotherapists are headed for yet deeper and deeper trouble. The dual nature of psychotherapy cannot be denied or minimized and the active role of the therapist required in working with earlier developmental layers of the personality moves the dynamic psychotherapist inexorably toward an ill fate. Deep-working, well-intentioned psychotherapists face the danger that their best-conceived efforts to help will be experienced as violent or incestuous intrusions that they should have known about in advance and should have taken measures to forestall.

But where does the phrase "should have known" appear in any single piece of responsible therapy research or even in a single theoretical tract on the nature of psychotherapy? Such a claim is completely untenable and unsupportable. No one who seriously practices in-depth psychotherapy is likely to use such a phrase. What may evolve in psychotic transference is never known in advance.

The misplaced focus by licensing boards and ethics committees on dual relationships when damaging exploitation is the issue has meant that therapists can no longer simply consider what such events as attending a client's wedding, attending a lecture or social event in a client's presence, offering a helpful book or cassette, giving or receiving token gifts or touch, or sending a birthday or sympathy card may mean to a client in the context of the therapy. Our spontaneity, the only tool we have at our disposal in psychotherapy, is thus in serious danger.

Fortunately, as the pendulum has begun to swing back, we can begin relying once again on clinical considerations rather than naive moralizing and absurd misconduct rulings to guide our therapy, but we are still by no means safe. Our growing expertise in elucidating the deepest, most primitive and crazy aspects of our clients and of ourselves is expanding at the very moment when the therapeutic dimension we most depend on—dual relatedness—has come under social, legal, and ethical censorship. It is by no means clear how we will come to grips with these and many related issues. Regulatory boards and ethics committees in their eagerness to provide rules for the practice of psychotherapy have rapidly moved toward positions that, if allowed to continue unchallenged, threaten to obliterate the essence of clinical work, which relies on the spontaneity of the therapist and the dual relationship.

The essential duality required for the successful practice of psychotherapy can be considered from many angles.[2] The views on duality presented here serve to contrast (1) the real, moment-to-moment, spontaneous, mutual need-fulfilling aspect of the contractual relationship that evolves over time between two people, with (2) the symbolic, interpretive relationship in which the two gradually come to stand apart, as it were, from their real, spontaneous relating and speak in such a way as to characterize from a third-party point of view the manner and quality of their relating. The two create pictures and stories that describe (as if from an outside or objective point of view) what is happening between them and why. This interpretive, third-party, symbolic relationship that the two share enables each to speak his or her subjective reactions arising from within the real relationship in such a way as to consider the emotional load (left over from past emotional relationships) that each may be adding to his or her ongoing appreciation of the other and of the relatedness.

In *Beyond Countertransference*, Natterson (1991) illustrates how patient and psychotherapist achieve through communication an intense oneness and fusion, how subjective features from the psychotherapist's past come into play in the countertransference, and how at the same time each is able to individuate and differentiate more completely from the experience than either was able to do before their work together. Natterson shatters the myth of the value-neutral therapist, exposing it as a fictive assumption. He makes clear that all human two-person transactions share fundamental meaning: "Each party attempts to influence the other with his or her view of the universe, to persuade the other of the rightness of his or her view. . . . This basic power orientation of dyadic relationships makes it natural for moral influences to be invariably significant components of the therapist's activity" (p. 28). Natterson's work highlights the duality between the real relationship and the emerging transference-countertransference relationship.

Transference, countertransference, resistance, and interpretation all rest on the existence of a dual relationship. All beneficial effects of psychotherapy arise in consequence of the dual relationship.

I offer the following suggestions for consideration in evolving safeguards against abuse while honoring the dual relationship inherent in the practice of psychotherapy:

1. When any direct or indirect contact outside the formal therapeutic setting exists between therapist and client, a consultant or third-party case monitor should be sought at regular (two- to six-month) intervals to evaluate and comment on the course of therapy. This is especially important in training programs where the trainee is likely to see or to hear much that will necessarily color the therapeutic relationship. It would also seem critical in small communities, where various forms of outside contact are inevitable.

2. Any dual or multiple roles that might be unavoidable outside the formal therapeutic relationship need to be kept in the public eye. Some provision for periodic review with a third party should be obtained to evaluate how the therapy is proceeding.

3. To protect privacy and confidentiality, all appearances of dual relationship that might potentially be seen by third parties and conceivably be reported to boards and committees for open investigation should be avoided. It is understood that pure work is to be preferred over complicated work, but that dualistic work with various outside influences and complications such as spouses, insurance companies, employers, and

government agencies, tends to be the rule rather than the exception. Complications cannot be assumed to be damaging exploitations. Multiple roles do not constitute unethical relationships that are exploitative and damaging. But avoidance of appearances and use of third-party consultation can help keep the distinction clearer and work to avoid negative therapeutic reactions and confidentiality breaks that inevitably occur as a result of investigation.

4. Qualified experts should render opinions to regulating bodies. At present most individuals serving on regulatory boards and ethics committees do not have advanced specialty training that qualifies them to make judgments about the subtleties of the dual relationship necessarily involved in depth transference and countertransference work without outside expert consultation. To the extent this is true, it would appear that professionals serving on boards and committees are operating unprofessionally and unethically. For most purposes, persons serving on regulatory boards and ethics committees need not have advanced expertise in the dual nature of transference-countertransference work in order to identify therapists' abuses of the professional relationship. But when subtleties are involved, when therapists have a sophisticated and enlightened rationale for various interventions based on the dual nature of transference work, or when therapists' professional reputation and personal life are to be profoundly affected by claims that they do not honor as valid, we cannot afford as a profession to allow people without advanced training and professional expertise in transference and countertransference analysis to stand in judgment on matters they are not qualified to understand.

One way to correct the current threat that therapists live under as a result of accusations of unethical dual relationship is for each board or committee to create panels of expert consultants who can demonstrate advanced understanding of the complexities of transference-countertransference relationships. These experts could be called on to evaluate areas of investigations in which subtle aspects of dual relationship are in play and to render expert opinion to regulatory boards and ethics committees regarding whether or not, given the facts of the case, the therapist has exploited or damaged the client. The existence of a dual relationship that forms naturally in the course of psychotherapy in and of itself tells us nothing.

5. An alternate approach to the expert consultant model is for the therapist to have recourse to settling the dispute in civil court, where full discovery and due process are guaranteed, as they are not under administrative law, and where malpractice insurance serves to protect the therapist from frivolous accusations that licensing boards are famous for prose-

cuting. We know that ethics committees and governing boards are prey to political and economic pressures and various preestablished biases, so that a therapist acting in good faith and upon sound professional opinion is not assured of a fair judgment.

While a judge and jury do not constitute peers in terms of depth understanding, at least with discovery and insurance resources there is some hope of an unbiased, unpoliticized, fair hearing. Some therapists have advocated that since a jury does not represent peer opinion, arbitration panels of persons sophisticated in aspects of depth therapy are to be preferred over civil courts. Arbitrators and professional jurors who deal with such matters daily and who are not paid by the state to prosecute us offer a refreshing alternative.

What is sorely needed is a more careful examination of the nature of the dual relationship and not just for the therapist's protection but also because the client suffers when the psychotic transference accidentally goes awry, leading to an investigative process. Also, we must focus our attention on the dual nature of our work so that we can develop even further its importance and potency for the benefit of our clients.

TAKING RECOVERED MEMORIES SERIOUSLY[3]

Psychotherapy as we know it today began when Freud first had occasion to doubt the veracity of certain molest memories recovered through hypnosis and free association. He was thus forced to reconsider his hypothesis that psychological disturbance was inevitably and directly related to traumatic seduction experiences that were repressed in childhood. Freud's abandonment of the seduction hypothesis has been widely misunderstood to mean either that he denied that childhood seductions had actually occurred or that he held recovered memories are not to be believed. Neither is true. Hedda Bolgar, a psychoanalyst and native of early twentieth-century Vienna, has assured us that there was at least as much incest in Vienna at that time as there is in any American city today (personal communication), and that Freud knew about it. Rather, Freud's critical discovery that has fueled psychoanalysis and psychotherapy up to the present is that, *from a treatment standpoint*, understanding the nature of internalized personal experience and its effects on a person's present life takes precedence over understanding the details of past experiences as remembered or related.

A century later, grassroots therapists and the public are encountering the same set of issues. How are we to consider recovered memories of past lives, birth trauma, multiple selves, dissociated experiences, childhood violence and seduction, satanic ritual abuse, and abductions by aliens?

Popular imagination holds a video camera theory of memory. We tend to be committed to the belief that our memories impartially and accurately store pictures of daily events as though we were walking camcorders. But it takes no more than simple reflection on our everyday domestic disagreements to conclude that even if our memories do function like sophisticated video cameras, there are widespread discrepancies between stories and pictures recorded by cohabiting cameras! In short, we see what we want to see and we remember things the way we want to remember them.

As early as 1914 Freud formulated that "screen memories" from early childhood function to gather many emotional details into a single picture or narration. Many emotional events or a whole emotional atmosphere becomes condensed and projected onto a screen, as it were, so that a certain picture or story remains as an emotionally salient "memory." The picture an individual recalls is likely to be vivid and compelling, and it is clung to tenaciously as certain truth, even in the face of reliable contradictory evidence. A screen memory may also be a reasonably accurate rendition of what actually happened on a given occasion. But it is vividly recalled, says Freud, because of its power to condense a whole emotional complex of the child's life so that the person, through pictorial and narrational means, retains a clear sense of where emotional dangers come from. Freud believed that what is essential to remember from early childhood has been retained in screen memories and that the psychotherapist's task is one of knowing how to extract that critical information. But regardless of whatever objective accuracy a given screen memory may or may not possess, its true value in psychotherapy, like that of dreams, is primarily subjective and its images are subject to the primary processes of condensation, displacement, symbolization, and the requirements of visual representability, so that screen memories can never be understood concretely or literally.

Kohut (1971, 1977) notes a special type of screen memory, the "telescoped memory," which serves to collapse a series of emotionally similar events that have occurred through various time periods of one's life into a set of vivid and compelling pictures or narratives. For example, one recalls a convincing memory of a certain event in a relationship that can clearly be placed in one's adolescence. But the emotional themes of that picture may serve to summarize, collapse, and represent the subjective truth of a series of experiences, dating perhaps from puberty, grammar school, and even earliest infancy. The memory of what happened in the back seat of a parked car in adolescence may then serve as a pictorial and narrational representation of a series of emotionally similar prior traumas that have become collapsed into this single remaining image, just as the full length of a small hand-held telescope is collapsed. Therapists are familiar in the working-through process with the emergence of dreams, memories, and transference experiences that indeed do stack up as an emotionally similar and subjectively familiar series.

Recovered memories and dreams spontaneously emerge in psychotherapy as therapist and client struggle to define hidden aspects of the here-and-now psychotherapeutic relationship—both real and transferential. The importance of screen and telescoped memories from childhood lies in the way lifelong emotional themes are condensed and displaced in much the same way as primary process material emerges in the dream, transference, and resistance remembering that characterize the therapeutic relationship.

Memories thus generated or "recovered" are most profoundly appreciated if they can be considered less as representations of actual events and more as ongoing and creative dreamwork that represents the transference and resistance themes as they emerge in the course of the development of the therapeutic relationship. It is for this reason that psychoanalysts since Freud have greatly valued the recovery of memories from early childhood. Unfortunately, the psychoanalytic interest in early childhood memories has been widely misunderstood as a frivolous and gratuitous journey into the past, whereas analysts in fact have always been militantly concerned with the here-and-now transferential moment of a person's relationships as it can be understood and interpreted through living creations of unconscious primary process thought that can be observed most clearly in the formation of dreams and early memories.

Four distinctly different psychological processes, listed here in developmental order, have been postulated in the history of psychoanalysis to account for the various conditions of remembering and forgetting:

1. *primary (neurologically conditioned) repression (or primitive dissociation)*, which acts to express a foreclosure of the possibility of reengaging in intimate relationship activities that have been formerly experienced as physically painful and mentally anguishing;

2. *ego splitting (or affective splitting)*, in which mutually contradictory affect states give rise to contrasting and contradictory self and other transference and resistance memories that represent early symbiotic or bonding relationships;

3. *dissociation (or vertical splitting)*, in which certain sectors of internal psychic experience have become unrealized or (defensively) walled off from the main personality due to overstimulating (traumatic) experience that it has not been possible to integrate into the overall span of the main personality; and

4. *secondary (defensive) repression (or horizontal splitting)*, brought about by self-instruction against socially undesirable, internally generated, instinctually driven activity and thought.

The layman's notion (which judges, jurors, and survivors' groups are most likely to hold) that presupposes massive forgetting of an intense social impingement and the later possibility of perfect video camera recall, is *not* a part of any existing psychoanalytic theory of memory. A century of psychoanalytic observation has shown that the commonsense notion of forgetting, derived as it is from the everyday experience of lapses in memory with sudden flashes of recall, simply does not hold up when fully emotionally charged interpersonal experiences from early childhood are involved. What appears to the layman as forgetting is considered by psychoanalytic theory to be the result of the operation of selective forms of recall that are dependent on the nature of the relationship context in which the memories are being recalled.

Nor do psychoanalytic theories regarding how emotionally charged memories operate support the common prejudice that human beings are accurate recorders of the historical facts out of which their personal psychic existences are forged! Human memory is not an objective process, but rather a calling forth or creation of subjective narrational images within a specific and highly influential relational context that the representational memories themselves seek to define.

Childhood memories generated, recovered, or constructed in the therapeutic development of transference and resistance to the psychotherapist and to the psychotherapeutic situation fall into four general classes characteristic of four general levels of relationship development, which are elaborated more fully in a later chapter:

1. *expressions* of the search for and the rupture of potential channels or links to others (characteristic of the organizing developmental period of four months before to four months after birth);
2. *representations* of self and other scenarios—in both passive and active (good and bad) interpersonal replications (four to twenty-four months);
3. *realizations* of self-to-selfother resonances (three years); and
4. *recollections* of wishes and fears of oedipal triangular relating (four to seven years).

These four types of transference remembering all have their own particular forms of resistance memory and are directly related to the four theories of memory just mentioned that have evolved in psychoanalysis—(1) primary repression, (2) ego-affect splitting, (3) dissociation, and (4) secondary repression. However, what usually pass as recovered memories in the popular mind most often are seen to express the earliest transference and resistance memories from the number one above, the organizing period of relatedness development (Hedges 1983, 1994b). How does this process work?

In utero and in the earliest months of life, the fetus and neonate have the task of organizing channels to the maternal body and mind for nurturance, evacuation, soothing, comfort, and stimulation. Infant research (Tronick and Cohn 1988) suggests that only about 30 percent of the time are the efforts made by an infant and mother successful in establishing mutual channels of connection that permit what Tustin (1986) has called "the rhythm of safety" to develop that is required for the two to feel satisfactorily connected. The many ways in which an infant fails in securing the needed contact from its (m)other become internalized as transference to the failing, rejecting, neglectful, or hateful (m)other.

Because the biological being of the baby knows just as every mammal knows) that if it cannot find the maternal body it will die, any serious impingement on the infant's sense of continuity of life, of going-on-being (Winnicott 1965), will necessarily be experienced as traumatic. As it were, an internalized terror response marks that failed possible channel of connection with a sign that reads, "Never reach in this way again." The range of possible infant difficulties goes from the traumatically understimulating or depriving environmental response to infant reaching, which leads to slumping, withering, and withdrawing responses, to the traumatically overstimulating or hurtful environmental responses, which lead to mentally impairing contractions and body-crippling constrictions. Such traumatic organizing level transference memories are not only presymbolic but preverbal and somatic and lead to chronically held intractable mental and physical attitudes. Resistance to ever again experiencing such traumatic, life-threatening breakdowns of linking or connecting possibilities is expressed in somatic terror and pain that mark where mother once was and then was not.

It is to this organizing experience and the reluctance to permitting or to sustaining deep, here-and-now connectedness experience that we will later return in order to show how recovered memories operate in the therapeutic relationship. A brief example will suffice at this point.

A therapist working with a multiple personality presents her work to a consultant. After she has presented an overview and general considerations, the consultant asks the therapist to bring "process notes" (event by event) of the next session for review. The therapist begins reading the process notes, telling how her client, Victor, began the hour and how he gradually zeroed in on a particular emotional issue. The therapist hears the concerns and very skillfully empathizes with the client's thoughts and feelings. Suddenly "little Victoria, age 4" appears in the room. The personality switch is significant in all regards and the therapist now begins listening to what the alter personality, Victoria, has to say. The consultant interrupts to ask how the therapist understands what has just happened. The answer is that Victor felt very understood in the prior transaction, and in the empathic safety and understanding presence of the therapist a more regressed voice (Victoria) can now speak.

This kind of critical event is ubiquitous in the treatment of organizing experiences—an empathic connection is achieved by the therapist and there is a smooth, seemingly comfortable shift to another topic, to a flashback memory, or to an alter personality. The therapist had worked hard to achieve this connection and feels gratified that her interpretive work has been successful. The therapist feels a warm glow of narcissistic pleasure that is immediately reinforced by the client's ability to move on to the next seemingly deeper and more guarded therapeutic concern. Wrong! When organizing or psychotic issues are brought for analysis, what is most feared on the basis of transference and resistance memories is an empathic interpersonal connection. This is because in the infantile situation the connection with the (m)other was experienced as painful and terrifying in some regard. That is, it was *the intimate I-thou or interactive connection itself* that was perceived by the infant mind to be the agent of the trauma. The client is then obligated to sever the link or rupture the connection just forged by some sort of turning way, changing the subject, or switching the focus in order to regain his or her position of unconnected safety.

The most therapeutically viable way of viewing the interaction just cited is to realize that the successful empathic connection was immediately, smoothly, and without notice ruptured with the personality shift! I like to think of the little white butterfly of the human soul safely fluttering out of the room.

The therapist fails to note what happened for perhaps several reasons:

1. The therapist is a well-bonded person and assumes unwittingly that empathic connection is always experienced as good by everyone.
2. The therapist doesn't understand how organizing transference and resistance operate and so is narcissistically pleased by the apparent connection he or she has achieved.
3. The client is a lifetime master at smoothly and efficiently dodging interpersonal connections—across the board or only at certain times when organizing issues are in focus.
4. A subtle mutual seduction is operating in the name of the doctrine of "recovery," in which resistance and counterresistance are winning the day with both parties afraid of personal and intimate connectedness, presumably because of its intense emotional demands.

5. The personality switch, sudden flashback, recovered memory, or change of subject allows relief from the developing interpersonal intimacy by focusing both therapist and client more comfortably on the historical causes of the dissociation or other red herrings.

6. The search for memories and validation successfully forecloses the possibility of here-and-now transference experiencing of the painful emotional horror of a traumatic infancy and how the therapeutic connection with the therapist is causing it to be replicated in the here-and-now of transference remembering.

Thus, the very real possibility of bringing to life and putting to rest traumatic modes of experiencing relationships that have been transferred from childhood is totally lost by the therapeutic technique being employed!

In the early 1990s I had puzzled considerably over how best to think of taking recovered memories seriously—not from a theoretical armchair but as a witness to years of listening to various kinds of recovered memories and as consultant to numerous therapists who had witnessed recovered memory experiences. Then one day a deeply distressed and horrified therapist appeared in my consultation group. Her horror? "Tomorrow a client I have worked with for two-and-a-half years has arranged, with the aid of members of her survivors' support group, a full family confrontation of her childhood molests."

I asked, "Survivors' groups encourage this kind of thing all the time, so what's the problem? Surely you're not involved in all that."

"No, of course not," she responded. "But after six months of therapy, when all of these abusive memories began coming out during sessions, she became quite fragmented and was having a hard time functioning. I sent her to a psychiatrist who put her on Prozac, which helped. She is on a managed health care plan so her psychotherapy benefits ran out rapidly. I continued to see her once a week for a low fee but she clearly needed more. I suggested she check out the Community Women's Center for a support group. At the center she was referred to an incest survivors' group. I thought, 'Oh, well, she is working on those issues so maybe they can help her.' Over the last two years of group participation numerous memories have emerged of absolutely terrible things that happened with her father and brothers. She was adamant that I believe all of the memories that came up in group and in session."

I asked, "And were the things believable?"

"Well, that's hard to say. She is clearly very damaged, borderline at best with organizing pockets around all of this abuse. I don't question whether she has been somehow badly abused. But I have no idea about the actual memories—there are so many of them and they are so grotesque."

"But she insisted on your believing all of them?"

"Yes, she did."

"And how did you handle that?"

"Well, I did my best to get out of it. You know, to tell her that I know some horrible things must have happened to her, that we would do our best to figure things out and find ways for her to face whatever happened and to find new ways to live—I said it all. But she had to establish in her own mind that I believed her. Then the memories began to be more explicit, things an infant can't possibly imagine unless they had actually happened to her."

I asked, "And so you believed her?"

"Well, in a way, yes. I mean, I don't know about all of the memories but clearly something awful happened to her. I let her know I believed that. But I'm sure she thinks I believe it all, just like her survivors' group does. But what I'm worried about now is she has all of this energy and support gathered for the grand confrontation tomorrow. She wants them all to confess, to say that they did all of these horrible things to her, to say they are sorry, that they are horrible people to have ever done such things, that they can never forgive themselves, and that there is no way they can ever make it up to her."

"Is that what she wants, some form of recompense?"

"I don't really know what she wants. Her father and her brothers do have money, maybe she wants some kind of payment. And there is a lot of household insurance money available. Her survivors' group has educated her to that. But that's not the main thing. Or at least I don't think so. *It's like her sanity is somehow at stake.* She now has amassed all of the believers she needs to validate her experiences and her memories in her own mind. She now feels absolutely certain that these many things happened. And if they don't confess, if they don't grovel, if they don't agree that she's right and they're wrong, I'm afraid she'll have a psychotic break! But what's got me scared is that I have somehow colluded in all of this without really meaning to. She's going to confront the family about all of these things, things that I have no way of knowing ever happened. And she's going to say that she remembered all of this in therapy and that her group helped her get the courage to finally speak the truth. You see, it's awful. I don't know how I got into this jam. And just yesterday I read about a group [the False Memory Syndrome Foundation] that's helping families fight back. They're encouraging families to sue the therapist for encouraging their clients to believe false memories. And, of course, therapists have lots of money to sue for too. I have three million dollars in insurance this family could come after. And do you know what's scariest? I have all of those memories written down in my notes. Sure enough, with her shaking, sobbing, and writhing as she remembered it all—event by event. Her family—at least on the surface—appears ordinary and normal. I don't think they're going to take well to being told they're criminals, and to being threatened with lawsuits for crimes they supposedly committed twenty-five years ago. It's all one horrible mess and I have no protection in any of this. If the family contacts me for information, I am bound by confidentiality. I can't tell them anything or help mediate in any way. The bottom line is, I'm fucked!"

I responded: "Follow me for a minute as I throw out some possibilities. When I listen to your dilemma from the perspective of borderline or symbiotic personality organization, I hear the bottom line is that your client has created a role reversal of the transference scenario. She has succeeded in molesting you, violating your personal and professional boundaries in much the same intrusive or forceful way she may once have experienced herself as a very young child—for whatever reason. According to this way of considering your dilemma, you are telling me that your life is now in as much danger as she may have felt in as an infant or toddler when all of whatever happened took place. The flashback dream memories are vivid and intensely sexual. What she experienced may have objectively looked very different. But the grotesque sexualized memories undoubtedly represent in a metaphorically true sense how she felt then, or at least how she feels now when attempting to express intense body memory-sensations arising in the course of the therapeutic relationship. According to this view, you are saying that all this time you have been feeling held emotional hostage in a similar helpless and vulnerable position to the one she felt she was in as a child—without having the slightest idea of how to extricate yourself from this intrusive violence."

"Oh, God, I'm sick in the pit of my stomach just realizing how true what you're saying is. I'm feeling all of the abuse in the symbiotic role reversal of the countertransference."

The therapist I have described here is bright, well trained, sincere, and well intentioned. Her course was carefully thought out and managed, but nevertheless has proven dangerous. Her training, like that of the vast majority of therapists practicing today, did not include how to work with primitive transference and resistance states so as to forestall massive acting out. By the therapist's own report her client was in danger of a mental breakdown.

When we believe clients, are we perpetuating a fraud? When we fail to believe them, are we refusing to help them with their recovery? What will ethics committees, licensing boards, and malpractice judges and juries be saying about how we conducted ourselves when the psychotic transference finally slips into place and it is we who finally, and publicly, stand helplessly accused of abusing this person in any of a variety of ways—by believing, by not believing, by molesting, by seducing. "It looks like we're all fucked!" was the response of the consultation group.

This therapist's horrifying vignette brought abruptly to my attention a key feature of the recovered memory problem. She feared that if her client did not get her way in the family confrontation she would have a psychotic break-down. The therapist herself was afraid of a malpractice suit or disabling ethical complaint. Therapists touched in any way by the phenomenon of these popularized recovered memories are afraid that something uncertain but catastrophic is going to happen to them in the vague but foreseeable future. What can it mean fearing that something mentally catastrophic is going to happen in the near future that is somehow related to the distant, unknown, and unrememberable past?

In "Fear of Breakdown," Winnicott (1974) convincingly demonstrates that when people in analysis speak of a fear of a psychotic break, a fear of dying, or a fear of emptiness, they are projecting into the future what has already happened in the infantile past. One can only truly fear that which one has already somehow experienced. Terrifying and disabling fears of breakdown, death, and emptiness are distinct ways of remembering agonizing mental and somatic processes that actually happened in a person's infancy. This nugget of an idea and all that has followed in its wake has changed the face of psychoanalytic thinking. What is dreaded and seen as a potentially calamitous future event is the necessity of reexperiencing in the memory of the psychotherapeutic transference the horrible, regressive, once life-threatening dependent breakdown of functioning that one in fact experienced in some form in infancy.

The fear of breakdown manifests itself in many forms as resistance to reexperiencing in transference the terror, helplessness, loss of control, somatic agony, and murderous rage once known in infancy. Therapists and clients alike dread disorganizing breakdowns, and there are many ways in resistance and counterresistance that the two can collude to forestall the curative experience of remembering by reliving the breakdown experience in the therapeutic situation and in the relationship with the therapist. One way of colluding with resistance to therapeutic re-creation of the breakdown experience is to focus on external perpetrators or long-ago traumas to prevent having to actually live through deeply distressing and frightening out-of-control experiences in the here and now together.

It is possible now to make sense of the strange and compelling nature of recovered memories. Environmental failure in infancy has led to a breakdown of early psychic processes with accompanying terror and the active threat of death (as the infant mind experienced or feared it). Having subsequent breakdown experiences is blocked by a primary neurological repression that says, "Never reach that way, never connect, never go there again." The breakdown fear lives on as a somatic underpinning that manifests as a dread of all subsequent intimate emotional relatedness or at least all I-thou experiences emotionally similar to those in which infantile trauma and a sense of breakdown (death, emptiness) occurred. The full horror of the breakdown experience cannot be directly recalled because: (1) no pictorial or narrational memory of the experience per se was recorded—only a nameless dread of dependence in trust relationships that are feared to lead to trauma; (2) the memory of the breakdown experience itself is guarded with intense signal pain, somatic terror, and physical symptoms of all types that function to pull the person safely out of the anticipated harm that intimate relating is believed to produce; (3) the memory of a shattered, injured, or destroyed sense of the earliest self is often expressed or represented in self-effacing, self-destructive, life-threatening gestures such as cutting or burning oneself, taking drugs to escape the consciousness of stress or other dangerous activities; and (4) the trauma occurred before it was possible to record pictures, words, or stories, so it cannot be recalled in ordinary ways but only as bodily agony and terrors of an approaching emptiness, breakdown, and/or death.

Most people have no trouble understanding an infant's fear of psychological breakdown or even possible or anticipated instinctual fear of death from lack of adequate and responsive care. But it was Winnicott's genius to see that from the infant's point of view it was an unresponsive and empty environment that preceded the breakdown and psychic death, and that an entire emotional sequence beginning with a sense of emptiness in the environment became systematically conditioned (internalized) in response to understimulating or overstimulating infant experiences of focal trauma or to longer-term experiences of having to adapt to difficult circumstances that produce a cumulative strain trauma (Khan 1963) with similar effects. It should be no mystery why the kinds of disjointed and fragmented mental and physical symptoms often associated with PTSD regularly emerge in the course of therapeutic transference and resistance remembering when working with organizing level transference, or that the death fear is often expressed in a variety of (counterphobic?) life-threatening and/or self-destructive, self-effacing and painful gestures or experiences.

The mythic themes of recovered memories (incest, violence, multiple selves, cult abuse, birth trauma, kidnapping, and alien abduction) have been present in all cultures since the beginning of recorded time. Archetypal images of those atrocities can be called upon by the creative human unconscious to allow for a creative narration to be built in psychotherapy that conveys the emotional essence of the infant's traumatic experience that is now being relived or threatening to be replicated as a direct result of building intimate connections with the therapist. The demand to be believed represents in some way the sense of urgency inherent in the violation of infantile boundaries. The primordial boundary violations that are registered in such transference memory role reversals can be interpreted through the role-reversal countertransference as the therapist feeling put upon or violated by the demand to "believe me" or "validate my pain."

Disturbing communications and bizarre or demanding symptoms function to rupture the trusting and intimate emotional connections forming with the therapist by forcing some sort of alienating response, perturbation, or disjunction into the relationship. The working through of the repeated ruptures of interpersonal contact by flashbacks, sudden physical symptoms, bizarre thoughts, panic attacks, personality switches, and boundary violations can be accomplished through the therapist's according some priority to the apprehension and fear that regularly accompanies each step toward greater intimacy, thus securing the organizing transference and resistance for analysis. Elsewhere I spell out in detailed analysis and vignette the theory of the organizing transference and the expectable alienated countertransferences (Hedges 1994c). A series of illuminating long-term cases are discussed in Hedges 1994a. My colleagues and I later demonstrate in a dozen in-depth case studies the nuts and bolts of transference and countertransference development and the working-through process—especially vivid in the case of Paul (Hedges 2000b). In that book I come to speak of the incessant symptom picture, whatever forms it may take, as "the clamor." This term simultaneously serves to indicate the desperate clamoring need once experienced in infancy and to stigmatize the function of the reoccurrence of the need in therapy as an alienating one to ensure that the other never risks coming close enough to truly connect.

Memories recovered in the course of psychotherapy can be taken seriously if one keeps in mind what kinds of early life events are subject to what *forms* of later recall, and how the recall can be meaningfully accomplished through transference and resistance analysis. We have studied the way human truth gets projected into creative and expressive images, narrations, and narrative interactions that capture the essence of the lived psychic experience. We know that plausible narrations demand a beginning, a middle, and an end. Characters must have motives and act in believable ways with purposes and affects. In a plausible narrative various gaps or inconsistencies in the story, the character structure, or the cause and effect of purpose are glossed over, filled in, and seamlessly woven together in ways that are vivid, flow naturally, and are emotionally compelling and logically believable.

We are taken in by the story of Dr. Jekyll and Mr. Hyde because we all know what it means to experience ourselves in various convincing and contradictory parts. Every time *Sybil* is on national television or a talk show airs live appearances of satanic ritual abuse victims or people abducted by aliens, our clinics are flooded with self-referrals. After the atomic bomb we looked to the skies for danger and sure enough our efforts quickly brought us flying saucers. We begin affirming more rights for women, children and other marginalized people and soon our culture begins noticing actual abusive incidents as well as many other violent and molest stories that seemed to have other sources. When our culture could no longer believe in conversion hysteria, we saw peptic ulcers, then stress, and now viral contagion as our public enemy. When we could no longer believe in Bridie Murphy's past lives, we turned to multiple selves, alien abductions, and satanic ritual abuse as archetypal themes to express primitive fears. The list of possibilities goes on, and will keep expanding as our collective imagination continues to generate believable images that can be used in our screen, telescoped, and narrative constructions to clarify what our infancies were like and what the structure of our deepest emotional life looks like.

"My parents in raising me were more concerned with creeds and ritual than they were with my needs to love and to be loved by them. The reverence they kept was like a cult. My father was the high priest, my mother a priestess who looked on, emotionless, while I was led to the altar and forced to kill a baby (me?) and drink its blood. Then I was placed on the altar as a sacrifice to the carnal wishes of all of their friends, the other participants who supported their dogmatic belief system. But the most unbearable part of all is that I was forced to do the same things they did, to become like them, to sacrifice human life in the same manner they did, in the same cult, at the same altar. As a result, I am a deeply damaged person."

"There is a higher intelligence that comes into my sphere, that picks me up, puts me down, and exchanges fluids with me through my umbilicus. They want my soul, my fertility, and they want to impregnate me with their superior mental structure. I have no control over the coming and going of the higher intelligence that governs my life but I am frightened by it and suddenly swept away. It's like being lost in an endless nightmare that I can't make go away. Like losing yourself in a horrible science fiction movie you just can't shake off. I have no control over these higher intelligences that watch me."

"My father loved me too much. I remember when he used to come into my room. I remember my mother was somewhere in the background. My childhood longings were misread by him and he took advantage of me. If she had done her job in keeping him happy like a wife should, I would not have been given to him."

"My mother ruled my every thought. We were always close, we shared everything. My father was an irrational, alcoholic brute, no one from whom I could learn masculinity. He gave me to her because he didn't want to deal with her dependency and so I had to be parent to her, husband to her—no wonder I am what I am."

In all of these familiar stories, and others, we can suppose that what must eventually be expressed or represented in the affective and interactional exchange of the psychotherapeutic transference and resistance is the loss of power, the loss of control over oneself, and a personal destiny to continue experiencing emptiness, breakdown, and death as a result of internalized environmental failures. The kinds of stories that must be told and the kinds of painful somatic memories that must be relived vary according to the personal and idiosyncratic nature of the infantile breakdown experience.

As professionals we have not yet begun to assess the grave danger each of us is in as a result of recovered memories emerging into the therapeutic transference–countertransference relationship. Escalating law suits, increasing disciplinary action by ethics committees and licensing boards, and skyrocketing costs of malpractice insurance make clear that the problem is real and that it is serious. For these and other reasons I always advocate the inclusion of a third party case monitor whenever organizing or psychotic transferences are being worked on so that all parties are aware of the work and so that all parties are protected from accidental derailing of the psychotic process. (The Informed Consent for Long-Term Psychotherapy [on the CD-ROM] offers further management suggestions [also see Hedges 1994c].) It is not abusive or neglectful parents and families that are the proper therapeutic target of primitive abusive transference feelings. It is ourselves as transference objects and the hard work we do to build a relationship into which transference experiences can be projected.

The Organizing Experience Worksheet (on the CD-ROM) aids therapists in considering how the organizing transference is slowly emerging and focuses on a series of crucial dimensions in which organizing experiences regularly appear as clients approach us for connection and flee in disconnection.[4] This form can also be used in peer review groups to observe how primordial fear manifests itself in our lives and in our psychotherapy practices.

Here are some things to keep in mind when dealing with any memory that emerges in psychotherapy:

1. Clinical, theoretical, and experimental research fails to support the popularized video camera theory of memory. The widely held view that externally generated psychic trauma can produce total amnesia for many years and then be subject to total recall of fact is a Hollywood invention that is completely fallacious. As a dramatic device for generating horror and suspense, the specter of capricious memory loss in response to unwanted experiences has indeed been successful in convincing millions that such things can and do happen—as attested to by an utterly spellbound population.

2. Recovered memories cannot be counted as fact. Consideration from a psychoanalytic and psychotherapeutic point of view shows there to be too many sources of variance in recovered memories for them to ever be considered reliable sources of factual truth. Memories produced in hypnosis, chemically induced interviews, or psychotherapy are setting, technique, and relationship dependent. The most important recovered memories that attest to a history of trauma originate in the earliest months and years of life. Our knowledge of the way the human mind records experiences during this period makes it impossible for pictorial, verbal, narrational, or even screen images to provide facts that are reliable.

3. Memories recovered in psychotherapy cannot be considered as merely false confabulations. We have a series of viable ways to consider the potential truth value of memories recovered within the context of psychotherapy. Much has been said concerning screen memories, telescoped memories, and narrational truth. Little attention has been given in the recovered memory literature to the kinds of transference and resistance memories that can be expected to characterize each developmental epoch of early childhood.[5]

The terror that many infants experienced in the first months of life due to misfortune, misunderstanding, neglect, and/or abuse is recorded in painful aversions to dependent states that leave them at later risk for psychic breakdown. The effects of cumulative strain trauma in infancy can be devastating in a person's later life, though no trauma was visible and no overt abuse present at the time. People resist having to reexperience in transference (i.e., to remember) the terrifying and physically painful memories of environmental failure in earliest infancy. But externalizing responsibility for one's unhappiness in life onto people and events of childhood goes fundamentally against the grain of responsible psychotherapy.

4. A simplified recovery approach tends to collude with resistance to the establishment of early transference remembering, and, to the degree that it does, it is antipsychotherapeutic. In acceding to the clients' demand to be believed, to have their experiences validated, and to receive support for redress of wrongs, recovery workers foreclose the possibility of securing for analysis the transference and resistance memories mobilized in the here-and-now psychotherapeutic relationship or set off by outside demands for more intimate relating. Encouraging the acting out of multidetermined recovered memories in the name of psychotherapy is clearly creating liabilities for such therapists.

5. Studies of recovered memories cannot draw responsible conclusions when collapsing over diverse categories of memory, developmental levels, and modes of personality organization, nor can conclusions uncritically be

generalized from the psychotherapy setting, which is situation and relationship dependent, to other social and legal settings. Human memory is complex, elusive, and multidimensional, so that all attempts to arrive at simplified or dogmatic conclusions are bound to be faulty. This includes attempts to consider the physiological aspects of memory as well.

6. Taking recovered memories seriously involves establishing a private and confidential relationship in which all screen, narrational, transference, and resistance memory possibilities can be carefully considered over time and within the ongoing context of the psychotherapeutic relationship. Therapeutic transformation of internal structures left by childhood oversight, neglect, and abuse necessarily involves mobilizing in the therapeutic relationship a duality in which the real relationship with the therapist can be known in contrast to the remembered relationships from childhood that are being projected from within the client onto the person of the psychotherapist and into the process of the analysis as transference and resistance.

Responsible psychotherapeutic work with memories recovered from infancy and early childhood requires much time and a well-developed interpersonal relationship between the client and therapist. The temptation for a therapist to take recovered memories at face value and to encourage revengeful and/or restitutive action against presumed perpetrators is great. The current limited managed care approach means that help for the several million who suffer from infantile trauma will not be provided. How many billions of dollars will we spend on litigational activities and criminal prosecutions before relatively inexpensive prevention and treatment measures are realistically considered? How many lives will be ruined and families destroyed before we attend to the truly horrible problem of infantile trauma and its effects in later adulthood? How many therapists will yet be trapped into a collusive role in order to avoid here-and-now transference remembering? How many therapeutic processes will yet be aborted by outside fluke occurrences because therapists failed to set up preventative measures? When such a misfortune happens to someone you are treating, will you have been practicing defensively enough to have protected yourself from potential disaster?

FULLY UNDERSTANDING THE GENESIS OF FALSE ACCUSATIONS

The last and perhaps the most important consideration in practicing defensively is understanding the source of false accusations against therapists, which entails studying the effects of infantile trauma on later transference developments. It was only as I gained experience as an expert witness testifying on behalf of beleaguered therapists who I felt had been unjustly accused on the basis of primitive transference developments that I could see how crucial our understanding of the transference-based false accusations argument is for the way we listen to clinical material and the ways we respond to transferences born of early trauma. In a later chapter I give an account of my work with the California Board of Behavioral Sciences to save a psychotherapist's license.[6]

NOTES

1. This section is excerpted and adapted with permission from *The California Therapist*, May/June, June/July, August/September 1993, originally entitled, "In Praise of the Dual Relationship," and reprinted in Hedges 2000b.

2. A brilliantly conceived book edited by Arnold A. Lazarus and Ofer Zur (2002), features thirty-one chapters authored by many nationally known therapists and writers pointing toward the benefits of dual relating and warning therapists of various dangers.

3. This section is excerpted and adapted with permission from *Issues in Child Abuse Accusations*, vol. 6(1) (1994): 1–31, and reprinted in Hedges 2000b.

4. The Organizing Experience Worksheet is reprinted from Hedges 2000b based on the fundamental theoretical dimensions discussed in Hedges 1994c, and illustrated in the case studies of Hedges 1994a, 1996, and 2000b.

5. While I establish the historical basis and broad dimensions of the listening perspectives approach based on four stages of self-and-other relationship development in Hedges 1983 and summarize it in Hedges 1992 and 1994a, the most comprehensive treatment of the theoretical perspectives along with extensive case studies and countertransference analysis appears in Hedges 1996.

6. Elsewhere I have fully elaborated the "Genesis and Preventions of False Accusations" (2000a).

7

Linking Infantile Trauma, Terrifying Transferences, and False Accusations[1]

HOWARD'S PLIGHT

Howard left word on my voice mail requesting the name of an attorney who defends psychotherapists. I left the name of the best attorney I know on his recorder, adding that I hope this wasn't for him! A few weeks later on a Tuesday I received a call from an investigator employed by the State of California. She explained that she was investigating a complaint of sexual misconduct against Howard made by one of his former psychotherapy clients. Howard told her that he had consulted with me ten years previously regarding this case. Had I indeed supervised him at one time? Yes. Could she ask me a few quick questions over the phone about Howard and his work? I explained that I could not say anything to her until I had obtained a release from him. I also stated that I thought she and I needed to meet in person, considering the potential importance of our time together. We set up an appointment in two weeks to discuss her concerns.

I was immediately sick to my stomach. I knew too well how grave this situation was. I hardly slept for two nights—and I'm usually a good sleeper. I tossed and turned with tortured nightmares. I dreamed of being in Berlin in 1938 smelling burning flesh with everyone around me saying there was nothing they could personally do, thus choosing to blind themselves to the atrocities that were occurring right under their noses. I saw the Nazi Gestapo in high black boots knocking on doors in the middle of the night. I saw the lines of those waiting to be burned.

I know too well our administrative justice system. I know that therapists are tried daily under conditions totally lacking in civil rights. Licensing boards for psychotherapists have sadly become Courts of Inquisition in which bizarre complaints of highly disturbed, disgruntled consumers are allowed to wreck the lives of hard-working, honest, well-intentioned therapists. Administrative justice as it is practiced today in California and most other places strips therapists of their professional dignity, their right to discovery processes, their right to a trial by jury, their right to practice their profession, their peace of mind, and the financial security they have worked a lifetime to establish for their families and their retirement.

In agonizing over Howard's plight, I knew too well that people who sit in judgment on state licensing boards are political appointees to represent consumers and have absolutely no training or experience in long-term, intensive psychotherapy. There's no way they would ever be able to understand his case. The same is true for state investigators and attorneys general—no relevant training, no expertise, no professional supervision, no understanding whatsoever of processes they are being called upon to deal with and make judgments about. Even the handful of licensed therapists who are sprinkled in the boards and the "experts" hired by the boards to examine accused therapists lack systematic supervised training that would make them qualified to render opinion on the deep transferences stirred up by long-term depth psychotherapy. I have written textbooks, published numerous articles, and lectured endlessly on this topic to little avail. An administrative monster continues to grind out injustices that destroy lives of my professional colleagues—creating hopelessly untenable situations against which therapists cannot even be fully insured.

Howard is now being called upon to account for himself in this Inquisition kind of setting. A woman who undoubtedly would have been burned at the stake as a witch by the Grand Inquisitor has accused him of sexual misconduct! I'm a miserable wreck just thinking about it. I've seen too much of this to even hope it will turn out okay.

Howard's attorney accompanies him for a two-hour interview with the state investigator. Afterward he tells Howard the situation is grim. The accusations are serious. It's next to impossible to defend oneself against unsubstantiated claims before state licensing boards. How do you prove you didn't do something you are accused of when the licensing board has significant political motivations and financial incentives to find you guilty? Administrative justice is set up so that the licensing boards simultaneously serve as accuser, prosecutor, judge, jury, sentencer, and penalty collector. Howard's attorney sees no way out and advises him to prepare for the worst. Disciplinary actions for sexual misconduct usually result in loss of license or, at best, five years of probation with huge expenses for required therapy, supervision, and ongoing education as well as steep financial penalties—not to mention public humiliation.

In the past when I have witnessed firsthand such travesties of justice it has been as a hired witness for total strangers. This was strikingly different. Howard I know — very well, in fact. I trust his personal and professional integrity almost more than my own. I know the case well. I had heard about Francine off and on for eight years. Howard had presented his work with her to more than twenty professional colleagues in case conference seminars that I either led or attended. I heard him present his work to three visiting internationally renowned experts. His colleagues called her "Howard's case from Hell."

Suffice it to say that Francine had been stalked and raped on a nearly daily basis throughout her childhood by every member of her family including her mother. Not surprisingly, she later became the victim of numerous other sexual assaults. Every time she saw Howard she announced in one way or another that she wanted to "jump his bones." The infernal saga tormented Howard endlessly for years as Francine slowly began to trust, gradually learned to connect with him, and finally began to develop a personal life with some rewards and some sanity. Then Prozac came along to give her just the added boost to motivate her to stop therapy, though the decisive working-through process was by no means complete. Several years later when Francine ran into some difficulties at work her new managed care provider would not support her going back to see Howard, instead offering her time-limited in-house crisis counseling. When Francine began recounting her sexualized agony and torment in her previous therapy with Howard, her newly licensed counselor working for the managed care company advised her to report Howard to the licensing board for misconduct — no one should ever have to feel so sexually overstimulated or be so tortured in therapy. It apparently never occurred to the counselor that childhood trauma might be getting mixed up in Francine's accounts of her therapy.

Frantic after the disturbing call from the state investigator and two sleepless nights, I arrived Thursday morning at a case conference seminar that I lead. I knew I couldn't sit passively by and watch Howard burn, but I dreaded what might be entailed if I tried to stand up to the power of the state. I asked the group to give me their time today as I was in crisis. During the ninety minutes I allowed myself to free associate and ultimately to break down. Everyone there knew I had been suffering with these issues for some time. All were familiar with my writings and lectures on the subject. They could feel my distress and urged me to talk freely, to let it all hang out — and I did. I found my heart racing, my hands perspiring, and my voice tense and strained as I swore at the "fuckin' boards," at the farce of administrative justice, at the uselessness of all my books, at the needless damage that board stupidity continues to foist on patients, at the atrocities I have seen boards commit against therapists, at the misery of therapists and their families I have seen suffer, and at the utter audacity of the licensed profession-als—the "expert witnesses"—who unethically allow themselves to be used as pawns in this whole devastating process. Did I scream and yell? Probably. I don't know. But I began tearing shortly after John quietly said, "There's more, Larry, this runs deeper." I was thrown back to second and third grade to Butch Prather, the school bully who often targeted me. I vividly recalled the day Butch caught up with me on my bicycle on the way home. "He took me down, but none of his cronies were with him that day and I beat the shit out of him. I was mis-erable then just like I am now." Jane said, "He forced you to hit him . . . he made an animal out of you!" "Yes, and I cried all the way home and sobbed with my head on my mother's lap. I had bloodied him and left him alone crying in a ditch. I never wanted to hit him. You're right. There was no choice, he made me fight him. And now damn it, I have to do it again." I was feeling deep fear and dread. I recalled similar emotions when I finally had to stand against the abusive force of my father and others. I definitely did not want this task. But I could find no escape. I protested, "Those state guys all have a police mentality—blind, igno-rant, vindictive. They are dangerous. All I have to do is to make myself a target and I'll be crushed." "That's what the Germans said about the Nazis," someone who remembered my dream chimed in. "It's too late, Larry," John reminded me. "You are already a target because of your papers on dual relationships and false accusations." "Thanks for reminding me. But the investigators and boards haven't understood it so far, why would I think more protest would do any good?"

The group's support was strong and I begin to calm down, to relax. I was fighting an imperative I couldn't avoid. I was dreading the prospects of mov-ing forward. If the accusations against Howard were allowed to stand, who would be next? I thought of all the therapists who for nearly thirty years have brought to me their most difficult cases for consultation. Most of these cases were high risk. Every one of us is vulnerable to this type of accusation, the kind that emerges from deep transference work. As you know, I have already been involved in civil courts representing accused therapists on a number of these cases. But at least in civil court there is a discovery process, and a judge and jury to appeal to. In administrative law—after the politically and eco-nomically motivated board has made an accusation—and if the therapist has thirty thousand dollars, cash in pocket—an appeal can be made to a state-ap-pointed commissioner who will hear the case. But the commissioner's deci-sions are not binding and are frequently overturned by the boards. More than half of the judges' decisions were reportedly overturned in 1990 and the fig-ure has risen steadily since.

"In the past few years I have done considerable expert witness work at-tempting to help falsely accused therapists. In every case in which I have been given full access to the court's records and been given the time to study and to formulate, each accusation I have tagged as likely to be false on the basis of transference considerations has been dropped by the administrative law judge. I assume from those results that I have at least been successful in creating reasonable doubt. But in case after case the licensing boards of California and now twelve several other states have ignored the findings of the commissioner and have gone ahead to sustain the accusations and to mete out severe disciplinary actions against the therapists. That's the current state of things. Anyone who's not terrified by that isn't dealing with reality!"

As I talked freely in the consultation group I felt the relief of support from colleagues. I still felt dread, but I also felt the necessity of biting the bullet and forging out something that had the hope of being effective. Howard's case was in itself moving to us all, but more than that were the broader issues of patient care and therapist safety for us all.

> *John*: There's no one better prepared than you are to do this. You have the credentials. You've written the books and articles. You have the research data. You have the experience and the courage.

> *Jane*: If you don't do this, then who will, who can? There isn't really a choice. You're prepared. You can do it. And so you must. We'll all help you in any way we can.

> *Larry*: It scares the shit out of me. I feel fear and dread.

> *John*: Of course you do, that's appropriate. But there's also plenty of support. People know you. Your work is credible. You are articulate and people respect what you have to say. Your fundamental good will in this is evident and known.

> *Larry*: But how do I dare start to tackle this monster if so far my words have fallen on deaf ears?

> *John*: Your protest is falling on sympathetic but deaf ears now. You are in it too deep. We all see you're not going to be able get out of this!

I had less than two weeks to prepare before talking to the state investigator. Ventilating with the group underlined that I must act and act now—quickly, decisively, and effectively. Being able to air my feelings and to feel supported helped me clarify that my enemies aren't the boards, the attorneys general, the investigators, the ethics committees, or anyone else. My enemy is simple ignorance—a certain lack of knowledge in critical places. For more than twenty years I have been conducting clinical research into these deep transferences. It is clear that there is indeed a widespread knowledge gap, and that ignorance of cutting-edge thinking is hurting clients and therapists in many ways. In my role as a professional educator I deal every day with knowledge gaps and problems of ignorance. I began to see this as simply another educational challenge—and it was true that I was up for it. Something inside me began to calm and to take hold.

I could clearly see that I had two tasks before me that were separate but interrelated. The problem of getting myself ready to meet with Howard's investigator was one. And the broader problem of how to call for a widespread educational campaign was the other. The tasks were related in that the accusation against Howard was inexorably propelling me to get the road paved in Sacramento well in advance of Howard's case coming to the attention of the board.

The format I selected to begin the educational campaign was a letter to Sherry Mehl, executive director of the California Board of Behavioral Sciences, with copies to be sent to a number of key administrative people in California and national organizations. What the fallout would be I did not know. But it wasn't my job to speculate about that. I needed to simply get down to the business of clarifying the problem and calling for accountability.

For the next two weeks I pounded on my computer. I printed out numerous revised drafts to read to friends, colleagues, consultation groups, and classes for feedback. Drafts were faxed all over the country asking for ideas and suggestions. The response was swift and enthusiastic. Everyone saw the need to get this straightened out as soon as possible. It's great to be able to count on people when you really need them. I sought professional consultation from several experts in law and ethics. Especially helpful was Muriel Golub, chair of the California Psychological Association's Ethics Committee. Dr. Golub knows these issues well and gave up considerable time on a holiday weekend to fax follow-up memos back and forth, helping me to clean up and focus my arguments.

By the time of my appointment with Howard's investigator, I was imbued with a rare sense of high energy, inspiration, and purpose, a firm feeling of widespread support, and an absolute sense of the rightness of what I had to say to her. Fortunately, she was a wonderful woman with a lot of common sense who had done this kind of work for many years. She had somehow been spared the deadening effects of the "civil servant syndrome." She had just come from having her nails done at a beauty salon she was investigating. In the morning she had interviewed people in a chiropractor's office about a complaint there. Now it was sexual misconduct allegations against a therapist. The investigator was up front in saying that she knew next to nothing about therapy—so if I was going to get technical on her, I had to go slow and explain as I went! She immediately grasped the sincerity of my intent, my level of sophistication in what I was talking about, and my passion for what

I believed. To her credit she asked good questions and stopped me often to be sure she was getting what I was saying correctly. It was a good meeting and I was heartened. But I have seen too much to be optimistic. It was now her job to recommend that the board make charges against Howard or that the allegations be dropped.

You are about to read "the letter," as it came to be known locally. It was the powerful thinking of a hundred plus people in this letter that fueled my interview with Howard's investigator. But even with all the energy that went into this confrontation, I was still shocked and incredulous when, a few weeks later, I came home and heard Howard's voice on my answering machine. "I don't know what you said to that lady, Larry. But I received a letter today from her indicating that she was closing my case! The accusation will not go to the Board. God bless you and thank you so much. I'll be talking with you soon."

And God bless everyone who has helped me in this journey over the years. When something is wrong we have to stick together and stand up for what's right. Yes, I'm still scared. And the educational campaign has just begun. But I'm breathing much easier now that the problem is clearly articulated and out in the open. Having loving support makes all the difference.

As you will shortly see I don't believe this is simply a case of bad justice for therapists, but of grave misunderstanding even by most therapists about the nature of deep transferences and the terrors and dangers they stir up. The ultimate concern here is for the well-being of the client and for the usefulness of the therapeutic process in helping to resolve issues of childhood trauma. I hope you find the letter interesting and that you pass copies of it along to your friends and colleagues who might be interested. You will feel as you read the letter the power of many voices behind me enriching, clarifying, and sculpting the final text. I hope you enjoy it.

LETTER TO THE CALIFORNIA BOARD OF BEHAVIORAL SCIENCES

June 24, 1997
Sherry Mehl, Executive Director
Board of Behavioral Sciences
Department of Consumer Affairs
400 R. St. Suite 3150
Sacramento, CA 92814

Re: Increasing awareness of how the "organizing" or "psychotic" transference operates in the accusation and investigation processes.

Dear Ms. Mehl:

As we discussed on the telephone, I am writing concerning a matter that has weighed heavily on me for some time. It is my belief that consumers as well as psychotherapists are currently being misled and damaged by a critical gap in knowledge about the nature and operation of transferences caused by infantile trauma. My primary professional activity for twenty-five years has been coaching therapists through their most difficult cases—in individual tutorials as well as in case conference groups. I have consulted on more than fifty cases involved in some type of complaint process in five states and have served as an expert witness on a series of cases brought before licensing boards. I have tried (not always successfully) to limit my work to cases in which I believed the therapists were doing an average, expectable job with their clients, and in which the therapy process had fallen prey to primitive transferences giving rise to distorted, faulty, and/or false accusations against the therapist. In the course of my work I have witnessed many serious breaches in law and ethics on the part of therapists who were abusing and taking advantage of their clients. I wholeheartedly support our investigation processes and believe that prompt and effective disciplinary measures should be taken against all who violate our legal and ethical standards.

It is clear to me that licensing boards and ethics committees have a very difficult task. It is also clear that the current knowledge base and operating policies allow most circumstances to be handled effectively and appropriately. For this I congratulate those who devote their time and energy to ensuring that psychotherapy remains a viable, effective, and safe professional enterprise in our society. However, a glaring gap in one particular area of knowledge and expertise needs to be addressed.

The Knowledge Gap

There exists a widespread lack of awareness regarding a psychological structure referred to as the "organizing transference." This transference structure is formed in early childhood in response to infantile trauma during the organizing period of development. In our literature this phenomenon has been assigned the label "transference psychosis" because it emerges as a deep transference structure in long-term, intensive psychotherapy, and called "psychotic transference" because, when the client transfers this early emotional scar into the psychotherapy situation and onto the person of the therapist, the client's capacities for ordinary perception and reality testing are eclipsed. *Under these conditions the person experienced in the past as perpetrator of the infantile trauma is confused with the object of the transference in the present—the therapist who has worked hard to elicit the transference.* The current acute distress at having to reexperience in therapy the deep psycho-physical trauma is "blamed" on the therapist—for, after all, it is he or she who has been active in bringing the long-forgotten past agony into the experiential present.

Since many otherwise sane people have a history of some kind of infantile trauma and are occasionally subject to such deep transference-memory regressions, I do not like the term *psychotic*, which implies some sort of wild, crazy madness. The terms *organizing experience, organizing memory structure*, and *organizing transference* better describe the origin of the experience that is being revived for therapeutic work. That is, a fetus or an infant while "organizing" psychological channels to the environment for nurturing, soothing, and tension relief is met with some form of invasive trauma. A traumatized infant typically reacts with agitation and, in extreme cases, terror. Intense fear in infancy is painful and accompanied by physical constrictions, diffuse physiological stress, and severe emotional withdrawal. It is the revival and working through of these regressive psycho-physical experiences in the present psychotherapeutic transference that permits eventual recovery and growth.

Most licensed therapists may never encounter the organizing transference because they are doing short-term work, cognitive or behavioral interventions, family or couple counseling, industrial or forensic consulting, or support groups of various types. But any therapist who has been seeing individual clients for very long inevitably attracts some people who need extended care. Psychotherapeutic relationships that last for more than a few months raise the likelihood that in time a significant emotional relationship will develop. It is the deepening of the therapeutic relationship that makes possible the perception and analysis of the well-known narcissistic and borderline transferences as well as the little-understood organizing transference.

Many competent therapists doing long-term work have, in the course of their professional development, made it a point to seek out additional supervision and continuing education as needed in order to successfully bring out the merger fantasies, split affects, dissociations, and projective identifications involved in deep work. And ethics committees and licensing boards are becoming accustomed to dealing effectively with complaints arising from narcissistic and borderline transference structures. However, in areas of deeper regression to the organizing transference, understanding remains limited.

Transference Memories of Infantile Trauma

There exists a significant and growing group of clients whose therapeutic needs press them to explore deeper or "more primitive" transference structures that contain the memories of infantile trauma. Infantile trauma or severe trauma later in life can result from the many kinds of overt or covert molest, abuse, or neglect that we already know about. But infantile trauma—either experienced in utero or in the earliest months of life—can also result from such things as toxemia in pregnancy, fetal exposure to alcohol and drugs, premature birth, birth trauma, birth defects, separation from the biological mother, adoptions, incubators, foster placements, medical procedures, parental or familial distress, holocaust conditions, maternal depression, and a myriad of other highly stressful conditions. Infantile trauma can be focal and acute, or it can be diffuse and cumulative in its effect on the developing child.

The Terror of Human Connections

What is it that characterizes this group of clients who have experienced severe infantile trauma? Terror—deep-seated, nonconscious terror that if they reach out for interpersonal emotional connection they will be retraumatized. The transference expectation insures that they will experience terrifying, body-shaking, soul-wrenching trauma in response to close emotional contact. The very nature of this transference alerts these people to the threat that, if anyone approaches them in emotionally significant ways, they will once again feel injured. Every cell in their bodies yells out, "Danger! Danger!" whenever they dare to experience the possibility of the human connections that have the power to heal them. Since intimacy was the original instrument of the abuse or trauma, it is deeply feared.

I frequently travel and lecture, conduct classes and seminars, and I meet privately every day with groups of therapists, teaching them about the effects of infantile trauma. I attempt to show them the ways that the organizing transference asserts itself as a terror of empathic connections. The knowledge expansion in the field of psychotherapy over the past three decades has taught most therapists the empathic skills involved in "connecting," "holding," and "containing" techniques appropriate for narcissistic and borderline transferences.

But therapists generally do not know, nor is it intuitively obvious, that many clients who were traumatized before ordinary forms of communication and memory developed have no choice but to experience the connecting overtures of the therapist as seductive, frightening, and painful. Nor is it intuitively obvious that ordinary empathic connections—which most therapists have been taught to value—paradoxically function in the organizing transference as intrusive retraumatizations that the client must avoid as much as possible, fend off, and eventually rage about and/or flee from in terror.

Is it any wonder that so many of these clients cry out in pain and seek public redress for their experienced injuries? Therapy promised them healing.

The therapist promoted relationship. And relationship led to terrifying and painful regressive transference experiences that they could not bear. Reality testing weakened. Then, in the revival of the confused and traumatized state of infancy, the therapist became experienced as the perpetrator.

I coach therapists daily as they struggle with their clients through this most treacherous of passages—through deep body-mind terror on the way toward learning how to make and to sustain human connections that have the power to cure. Much of our work is devoted to learning how the specific client characteristically desires and approaches the therapist for the human warmth and connection that he or she has been deprived of for so long. We study week after week, month after month, exactly how each client begins to experience the connection to the therapist. Then we wait and watch exactly how the client instinctively falls into deep fear, physical symptoms, disorientation, and contact avoidance. Studying in each client the operation of the predefense fear mechanisms common to all mammals—freeze, fight, or flee—aids us in the discovery and working-through process toward safe interpersonal connections and emotional interactions that allow growth and healing. Accusations of therapists are a regular part of reviving the accusatory cry of infant trauma for psychotherapeutic study.

There is no way we know at present to determine in advance the exact nature of the trauma experienced at the base of a person's psycho-physiological being. Nor is there any way known to predict exactly how that trauma will reassert itself in the approach-avoidance matrix of the therapeutic situation as the transference-countertransference struggle unfolds.

It is clear that the terror of interpersonal connection these people experience is distinctly different from the fear of abandonment that people working on narcissistic and borderline transferences experience. Also clear is the agony of the accusatory cry revived from the traumatized infant self, "You hurt me when you came near me—when you touched me!" Or, in the reverse, is the fighting clamor to the effect that the therapist did not give or do enough. A harshly accusatory or incessant cry and struggle for "more," of course, can serve to alienate the affections of the therapist so that deep emotional connections do fail—thus replicating the infantile trauma afresh. The struggle to get the therapist to be more attentive, or to do more, often purposefully functions to disturb or rupture the therapist-client empathy ties—the exact thing that produced the original trauma.

At the moment of confused, regressive, psychotic transference reexperiencing, the perception and reality testing of the client are sufficiently eclipsed so that the traumatic psycho-physical memory resurfaces in the present in a form that contradicts reality. That is, it is caring, reaching out, and the desire for compassionate healing connections that the therapist is offering. This offering elicits the impulse to reach out to find human connection. But then, because of the nature of the organizing transference, the emotional connection will necessarily be experienced as terrifying and painful. At such moments clients can actually perceive and believe that an abusive violation has occurred when in reality there was no such violation. Rather, early trauma was reawakened and distortedly attached to what the therapist did or did not do.

The transferred infantile experience of sensual connection being traumatically intruded upon is thus, "You were loving me, encouraging me to open up to you, insisting that I trust you, and then you hurt me." The "then you hurt me" takes endless forms as the historical specifics of the client's infantile trauma emerge. But the archaic, sensual body memory of trauma is now emerging in an adult with a fully sexually charged body. And, given the sensuality of the original experience, the transferred experience is often felt to be a sexual or quasi-sexual intrusion.

Staying with such persistent and traumatic structures takes stamina on the part of both therapist and client. At any point in the process, therapist or client could, for any of a variety of reasons, falter in intent or determination. Or an outside, unforeseen event could interrupt the working-through process with disastrous consequences. This is often the point at which complaints are filed. There is a significant knowledge gap about the nature of this kind of transference remembering. And there is a knowledge gap regarding how therapeutic technique for this kind of work necessarily differs in major ways from work with narcissistic and borderline transferences.

The Damage Created by the Knowledge Gap

Consumers who approach psychotherapy with the hope of having their deep trauma wounds healed are being misled because many therapists haven't the slightest idea how even to identify the organizing or psychotic elements in deep transference, much less how to work with them. For example, many "recovered memories" attributed to later events can undoubtedly be traced to transference effects of infantile trauma that has been misunderstood by therapists. This is the subject of my text, *Remembering, Repeating, and Working Through Childhood Trauma* (Hedges 1994b). Licensing boards have an obligation to consumers to address this knowledge gap in an aggressive and creative way before more damage is done.

When training therapists, I often say, "It's not just your own neck that's at stake if you naively conduct yourself in such a way that allows you to be the target of a transference accusation, but the progress and well-being of the client as well. No client was ever cured of infantile trauma in an investigation process or in a courtroom. If you don't know what you're doing you will bring disaster on yourself. And you will have failed in the trust relationship and the cure you had worked so hard to achieve."

A Brief History

The organizing (or psychotic) transference was first extensively studied by Sigmund Freud in his famed Schreber case of 1911. Schreber, a well-known civil magistrate in Vienna, had published his scandalous memoirs of several hospitalizations for a severe and continuing paranoid psychosis. Among his many confirmed false allegations were claims of repeated violent and sexual assaults in the hospital by his treating physician and caregivers, which Freud successfully traced to transferred infantile trauma.

Freud had earlier shown how the same kind of deficit in reality appreciation in the 1882 treatment of Anna O. had led her to blame her therapist for her false pregnancy. In Freud's (1895) "Project for a Scientific Psychology," he clarified the dynamics not only of how childhood molestation leaves a person vulnerable to later molestations, but also of how later intimate contacts can be psychologically confused with infantile intrusive trauma.

I first summarized the basic literature on the organizing or psychotic transference in my 1983 book, *Listening Perspectives in Psychotherapy*. I have subsequently published (with Jason Aronson of Northvale, New Jersey) six additional textbooks for psychotherapists with clinical contributions from more than 200 therapists, addressing this subject. Most relevant to this topic are *Working the Organizing Experience* (1994) and *In Search of the Lost Mother of Infancy* (1994). Dr. James Grotstein, a Beverly Hills psychoanalyst and an internationally recognized expert on psychotic transference, wrote a review of the literature with an extensive bibliography as a foreword to *Working the Organizing Experience. Therapists at Risk* (1997), coauthored with Robert Hilton, Virginia Wink Hilton, and attorney O. Brandt Caudill Jr., further elaborates the dangers to consumers and therapists.

The Need for Expertise in Closing the Knowledge Gap

Enclosed please find a series of papers in which I have specifically addressed the knowledge gap. "In Praise of the Dual Relationship" looks at dual relationships somewhat differently than you may be used to. I take the position that the heart and soul of depth transference interpretation rests on a principle of duality in which the real relationship is revealed to be distinctly different from the fantasized transference-countertransference relationship. On the opposite end of the duality spectrum lies the exploitation and damage created by engagements such as sexual acting out. There are many actions of therapists that clearly violate clients' boundaries in exploitative and damaging ways. Such violations should be disciplined firmly and appropriately.

But in the "gray area" of the duality spectrum between useful transference interpretation and destructive boundary violations lie many activities engaged in by therapists and clients aimed at (1) developing the real relationship and (2) elucidating the transference-countertransference relationship. The intent and effects of activities and events in the gray area of the duality spectrum in long-term therapy can easily be misunderstood by outside observers. I take the position that ethically responsible professional opinion regarding the organizing or psychotic transference requires careful and studied thought. Responsible and ethical opinion can be rendered only by properly trained professionals who possess such expertise—*which includes many years of personal experience in actually doing and supervising long-term, intensive therapy.*

In my paper studying dual relationships I specify the psychodynamic issues at stake and what such consultative expertise might look like, using the California Research Psychoanalyst Law as an already existing codified model of expertise. I asked if we could name even one licensed therapist who currently renders opinions on a licensing board or who is routinely hired as an expert witness by a licensing board that possessed such expertise. I expressed my belief that a great many therapists are operating unethically in board-related activities by rendering professional opinions in areas outside of their training and expertise.

Further, I called for the establishment of agreed-upon standards regarding what constitutes expertise in understanding the workings of organizing or psychotic transference. I suggested forming a preselected panel of such experts who could be called upon to provide education, advice, and experienced opinion to licensing boards and administrative law judges. Following the newly proposed requirement that the decisions of the administrative law judge be held binding in cases in which the credibility of the accusing consumer is in question, I would now suggest not only that such expertise be available to support the work of the licensing boards, but also that it be a regular and mandated part of the administrative hearing in such cases.

Perhaps a task force composed of members of the various boards and professions should be formed to study the situation, to seek out expertise, and to make recommendations. Infantile trauma is here to stay, and consumers who seek out therapy for such deep wounds have a right to know that this branch of psychotherapy is being appropriately monitored by the professions and by the state boards. Perhaps an in-service training or consciousness-raising day sponsored by each state board and ethics committee might be a first step in the recognition of the problem.

The Goal is an Educational One

I realize that my opinions and conclusions as well as my recommendations are offered before the state boards and ethics committees have had an opportunity to assess the nature and seriousness of the problem I am pointing to. I further recognize that many professionals practicing psychotherapy may not even be aware of this knowledge gap. This is because only a relatively small sector of the therapist and client populations has as yet been impacted by the problem.

I wish to make clear that as an educator, my primary concern is the dissemination of information and knowledge. As a trainer and as a consultant to psychotherapists, I am concerned about a knowledge gap that is widely affecting therapists and consumers alike.

The Magnitude of the Problem

Let me close by expressing my opinion as to the magnitude of this problem. I think of an avalanche slowly accumulating weight over a long period of time until one sparrow quietly settles on a small twig—adding just the right weight in the right place to precipitate an enormous disaster. I believe the avalanche is in place and that it is precariously balanced at present.

First, we have a large and frightened community of psychotherapists whose consciousness about these matters is slowly rising. Many are slowly aiming their sights toward licensing boards, which they believe to be the source of a serious danger that is not being addressed and that threatens them personally, their professional practices, and affects their decisions about what clients they feel safe working with.

Second, we have a large, politically powerful and incensed population of seriously mentally ill consumers who, first because of unenlightened treatment approaches, then because of the managed care industry, and now because of frightened therapists blaming licensing boards, feel that they are being denied treatment. These people have organized nationally and locally to lobby for protective legislation and are increasingly targeting the licensing boards as the current cause of their inability to obtain treatment because therapists are afraid of the serious liability involved in taking them on.

Third, we have a formidable group of prelicensed trainees, graduate school educators, and training clinic personnel who are in acute distress because of the sudden drastic diminishment of apprenticeship opportunities. Many supervisors, even senior clinicians who have been involved in supervision and training for years, are now loath to involve themselves with prelicensed training, or even to engage in case supervision of licensed therapists, because of disturbing disciplinary actions of state boards, which have held supervisors accountable for the inappropriate actions of people they are helping to train. Professionally responsible supervision and training is slowly grinding to a halt until more safety nets are in place for supervisors.

Finally, we live at present in a supercharged social atmosphere. Whether we choose to speak in terms of a litigious society or in terms of an era of increased accountability, legislators, judges and jurors, governors, and the public at large are all concerned about liability and about damage to innocent victims. Therapists are running scared because they have no reassurance that their deep transference work will be understood and respected if an accusatory situation arises. Therapists are becoming innocent victims of an unknowledgeable board.

The State Boards Must Be Accountable

It is my purpose in this letter to begin a calling to account of the state boards and the ethics committees of the various professions by pointing out the serious liability that currently exists because of a critical knowledge gap regarding the dynamics of organizing or psychotic transference. Liability through ignorance is sometimes excusable, but continued thoughtless practices after one has been informed of their damaging consequences are not excusable. Boards and ethics committees now stand informed. How they will choose to curtail the ongoing damage being done by the knowledge gap remains to be seen.

In my lectures around the country on the subject of false accusations and the existing flaws in administrative law, I am regularly met with angry shouts of protest. Some say, "Let's sue the licensing boards!" And, as we know, suits against state boards regarding issues of discipline have begun and will likely increase. It seems only a matter of time before we have some class action suits involving millions of settlement dollars and widespread public embarrassment for licensing boards.

Others say, "We must take legislative action at once!" And as we know, this has already happened in Arizona where a grass-roots movement of patients and therapists appealed to the legislature at "sunsetting time," successfully blocking a scheduled reauthorization of the state board. Sunset time in California is just around the corner and a massive letter-writing campaign to the legislature or to the governor could have disastrous consequences.

My Appeal

I am appealing to you and to all people involved in the investigation and disciplinary processes for psychotherapists to help in closing the knowledge gap.

It is my impression that the ethics committees of the professions have long practiced obtaining appropriate outside expert opinion on these matters so their position seems less critical. The professional organizations at present are so beleaguered with issues brought about by managed care that they may be slow getting around to this set of issues. The welfare of many consumers is at stake as well as the board's liability for enforcing fair and appropriate disciplinary standards on therapists.

The reality is that one disgruntled consumer or therapist could file an ethics complaint against all of the clinical members of all of the boards and all of the expert witnesses working for the boards who do not clearly possess the training and experience that would constitute expertise in this area. An ethics complaint against a number of licensed therapists would serve to create immediate pressure within the disciplines and within the boards to find ways of addressing the knowledge gap, but not without unfortunate consequences to the individuals involved.

In discussing my concerns with Muriel Golub, Ethics Chair for the California Psychological Association, she suggested that this problem area be addressed in the most professional, ethical, and constructive manner possible. This would clearly involve educative efforts aimed both at individual licensees and at all participants who carry out the investigative and disciplinary processes. I completely agree.

It is my intent that this statement be the beginning of a dialogue to better understand the nature of infantile trauma and the way it affects the transference-countertransference relationship of long-term psychotherapy.

The goal is to initiate educational measures to help therapists deal more effectively with the organizing transference and to help investigative personnel at all levels discern its operation, seek appropriate consultation, and make the best decisions possible.

Thank you for your consideration of my concerns. I hope to be able to speak with you soon. In our brief telephone conversation several weeks ago you invited me to send you my papers on the subject. My offer to come to Sacramento for the purpose of discussing with you further the nature of the "organizing" or "psychotic" transference as it affects accusatory processes still stands.

Yours very truly,
Lawrence E. Hedges

Enc:
"In Praise of the Dual Relationship"
"False Accusations Against Therapists"
"Prevention of False Accusations Against Therapists"
Curriculum Vitae

Several weeks later I received a letter from Ms. Mehl thanking me for my materials, which would be put in the library of the board. In a subsequent letter I requested some assurance that board members be notified of my concern and requested further opportunities to speak with her in person or by telephone. No response. So that's where we stand today. My interpretation is that there is a total lack of interest or concern for this serious matter at the board level. I sent copies of this letter to other California and national licensing boards and ethics committees and received no response except a letter from Dr. Golub, thanking me for at last bringing some clarity to this very difficult set of issues. Recently, I resent the letter to Tom O'Connor, head of the California Board of Psychology along with a copy of my most recent book, *Terrifying Transferences: Aftershocks of Childhood Trauma* (2000b) Again, there was not even so much as an acknowledgment of his having received my letter, papers, or book. The state doors seem closed to any new information that would ameliorate our plight.

NOTE

1. This chapter is reprinted from *Terrifying Transferences: Aftershocks of Childhood Trauma* (Hedges 2000b).

8

False Accusations and Where They Come From

AN IMAGINARY PROFILE OF A FALSE ACCUSER

This chapter presents my impressions of what I think is causing us so much trouble in our field today, based on my review of hundreds of cases of transference-based false accusations that have come up in the course of psychotherapy—a great many of which have become acted out in legal-ethical settings. Unfortunately, it is impossible to provide real case examples because they are always shrouded in client confidentiality and/or licensing board secrecy. But I can create a general profile of the kinds of features often associated with the people and circumstances that do give rise to false accusations.

First, there is more often than not a clear history of severe early intrusive abuse—physical, sexual, neglect—or some developmental trauma that may or may not be known about at the outset of treatment. In therapy what may be immediately evident are the typical symptoms we associate with posttraumatic stress disorder (PTSD)—anxiety, disorientation, dissociation, confusion, sleep interruptions, somatization, obsessions, eating disorders, addictions, suicidal gestures, self-abusive acts, intrusive dreams, and memories or visual fantasies of various forms of trauma and abuse. Or we may see a more frankly psychotic or dissociative clinical picture. There is additionally the seemingly incessant demand (in a myriad of forms) that the therapist help the client get to the bottom of the stress or symptom pattern and then somehow make it all better.

As we slowly peel away the layers of clamor and begin to get a clearer idea of what the client's life has been like, we see that the ways the client has experienced traumatic events take on a certain regular character or motif that can gradually be traced to specific developmental events that began in very early childhood, usually during the earliest months of life. There are, of course, many people who are much better organized than this but move to a more primitive place as the organizing transference clicks in.

Two worn-out and horribly distraught parents traveled more than a thousand miles to consult with me in the early 1990s regarding the accusations of neglect and molest their grown daughter, Amy, had hurled at them several years before. Memories of repeated sexual episodes in her early childhood, allegedly perpetrated by her father during the night and ignored by her mother, had emerged in her eating-disorder psychotherapy and survivors of abuse group. The parents' lives and those of other family members had been wrecked over a period of several years as they tried in good faith to respond to their daughter's plight, which they had absolutely no way of understanding. Both parents had immediately gone into intensive therapy themselves and the father had even submitted himself to hypnosis and a sodium pentathol interview—with all the experts concurring that the molest as remembered had never occurred. The father's questions then to me were, "What is going on? Why would Amy make such a thing up? Isn't it possible if I had done such heinous things that I could repress them completely? Isn't it possible that even the truth serum isn't picking up my denial?"

Amy's mother was in a total quandary. At first when the accusations had come out she had immediately left her husband of thirty-seven years, and then she realized that that was wrong. Now she truly believed that he had no memory whatsoever of anything inappropriate ever happening and over time she had come to totally disbelieve that anything inappropriate had ever occurred. But what *had* happened to Amy that was coming out in therapy in such a traumatic way for everyone?

I explained to them that developmental trauma that happened so early it cannot be remembered in ordinary ways—pictures, stories, and relationship repetitions—is often remembered in psychotherapy through physical constrictions and agitations and through vividly constructed archetypal memories and dreams of such things as past lives, molest, ritual abuse, and abduction. Suddenly the parents' eyes locked in on one another and the mother began welling up with silent tears and chest heaving. We three sat in silence until the father quietly told me the painful story that had never even occurred to them as relevant, of a baby nearly born dead due to placenta abruptio that had been interpreted by their obstetrician as the mother's body rejecting the baby by sloughing off the placenta before birth so that the baby had been starving to death when a cesarean section was performed to save Amy's life. The mother had carried heavy guilt all these years for her body's rejecting this daughter, the second-born she had wished would be a boy. The child had indeed formed a close affectionate craving for her father very early on. After this breathtaking moment of truth had subsided, the father said, "I think now I know how this nightmare we're all involved in began."

It seems Amy and her sister were discussing their therapy experiences while driving together a long distance through the countryside while returning from a large family Thanksgiving gathering. Amy was telling her sister that what kept coming up for her in therapy was the strong sense that she had been molested as a child. Her sister, also in therapy, said that at times she had wondered about that for herself and then added, "But, really, who in our past could have done such a thing?" This question set off a violent agitation in Amy until she finally gasped, "It could have only been Dad," and she began convulsive vomiting. They had to pull off the road into a deserted park as Amy went into wild, uncontrolled flailing, sobbing, and gasping convulsions for nearly three hours with no help available. Her sister held her, got the hyperventilation under control, and tried in vain to comfort Amy, to calm her down emotionally. "But," continued the father, "the one thing that never made sense to any of us was that throughout this entire time Amy was wildly clawing at the earth, tearing at the grass and weeds, and eating it in seemingly starving desperation. And this, right after she had just eaten a large turkey dinner—it made no sense."

This story needs no further interpretation except to say what an enormous disservice her therapist had done to Amy and to her entire family by colluding in the resistance to bodily transference-remembering in therapy and by encouraging her to take her recovered memories of abuse literally (rather than seriously) and then to externalize them by acting out the infantile accusations against her parents, who had done their best to respond to her seemingly boundless childhood cravings for affection and her frequent rages that it was their fault that she didn't ever get enough.[1]

The second feature in the profile of people who develop transference-based false accusations in therapy, based on my experience, is that almost all—certainly at least 85 to 90 percent—are women. One can only speculate about why. Girls in general have certainly been less valued and more neglected and subject to all forms of abuse in our culture for the last 3,000 years than have boys. Are men, then, less likely to have suffered early traumas? Or has our culture made it easier for women to move into their victimization miseries in psychotherapy today than for men? Is it threatening to men's sense of virility to identify themselves as passive victims? Or is it possible that as the veil of cultural denial about the victimization of women, children, and minorities has been slowly lifting during the past few decades, women have felt freer to raise their voices about what has been done to them? Since the abuse and trauma began so early in life, is it that somatopsychic memories can only be sensibly represented in dream-like constructed narrations of archetypal horrors? Or is my population a systematically biased sample because of my referral base? I am completely unable to address the question of minority abuse since I have operated primarily in a white, male-dominated system. But Alice Walker, Toni Morrison, Sandra Cisneros, Maxine Hong Kingston, Arundhati Roy, Lisa St. Alban de Téhran, and Leslie Marmon Silko represent strong voices for similar abuses being experienced among a wide racial range of marginalized people.

Whatever the answers might be to these questions, the typical profile I am drawing would be of a young to middle-aged woman who has been involved in some type of hypnosis, psychotherapy, or group work that has stimulated her to feel her deep sense of having been abused as a child and to cause her to begin searching for images and narrations that seem to make some clear sense out of her otherwise disjointed, confused, and terrifying feelings. A psychotherapist or consciousness-raising group member taking the stance that "if you think it might have happened, then it probably did and you have repressed it," offers a quick and easy answer, so that the process of transference remembering becomes aborted. Such an approach, rather than elucidating the accusations that "you weren't there for me," "you failed to protect me," or "you did it to me" in the ways they are now coming up in transferred feelings, aids in the resistance to the full experiencing of memories of body pain and mental terror in the here-and-now process of psychotherapy.

The third feature of the false-accusation profile is a regular and reliable pattern or motif of experiencing neglectful, traumatic, and abusive moments. There is nothing strange about consistency in personality makeup. Each of us has developed from earliest childhood a number of characteristic ways of organizing our perceptions and experiences. Psychologists have studied individual patterns of character formation extensively and have developed many ways for identifying and testing for enduring patterns of experiencing and relating to others (Johnson 1991). Great literature, such as Dostoyevski's *Crime and Punishment* or *The Brothers Karamazov*, illustrates clearly the expected regularity of our individual patterns of experiencing life, and how readily we distort perception and action to fit our personal preestablished characterological patterns of experience.

For example, we might have a psychotherapy client who has experienced a series of strikingly similar date rapes that she and everyone else are certain she is not setting up, asking for, or causing. She has a pattern of having been abused in certain ways in childhood with vivid and terrifying memories of yet earlier and/or more shadowy forms of intrusive trauma. In psychotherapy we are often able to trace even further back through reports of family members, neighbors, and hospital or police records events that date the first modes of traumatic experiencing to near and even before birth. Expectably, one can discern a psychological profile from all of these various sources of data, much as one might draw a picture of characterological functioning based on an extensive battery of psychological tests. A unique picture emerges that serves almost as a fingerprint of the individual's personal modes, styles, and patterns of experiencing and relating. The regularity and reliability of such patterns is well familiar to us, as we have all drawn similar character profiles of ourselves and others with whom we have close and intimate relationships. As parents we watch personality profiles form from the first day of life and are constantly amazed at the uniqueness and creative individuality of each of our children compared to others.

Thus, anticipating the question of how an expert witness might feasibly work when the truth or falsity of accusations is in question, a life profile of expectable responsiveness under conditions of interpersonal trust and intimacy begins not so mysteriously to emerge from the available life history data and the documented experiences of the therapist, previous reports of hospitals and therapists, and communications from others who know the person well. And presto, the history and profile amazingly match the events and experiences leading up to and including the accusations themselves! False accusations that stem from transference do not spring up casually or suddenly from a vacuum, but instead emerge gradually over a long period of time within the context of an extensive and robust trust relationship—though some trigger event may well precipitate a sudden acting out of the transference-based hurt and rage.

THE SURPRISING LEGAL SUCCESS
OF THE FALSE-ACCUSATION ARGUMENT

Whenever I have been given the opportunity to study the full clinical record, have addressed the theory of transference-based false accusations, and have drawn up a personalized characterological profile to show how the particular bent of the relationship and the accusations fit a long-standing pattern based on the person's life history, administrative law judges and civil settlement conferences have invariably dropped the questionable accusations in the face of probable or at least possible doubt.

I was at first surprised when judges took such an interest in the false-accusation argument and asked me to clarify and to elaborate the various points of my opinions. Then I began to realize why. If you are a judge and sit all day long, day after day, hearing complaints against professionals and business people, you have to continually be asking yourself whether these people are dissimulating, distorting, or fabricating, and for what reasons. Attorneys and judges are skilled at ferreting out most sources of deliberate misrepresentation and purposeful lying. But when a person seemingly with full heart and sincere conviction levels the finger of accusation at someone for crimes they appear not to have committed, on what basis does one account for it? I soon realized that judges and attorneys were eager to understand from a perspective of depth-psychological research some fresh ideas on where these particular kinds of false accusations were coming from. I realized that these kinds of accusations arose primarily in the context of trusting relationships, and that the trusting relationships had not simply gone awry or been disillusioning, but that they had provided the basis for the reemergence and projection of prior experiences of abuse, exploitation, and damage. Something truly vital to understand about human nature has emerged from depth-psychotherapeutic studies of the effects of trauma on the origins of personality.

In my legal and ethical studies I have included in my sample only those cases in which, through careful prescreening, I had reason to believe the transference-based accusations of the therapist were false. By false accusations I am not referring to deliberate dissimulation or to manipulative use of the justice system for money or revenge on the client's part, but rather to scars left by deep, early trauma that have manifested themselves in later life as some form of terror of intimate connections. These accusations are almost invariably offered in conscious sincerity, emotional determination, and good faith—"You have used your sacred role and the power differential in our relationship to hurt me and I want to ensure that you do not hurt me or anybody else in this way again."

In hindsight, the success and plausibility of the transference-based false-accusation argument can almost be viewed like a Shakespearean tragedy in which the tragic flaw is a character deficit from the beginning that leads to an inevitably tragic and destructive end. That there are so many cases with histories of severe infantile trauma and abuse that do undergo meaningful and helpful transformations safely is the amazing thing. Our many successes as a profession can be attributed, to a century of psychotherapeutic research and to the timely advent of psychotropic drugs that slow and contain agitated, depressive, and fragmenting processes so they can be effectively worked with.

THE PROBLEM WITH CONSIDERING
TRANSFERENCE-BASED ACCUSATIONS FALSE

To speak of false accusations is to take a seemingly arbitrary point of view regarding an event that is happening between two people. One person points the finger and says, "I trusted you in your professional role of therapist and you have misused that trust to exploit and damage me." The accused may be able to acknowledge that such and such events occurred, but not be able to agree on the meanings of those events or that exploitation or damage was involved. If we had a neutral or objective way of observing the events in question and the alleged negative results, we might indeed see a damaged person. But would we be able to agree beyond the shadow of a doubt that the observable damage is a direct causal result of exploitative acts by the accused? And would it be clear that exploitation of some sort was involved?

In the type of allegation I am defining as a transference-based false accusation, it is not possible to establish a direct causal link between actions of the therapist and the damage claimed or sustained by the client, nor is it possible to establish beyond a doubt that the activities of the therapist in his or her professional role were exploitative. I am aware that in certain ways this definition may beg the question of what is to be counted as false when separate points of view are being considered. But accusations as serious as professional misconduct must carry a heavy burden of proof so that the question of true or false requires the establishment of a satisfactory standard of evidence that in my experience frequently seems to be lacking in accusations against therapists. So what is the nature of the damage being pointed to and where did it come from?

THE GENESIS OF THE ORGANIZING TRANSFERENCE AND THE FEAR OF BREAKDOWN

Clinical research shows that earliest transference and resistance memories are those from the organizing (or psychotic) period of relatedness development (Grotstein 1994; Hedges 1994a, c, 2000b), as discussed in the previous chapter. Winnicott (1965) points out that early impingements into the infant's sense of continuity with life oblige the infant to react to environmental failure before the infant is fully prepared to begin reacting and thinking. The result of premature impingement is the formation of a primary persecutory mode of thought that forms the foundation of subsequent thought processes. That is, traumatic impingement on the infantile (omnipotent) sense of "going on being" ensures that the first memory sense that is destined to color all later memories is "the world hurts me by intruding into my mental space and over- or understimulating (traumatizing) me. I will forever be on guard for things coming at me that threaten to destroy my sense of being in control of what happens to me in these ways again." As a lasting imprint this earliest memory is essentially psychotic or unrealistic because the world at large presents many kinds of abusive impingements. Searching the environment tirelessly for the particular kind of primary emotional intrusion that once forced the infant to respond in a certain way not only creates perennial paranoid hazards where there may be none, but also causes the person to miss other realistic dangers that are not being scanned for because of this prior preoccupation of the perceptual system.

A person living out organizing states will do so without her or his usual sense of judgment, perception, or reality testing capabilities. This is likely to mean that inner fears and preoccupations cannot be reliably distinguished from external features or forces, and that the person may be temporarily or perennially living in frames of mind that are in essence psychotic in nature, though this may not be at all obvious. Infantile thought modes that have been revived for therapeutic investigation are not generally reality oriented in the ordinary sense and are extremely limited in what can be focused on at a given point in time, so that we cannot at such moments count on a person's ordinary ego functions to be available to mediate and moderate the prevailing emotional sense of persecution that inevitably colors the person's entire experience at the moment. This is equally true for people living only limited pockets of organizing experience as it is for people pervasively living out their organizing experiences.

Whether the organizing experience has been a client's pervasive way of living in the world or whether it exists as only a small pocket of a person's overall personality structure, when it manifests itself as transference in a long-term psychotherapy process both participants are in for a rocky ride! Elsewhere I have detailed the expectable kinds of subjective complaints and concerns that are often expressed by clients and the expectable kinds of countertransference often generated in therapists as two seek to frame this most primitive of transferred experiences for psychotherapeutic study and transformation (Hedges 1994c). My colleagues and I, working over a twenty-year period with organizing transferences from a variety of points of view, have put forward a series of case studies to illustrate the various kinds of therapeutic processes we have thus far encountered. In these case studies accusations of all sorts are ubiquitous and serve a number of purposes. We have found that empathy, attunement, and holding-containing techniques *do not* constitute optimal responsiveness (Hedges 1998). Rather, the working-through process must regularly include an interpretive awareness of the deep terror of emotional connecting that invariably accompanies moments of interpersonal relating and a way of working with the primitive countertransferences stirred up by the process. This kind of intensely interactive relational process requires that two people be highly motivated to achieve a mutually transformative experience. But we also have found that fluke occurrences inside or outside of the therapeutic relationship can easily tip the balance of the working-through process and precipitate a negative therapeutic reaction in which the terror-driven transference-based accusations become acted out in various ways, including law and ethics complaints. When such an event occurs it is vital that the therapist at all times has been practicing defensively, or two people will be plummeted into an adversarial relationship from which neither can easily recover.

TRUST RELATIONSHIPS RAISE THE
CLAMOR AND SET THE STAGE FOR A FLUKE

Since early interpersonal relations were experienced by the child as vehicles of trauma, abuse, or lack of protection from fear and pain, it is trusting emotional relationships that regularly revive long-conditioned fear and avoidance of intimacy. Trust relationships such as psychotherapy invite intimacy and connection that in turn gradually stir up primordial terror as emotional intimacy and/or dependency on the relationship increases. I have written extensively on the "clamor" that ensues in a myriad of forms in psychotherapy and the kinds of "fluke" events that typically precipitate a false accusation disaster. I have further pointed out the nature of "cumulative strain trauma" (Khan 1963) and how in these false-accusation cases prolonged adaptive strain on the part of a very young child can have the same effect in organizing a fear response to intimate relationships as various kinds of more intense and focal abuse and trauma.

In the actuality of the psychotherapeutic relationship, clients are usually complaining the whole time during intimacy development that not enough is being given or done, that frequent emotional abandonments and betrayals are being experienced, and that everything in the relationship would be okay if the therapist would only provide better holding and containment of their anxiety, depression, and terror (Hedges 1994b, 1997, 2000b).

NOTE

1. I am pleased to report that ten years later Amy's parents again visited me. They had remained in contact with her through her siblings all this time offering help, discussion, mediation—anything that might heal the family rupture. Amy had been through several therapists, had been able to establish herself marginally in a profession and was now requesting an invitation to this year's Thanksgiving dinner. Her parents were overjoyed but understandably anxious and wanted to discuss the upcoming even with me. Clearly healing was on the way.

9

Defending against Complaints
by State Licensing Boards

Pamela Ann Thatcher

The most stressful challenge mental health professionals can face is dealing with a complaint filed against them with their licensing board. Any person at any time can contact a professional's licensing board. Complaint procedures are now available on-line. A complaint form will be provided to that person, who can be a client, a spouse of a client, another professional, a spurned lover—the list is virtually limitless. Moreover, when civil actions are settled by professionals over a given monetary limit, there is a duty to report the settlement to the licensing board. Complaints based on therapists' actions from as long ago as twenty years have been lodged against professionals and have actually been investigated by licensing boards. Some states, including California, have passed laws limiting the time period during which a licensing board may pursue a professional.

A complaint impacts all aspects of a professional's life. The mere fact that a complaint has been filed can adversely affect one's status as a provider with many health maintenance organizations. Obviously, a professional suffers many emotions when wrongfully accused of gross negligence or intentionally wrongful conduct. The cost of defending against such an accusation can be financially devastating. The reputation of a professional can be forever damaged, even if the case is ultimately dismissed by the board.

The lack of due process in the administrative context presents an enormous danger to a professional. While the boards are focusing on protecting the public, a professional's identity and livelihood are not afforded protection by the procedures currently in place. This chapter is written in the context of administrative matters in the State of California but similar circumstances exist elsewhere.

THE ANATOMY OF THE LICENSING BOARD

What is the "Board"? There are numerous boards provided for under the Business and Professions Code.[1] Their purpose is to enforce the laws and regulations concerning different professions. For instance, in California, the Board of Psychology governs psychologists. It consists of eight members (Business and Professions Code §2920). Three of these are "public members" from outside the profession, while the remaining five are licensed psychologists (Business and Professions Code §2920). While the Governor appoints six members, including all professional members, the Senate Rules Committee and the Speaker of the Assembly appoint the remaining public members (Business and Professions Code §2922). Thus, all of these individuals are political appointees. The five psychologists chosen are supposed to "represent, as widely as possible, the varied professional interests of psychologists in California" (Business and Professions Code §2922). The only other requirement for Board members is that they be residents of the state (Business and Professions Code §2923).

The Board of Behavioral Sciences (BBS) consists of eleven members; five are public members and six are licensed professionals. The professional membership consists of two clinical social workers, one educational psychologist, and two marriage and family therapists (Business and Professions Code §4990.3). In the past, positions on the board remained vacant for significant periods of time. Until the Governor appoints people to fill these positions, professionals can be disciplined without adequate representation.

Once a complaint form is received by the licensing Board (hereinafter "Board"), it is reviewed to determine whether it warrants an investigation. If an investigation is requested, the complaint is referred to the State of California, Department of Consumer Affairs; Division of Investigation. This department is charged with investigating matters for a broad range of boards, such as the Horse Racing Board, the Funeral Directors and Embalmers Board, the Medical Board, and the BBS. A diagram of the administrative claim process is shown in table 9-1.

An investigator from the Department of Consumer Affairs interviews witnesses. Witnesses in these matters are usually the complainant, the complainant's current therapist, and the therapist who is the focus of the complaint. Usually the Board investigator will also obtain the complainant's medical records from both the current therapist and the therapist in question. Therapists can only release client records to the investigator, if they are presented with a release form signed by the client. After the completion of an investigation, a report is prepared by the Department of Consumer Affairs' investigator and sent to the Board. The executive director at the Board reviews

Table 9-1. Administrative Claim Process

Complaint to Board		→ *Reviewed and No Action Taken by Board*
Reviewed and Referred for Investigation to Department of Consumer Affairs ↓		
Investigator's Report to Board ↓	→	No Action Taken by Board; Matter Closed
Board Refers to Expert for Review ↓	→	Expert Opinion: No Violations; Matter Closed
Expert Opinion: Violation ↓		
Board Refers Matter to General's Office to File an Accusation ↓	→	Settlement by Stipulation with Attorney the Board
Administrative Hearing ↓		
Proposed Decision by Administrative Law Judge ↓	→	Nonadopted by Board ↓
Adopted by Board ↓		Further Briefing/Hearing ↓
Writ to Superior Court ↓		Board's Decision ↓
		Writ to Superior Court

these reports. A determination is made either to pursue further action or to close the matter at that time. This decision is usually made unilaterally by the executive director of some Boards. If the Board, usually through the executive director, determines that further action is warranted, the matter is reviewed by expert consultants. The Boards have a list of professionals willing to act as consultants to review matters for them.

These professionals have previously provided their resumés to the Board for consideration. Telephone interviews with the potential experts are conducted in many instances, rather than any face-to-face interview. These experts are usually compensated at a fraction of their typical rate to review matters for the Board. This service can still be very lucrative, however, given the fact that the Board frequently uses the same experts over and over in many matters. Moreover, those professionals who want to focus their practices in the area of expert testimony find this work helpful in establishing credibility.

Generally, these consultants receive minimal training. Any information about relevant laws and regulations is usually provided by the deputy attorney general who prosecutes the case. In past cases, the attorney general's office has relied on laws that were not in effect at the time of the alleged wrongful act. Obviously, the expert applied the wrong law in those cases. In other cases, Board experts testifying about the necessary elements of "gross negligence" have rendered testimony contrary to statutory and case law.

Basically, the Board utilizes psychologists to review psychologists, and so on. If they don't do this, one can challenge the qualifications of the expert. For instance, if the Board attempted to utilize a psychologist to testify regarding whether a psychiatrist had committed gross negligence, then a challenge to the expert's qualifications would probably be successful. In numerous cases, however, the Board of Psychology has referred matters for review to MFTs (marriage, family therapists) and LCSWs (licensed clinical social workers). This "technical problem" is useful to the defense in that it is essential to have a qualified expert's testimony regarding standard of care issues. For example, did the therapist commit gross negligence? In one case, the Board's expert admittedly had no knowledge of the experiential psychotherapeutic modality. Although he openly admitted this lack of knowledge in his written report to the Board, this did not stop him from criticizing conduct that was recognized as an acceptable therapeutic intervention in the modality (i.e., evoking a client's emotional response with limited physical contact).

Usually, the identities of both the respondent and the complainant are made known to the experts through the provided documentation. There is no proscription against an expert who has knowledge of one of the parties from being involved in a case. Any knowledge, however, may be used to show bias at a hearing. For instance, in one matter, the Board's primary witness was a long-time competitor of the therapist, who was the subject of the investigation.

In their review, the experts examine the investigator's report and other documents specifically provided by the Board to determine if there is any violation of laws and regulations governing the profession. These experts prepare a report for the Board. If the opinion is that there has been a violation, the matter is referred to the State Attorney General's office. The Attorney General acts as the lawyer representing the Board and prosecutes these administrative actions. The Attorney General then files an Accusation against the licensee. The Accusation is usually served on the licensee by certified mail. The Accusation sets forth the alleged wrongful conduct and the laws that have purportedly been violated by the licensee. In most instances, the Board requests a revocation of the license as the appropriate penalty.

Within fifteen days of service of the Accusation on the licensee, the licensee must file a Notice of Defense (California Government Code §11506). It constitutes a waiver of the licensee's right to a hearing if a Notice of Defense is not filed in a timely fashion. If the licensee fails to respond in any manner to the Accusation, the Board can revoke the license without a hearing

(Government Code §11505). By contrast, an individual is given thirty days to respond to a summons and complaint in a civil action. In both civil and administrative matters, however, there is a procedure for relief from an untimely response. In administrative cases, the Board, at its discretion, can accept a late Notice of Defense (Government Code §11506). A Notice of Defense reserves defenses to be raised later at the administrative hearing (Government Code §11506). Although a form Notice of Defense is served together with the Accusation, this form does not operate to reserve all the defenses that may be available. Normally, an attorney should be consulted to determine the viability of other defenses (i.e., statute of limitations, laches). Laches is a defense that allows a party to argue that his or her ability to present any argument has been severely jeopardized because of the passage of time, such as: witnesses and/or documents have been lost or destroyed, and/or memories of events have faded. An Accusation is often premised on laws and regulations that were not in effect at the time of the purportedly wrongful conduct. It is important to assert any and all defenses at this stage, or risk that they will be considered waived as well.

Prior to a hearing, discovery may be conducted by both parties. A form entitled Request for Discovery is exchanged between the parties (Government Code §11507.6). Names of witnesses, documents intended to be introduced into evidence, investigators, and experts' reports are subject to disclosure when this form is sent. Discovery is the formal gathering of information from witnesses and the obtaining of relevant documents. The discovery available in an administrative matter is extremely limited, which limitations are discussed in the next section.

Further, it is also possible to settle the matter with the Board prior to a hearing. Each Board has a published set of disciplinary guidelines. These guidelines are an attempt to set forth the terms and conditions of penalty that the Board would consider acceptable in resolving a matter short of a trial.

The Office of Administrative Hearings acts as the court in these matters. All pleadings are filed with them and any decisions are made by administrative law judges. Either party, the state or the respondent, can request a hearing date at any time during the process. This is particularly significant if a hearing is set early in the process because it leaves less time to prepare a defense. The Board, together with the Attorney General's office, could take a year to investigate a case and only leave months for the therapist to prepare a defense for the hearing. Most of the time, there is a significant time lapse between the initial contact with the Board and any notice that an Accusation will be filed by the Board. Unless a therapist specifically requests it, there is frequently no notice given to the therapist that an investigation has actually been closed by the Board, without any further disciplinary action.

The Office of Administrative Hearing sets the date for a hearing, generally, a minimum of six months from the filing of an Accusation to as much as four to five years. There is no law limiting this time period. Although the professional has to live with these pending allegations, it may be more beneficial to have the process take several years. If there are no new complaints while the case is pending, this can be introduced as favorable evidence for the defense (i.e., that the therapist does not present a danger to the public, that the complaint is false, or that any misconduct was a one-time aberration). On the other hand, the continuation of such proceedings can have a devastating impact on a therapist's practice.

These types of challenges to one's professional life can cause health problems, especially those induced by stress. Several professionals have stated that these proceedings have caused heart problems or the onset of cancer. Many organizations will terminate referrals of therapists who are the subject of an investigation, including certain HMOs and PPOs (preferred provider organizations). Normally, administrative complaints have to be revealed on applications for out-of-state licensure, staff privileges, insurance, and so forth.

The cost of defending against a Board hearing can run into tens of thousands of dollars, depending on the magnitude of the case and whether a party seeks the intervention of the superior court. Although discovery is significantly more limited in administrative matters, as opposed to civil matters, the cost is still significant. The risk of losing one's livelihood, however, is also significant, given the lack of safeguards in the administrative system to a fair and impartial process.

Cases involving claims of sexual misconduct where the complainant has seen several subsequent providers and has a long treatment history before, during, and after the respondent's care can cost up to $50,000 to $75,000 in attorneys' and experts' fees. Many attorneys request a significant retainer in these matters and in some instances will keep this money even if they are able to resolve matters early in the process. Civil matters involving the defense of mental health professionals in sexual misconduct cases can cost anywhere from $150,000 to $250,000. The difference in cost between the two is in the ability to conduct much more discovery in civil matters (i.e., to conduct depositions). The cost in an administrative matter usually involves retaining an expert to testify on whether the licensee's conduct constitutes gross negligence in treatment. Further, in sexual misconduct matters and others, it is best to retain a forensic expert to conduct an independent mental examination of the licensee. The forensic expert may be able to conclude that the licensee poses no danger to the public. Further, a licensee may want to seek out a personal therapist during the pendency of these matters as well as a supervisor for his or her practice. All of these professionals can then be called as witnesses at the time of the hearing to testify on behalf of the licensee. Of course these professionals must be paid for their expert services. Further, the longer the administrative process takes, the more attorney fees and costs are incurred in the defense.

Those licensees who do not have the resources to present a defense to an administrative charge obviously stand to lose the most. Individuals who usually suffer the greatest hardships are interns and/or psychological assistants. They usually have far more limited resources than licensed individuals. The results of the oral examination can be withheld as well as the issuance of the license, if there is even an initial complaint filed against them. Moreover, the time between the filing of the complaint and the ultimate determination can take years. During the entire period of time, the intern/assistant has to work as an unlicensed and supervised individual at a reduced rate. The Board, armed with this information, typically takes a harder line with interns. The overwhelming rationale for this conduct appears to be to send a message to other interns.

In California, an administrative law judge presides at the hearing. Administrative law judges are appointed by the Director of the Office of Administrative Hearings (Government Code §11502). The judges are staff members of the Office of Administrative Hearings and are employees of the state. Likewise, the deputy attorneys general prosecuting the case are also state employees. At the conclusion of the hearing, the administrative law judge issues a "proposed" decision (Government Code §11517). The Board, a state agency, then has the power either to adopt the proposed decision or non-adopt it. If the Board non-adopts the decision, then it must decide the case on the record. The record typically consists of the written transcript of testimony given at the hearing and the exhibits entered into evidence. Historically, if a favorable decision was received from an administrative law judge, there was a great likelihood that it would be non-adopted by the Board. A favorable decision in this context would be one recommending dismissal of the Accusation or imposing few penalties on the licensee (i.e., something less than revocation of a license). Boards now have a tendency to adopt favorable decisions. Decisions by administrative law judges are currently well-reasoned with numerous citations to the evidence introduced at the hearing. It makes their decisions harder for the Board's to challenge.

Politically and practically, administrative law judges take on the system when they rule adversely to the Board and in favor of the licensee. After all, why would a state agency use scarce resources to seek the revocation of a license if it is not warranted under the facts? Previous executive directors of certain Boards have stated that the reason they nonadopt some decisions is that the administrative law judges do not understand the law.

When the Board nonadopts an administrative law judge's proposed decision, it can simply order a copy of the transcript of the hearing, the record, and make its own decision. It has been discovered that sometimes when the Board orders a copy of the transcript, it doesn't even bother to order a copy of the exhibits that were admitted into evidence. Thus, the Board does not always have a complete record of the hearing.

There are other problems encountered when the Board substitutes its own findings, rather than relying on those of the judge who actually saw and heard the witnesses testify. One of the most obvious problems is that members of the Board typically have no legal experience. Thus, the objections to evidence at the time of the hearing may or may not be understood and addressed by members of the Board. For example, the Government Code provides that hearsay can be admitted in an administrative action. Investigators can testify to what a witness told them during an interview. Hearsay cannot be the sole basis, however, in support of the allegations against a professional. Board members have to recognize that testimony is hearsay, take into account that the information was probably allowed as administrative hearsay only, and then ignore it if it is the only evidence supporting a charge. The Board members also have no way of judging the demeanor of the witnesses from simply reading the written transcript of the hearing. This is often one of the most crucial elements in these matters, especially if the matter is about sexual misconduct, which determination is usually a battle of credibility. The licensee is at a disadvantage and the due process protections available in the civil and criminal courts are largely unavailable in this context. The Board acts as the accuser and the ultimate jury in all matters. It initiates the proceedings and is the final arbiter of the case. If the Board ultimately issues a decision imposing a penalty against the licensee, the recourse for the licensee is to file a writ of mandate with the Superior Court. Again, this is at great expense to the licensee.

In seeking the intervention of the Superior Court after losing at the administrative stage, the burden is on the licensee to show that based on the evidence, the Board's findings are wrong. Although the standard of review differs depending upon the issue presented to the Superior Court (i.e., whether one is addressing the imposition of the penalty at all or just the degree of penalty), the chance of obtaining relief from the Superior Court is very low. This is due to several factors. As to any type of relief, the Superior Court must review the entire transcript of the hearing. The same problem with the demeanor of the witnesses exists in that the Superior Court judge is unable to see the witnesses testifying but must rely on the written transcript. Realistically, the Superior Court is also short on time. Reviewing the entire transcript of an administrative hearing can be extremely burdensome, especially if the hearing took many days. In seeking Superior Court intervention, the licensee may ask it to use its own judgment in cases where the administrative law judge imposed no penalty but the Board ultimately did impose discipline. In matters where the licensee is only asking the court to reconsider the fairness of the penalty imposed, the administrative finding will not be disturbed unless there is an abuse of discretion. The abuse of discretion standard is broad. The rationale is that the Boards are better able to police their own. Thus, the licensee's best chance of gaining relief from the Superior Court is in a matter where the administrative law judge ruled in favor of the licensee by dismissing the Accusation but the Board nonadopted the decision and imposed a penalty. The probability of gaining relief from the Superior Court is determined on a case-by-case basis. Overall, the probability of Superior Court relief is small.

INVESTIGATION OR INQUISITION?

The investigators for the Department of Consumer Affairs may investigate matters for any Board under the jurisdiction of that department. As previously stated, this includes such diverse Boards as that of Cosmetology, Automotive Repair, Funeral Directors and Embalmers, and Psychology. Needless to say, it is essential that these investigators have a basic understanding of the laws and regulations governing the particular licensee at issue because if they ask the wrong question they get the wrong answer.

Many times, the investigators lack a basic understanding of the law governing these professions. In one matter, a supervisor had been accused of "aiding and abetting an unlicensed individual to practice." The case involved a marriage, family therapist and an unregistered intern. The intern had not timely received a registration number before seeing several clients. At the administrative trial, the investigator admitted he was unaware of the difference between a registration and a license as these terms applied to MFTs and interns. This lack of knowledge furnished the basis for the reasonable inference at trial that this investigator had caused confusion during the investigative interview. He had not asked clear questions. For instance, he asked the supervisor whether an intern could practice before receiving a *license*. The supervisor correctly stated that an intern could see clients before receiving a license. The investigator had meant to ask whether an intern could see clients before receiving his registration number, not his license. The Board attempted to use this information to show that the supervisor thought that an intern could see clients without a *registration number*. The wrong information was received because the investigator asked the wrong question. Thus, the wrong conclusion had been reached about the supervisor's knowledge in this regard. Although this may seem a simple distinction to a licensed professional, these types of mistakes formed the basis, in part, for the filing of an Accusation against the supervisor.

Even more critical, the investigator asked, "Did you know that the intern was not registered when he was seeing clients?" The investigation was conducted two and a half years after the alleged wrongful conduct. By that time, the supervisor had been made aware of the problem. He responded affirmatively to this question. The Board contended that this proved the supervisor knew, at time the intern was seeing clients, that the intern held no registration number. However, that was not the investigator's question, nor was it the supervisor's answer. The investigator *never* asked the question, "Two and a half years ago, while the intern was seeing clients, did you know he was not registered with the Board?" The supervisor had no concurrent knowledge of the unlawful activity.

The supervisor had transferred control of the office to another licensed individual and was unaware that the intern had even begun seeing clients at the office. The investigator had failed to elicit information about the date the supervisor had sold the practice. In fact, the Accusation stated that the wrongful conduct occurred after the sale date. The investigator, however, neglected to obtain this information or any of the transfer documents. We obtained a favorable decision from the administrative law judge. His proposed decision was to dismiss the accusation. He found no intentional wrongdoing on the part of the supervisor. Initially, the BBS nonadopted the decision, and reviewed the transcript. This matter was pending for almost two years, and generated over $20,000 in defense costs and fees. Ultimately, the Board adopted the judge's decision.

Generally, investigators conduct interviews of witnesses without tape-recording them. Many times all of the other witnesses are contacted before any interview is conducted with the accused mental health professional. Recently, investigators have begun to label these interviews "professional courtesy interviews." Further, if an interview cannot be scheduled in the immediate future, investigators will file their report without any input from the professional, evidence, once again, that these investigations are not meant to ascertain the truth. Rather, they are designed to elicit information that corroborates the complaint.

Any professional who is the subject of an investigation should contact an attorney familiar with administrative proceedings. A meeting with an attorney should always precede any contact with a Board investigator. On numerous occasions, professionals have been told that an attorney is not necessary. I have even had investigators send me letters indicating that it is not necessary that I attend interviews between them and my clients because these meetings are "interviews and not inquisitions." Professionals are always entitled to have an attorney present at the time of an interview or to consult with an attorney prior to any contact with an investigator. There are numerous reasons to consult an attorney.

Often, investigators will not inform the professional of the nature of the investigation, what the charges are in the complaint. I have been told by investigators that they will not inform us of the allegations in a complaint before an interview, even when it is acknowledged that an investigation of my client is being conducted. Prior to any interview with an investigator, however, one should *always* ascertain the nature of the complaint. Investigators will disclose limited information about the complaint prior to the meeting and additional details can be ascertained during the interview.

Again, if the investigator indicates that an interview is unnecessary, a letter should be sent confirming failure to conduct an interview. It is important to confirm this information because the therapist has a duty to cooperate in an investigation of a complaint and a refusal to meet may be viewed as an indication of guilt. In many instances, professionals have consulted with an attorney after they have met with a Board investigator, only to admit that they still did not know the charges after several hours of interview.

Further, the investigator's lack of knowledge can be the direct cause of inaccurate answers. In one matter, an intern was asked the nature and type of his supervision. The intern responded that it was individual and on a weekly basis. The investigator's next question was, "Well, isn't it true that you lead a group and that you were supervised in this group?" The investigator had confused the concept of individual supervision sessions between a supervisor and an intern with the concept of group therapy sessions conducted by the intern under the supervision of the supervisor. Of course, the intern was supervised for any services rendered, whether they were providing individual or group therapy to others.

Investigators also use the type of inquiry known as the "Are you still beating your wife?" category. A fact, usually not true, is assumed for purposes of the question (i.e., that one beats one's spouse). In one matter, an investigator asked a therapist why he had commented to the complaining client that a group coleader's conduct was inappropriate. The therapist was now contending during the interview that he saw no inappropriate conduct. The therapist, however, had never told the client that he witnessed any inappropriate conduct. This fact was simply assumed in the investigator's question. In another matter, the investigator asked the therapist what steps she had taken with regard to her suspicions of child abuse. The therapist, however, never had any suspicions of abuse while treating the client in question.

I have been contacted by numerous individuals who have met with an investigator without benefit of counsel. Many times these practitioners participate in an interview without knowing the focus of the investigation, even by the end of the interview. Therapists often write lengthy "responses" to an investigator without any clear idea of the focus of the investigation. Information in these long discourses can actually generate additional charges against a professional. At best, they furnish the basis for a myriad of questions from the Board's expert witness.

There is also the possibility that the investigator will tell the licensee that he or she is not the subject of the investigation. This is usually done in cases involving supervisors and their supervisees. When you interface with a Board investigator it is always best to assume that you are the subject of the investigation. If the investigator is contending that a supervisee has done something wrong, it may ultimately be shown to be the supervisor's fault as well. Likewise, if a supervisor has acted inappropriately, the Board is interested in knowing whether the supervisee has knowledge of the problem and has taken any steps to stop it, for example, if a supervisor is having sex with a client who is later referred to his intern. What are the intern's duties? The Board will want to know whether the intern informed the client of her options in pursuing the supervisor with the Board, and so forth. Further, if the supervisor is utilizing a technique that is not generally accepted in the psychotherapeutic community, the intern also becomes a target.

Another area of concern in providing information to an investigator occurs when the complaining party was not the only client seen in therapy. Many complaints arise out of the participation by the therapist in family law matters. There have been numerous reported cases in this area, which indicate just the tip of the litigation iceberg (see *Howard v. Drapkin* [1990] 222 Cal.App.3d 843; *Goottee v. Lightner* [1990] 224 Cal. App.3d 587). In *Howard v. Drapkin*, Dr. Drapkin had performed an evaluation of a family for purposes of determining custody issues. Both the husband and wife, through their attorneys, had agreed to retain Dr. Drapkin for this purpose. After the results of the evaluation were provided to the parties, the wife filed a civil action against Dr. Drapkin, contending that the psychologist's conduct during the evaluation constituted professional negligence (i.e., allegedly screaming at the wife during sessions). The Second District Court of Appeal held that Dr. Drapkin's conduct was protected, both by the judicial privilege of Civil Code §47(2), and by the doctrine of quasi-judicial immunity. Thus, Dr. Drapkin could not be sued by either party for the purported wrongful conduct. The doctrine of quasi-judicial immunity is premised on the theory that counselors perform essential functions (i.e., evaluations) to the family law courts, such that they should be extended the same immunities available to other judicial officers. Judicial privilege is established by statute and provides a privilege to judicial officers, parties to litigation, and others for acts taken during the course of a judicial proceeding.

The Fourth District Court of Appeal, however, rejected the argument of quasi-judicial immunity in a case with essentially similar facts. They were unwilling to expand the zone of protection as the court did in *Howard v. Drapkin*. They did recognize that a therapist's conduct may still be protected by the judicial privilege of Civil Code §47(2). Conduct would have to meet the following criteria: be by a participant to the judicial proceedings, occur during the course of such proceedings, and logically relate to them.

Even though a therapist's conduct may be privileged in the civil context, the Board can still pursue the therapist. Several claims against therapists have arisen when the therapist has attempted to collect from the responsible party in the family law matter. The complaining party usually says that the therapist's conduct was inappropriate in performing the evaluations. Usually, these complaints are successfully dealt with at the administrative stage. Investigators recognize that the claims are made in retribution for collection attempts by the therapist.

In other instances, parties to family law matters file complaints with licensing Boards to gain a tactical advantage in the litigation: for example, to have another court-appointed evaluator appointed, or to appoint another therapist to see the children. A pending licensing matter has a "chilling effect" on the acceptance of that therapist's opinions.

Several cases against therapists have been initiated by disgruntled lovers. When a therapist has a personal relationship with another individual, the two most likely discuss personal issues. These same topics are likely to be discussed in therapy. In one case, a therapist was having an affair with a married woman. In order to conceal their relationship from their respective spouses, they agreed that they would use a group therapy situation as a place to meet. Once the woman's husband found out about the affair, however, he threatened to report the therapist to the Board for "ruining his marriage." The husband was under the mistaken impression that his wife had been in therapy, rather than just carrying on a personal relationship with the therapist. There had been no therapy notes taken during the contact between the therapist and the woman. She had never paid for any therapy. The contact had originally started because she was a student in a program that the therapist was involved in at a school. The woman testified that she broke off the relationship with the therapist because she realized that he could not support her if he lost his license as a result of her husband's complaint. She also testified that she was aware during the entire course of the relationship that it was inappropriate for a therapist to have a sexual relationship with a client. After breaking off the extramarital relationship, she decided to sue the therapist for money. Her contention was that the "relationship" she had with the therapist was really therapeutic in nature because she discussed her personal issues with him. She also reported him to the Board. While the civil action was disposed of by way of a motion for summary judgment, the Board continued to pursue the therapist administratively. Ultimately, the therapist decided to stipulate to allow revocation of his license because of health and financial problems. A stipulation is a written agreement with the Board to resolve a matter prior to a hearing. It usually entails an agreement to certain punishment (i.e., taking courses) and admission of wrongful conduct.

Even though therapists may successfully defend themselves against a civil action, the Board can still take steps. In some instances, civil actions are disposed of on procedural grounds. One of these grounds may be that the plaintiff-client waited too long to bring a civil action against a therapist. This type of procedural win does not bar the Board from taking action. Prior to January 1, 2000, there was no statute of limitations applicable to Board proceedings. This meant that the Board could pursue matters as much as twenty years old, or older. As of January 1, the statute of limitations in licensing matters is three years from notification of a complaint (i.e., discovery of an act) or seven years from the act, whichever occurs first (Business and Professions Code §2960.05). Many states do not yet have such statutes of limitation.

The primary statute of limitations applicable to civil actions brought against health care providers is Code of Civil Procedure §340.5. This section states, in pertinent part:

> [I]n an action for injury or death against a health care provider based upon such person's alleged professional negligence, the time for the commencement of action shall be three years after the date of injury or one year after the plaintiff discovers, or through the use of reasonable diligence should have discovered, the injury, whichever occurs first.

Even though plaintiff-clients cannot successfully bring civil actions against mental health professionals after this limitation period, the Board can pursue licensees for up to seven years in some cases.

It is the therapist's burden to prove the defense of laches at the time of the administrative hearing to gain any relief from prosecution based on time. Essentially, laches is a defense that provides that the case is barred because the defendant has been deprived of presenting a defense due to the passage of time. The showing must be that witnesses cannot be located and/or that documentation proving one's innocence cannot be located or has been destroyed, or other exculpatory evidence that may have exonerated the therapist of the charge is now unavailable. Also, the passage of time allows the argument to be made that the licensee really poses no danger to the public because he or she has been practicing in the ensuing time period with no further complaints. Further, imposing a penalty at this late date would not serve to promote any legitimate public purpose.

Civil Code §43.93 indicates that a cause of action no longer exists between spouses. Several cases involved a therapist marrying a client, only to have the marriage terminate at a later time. After divorce, the spouse-client turned around and sued the therapist for professional negligence. These cases can no longer be pursued in the civil context. However, there is no prohibition from pursuing these claims administratively.

Professionals often believe that the investigator is in their corner because the investigator is affiliated with their Board. By training and sometimes by nature, mental health professionals want to help these investigators understand the pathology of their clients and why these professionals believe that their clients would misinterpret the therapeutic relationship: for instance, why a borderline client might sexualize a relationship.

In many instances investigators conduct their questioning to substantiate the allegations contained in a complaint rather than to ascertain the truth. I have had investigators refuse to conduct interviews with my clients if I state my intention to tape-record the interview. Other investigators have demanded that they maintain the original tape recording of the interview. If there is a problem with recording an interview, I always have a third party present, such as a paralegal, who will take notes.

QUESTIONABLE ACCURACY OF WITNESS STATEMENTS

Even though civil matters generally involve only monetary issues and administrative matters involve an individual's professional status, the professional is limited in the ability to present a defense in licensing cases. During administrative discovery, the respondent is entitled to the investigator's report, any consulting experts' reports, any statements made by witnesses, and any documents obtained during the investigation. In most cases, the statements made by witnesses are not under any type of oath, nor are they signed under penalty of perjury. In most cases these "witnesses' statements" are contained within the investigation report and are summaries of the interview conducted with a witness by the state's investigator. Frequently there are not even any quotes attributed to these witnesses in the reports. It is standard procedure for investigators to destroy their rough draft notes of interviews and to maintain only the typewritten final report. In rare cases, statements allegedly signed by witnesses attesting to their accuracy had to be corrected later by these witnesses because they were never given an opportunity to review them.

The tape recording of interviews would further ensure the due process rights of the accused professional. If the interview transcription were available, the questions, together with the exact answers of the witnesses, would be available. Any bias of the investigator would be subject to scrutiny. Many times there is a mindset that just because there is a complaint filed against an individual, the professional has done something wrong.

I have encountered several instances where the investigator in a matter has referred witnesses to the attorney for the original complainant. The rationale is that it is just one more step in protecting the public. This type of referral can negatively impact the credibility of witnesses. In most of these cases, the allegation of inappropriate sexual contact is made by the original complainant. Once these other witnesses are contacted and information is shared about what another client suffered at the hands of the therapist, it becomes very easy for the same allegation to be made by these witnesses. An example would be an allegation that drugs were used to obtain sex with clients. Moreover, if the therapist actually has had a sexual relationship with one client, details of the act, together with physically identifying features, can be shared by the other purported victims. Thus, a "pattern of abuse" is created based on the sharing of information.

Later, the Attorney General's office usually contends that the investigator's rough notes are not subject to disclosure during the course of discovery. The contention is that only the investigator's report, ultimately made available to the Attorney General's office, is discoverable. The inherent problem with the report is that it is usually a summary of interviews. Thus, the actual questions asked and the specific answers are not documented, except, perhaps, in the mind of the investigator.

The presence of counsel is also important to focus the investigator on relevant issues. For instance, where the complainant is a convicted felon, the issue of credibility is important. During an investigation, a Department of Consumers investigator stated that the criminal record of the complaining witness was on multiple felony counts for grand theft auto. The complaint was that the therapist had a personal relationship with the complainant as well as a professional one. The reality was that the complainant was a vengeful person with whom the therapist had the misfortune of having a personal relationship. In inquiring about proof that the complainant had furnished about his purported status as a "client," the investigator had only been given a copy of one check written to the order of the therapist. The credibility of these parties, obviously, was of paramount importance as to whether the complainant was ever a client. In many instances, the testimony of the parties is so diverse that the issue of credibility is of paramount importance.

Another instance concerned the determination of whether it was necessary for a therapist to file a child abuse report when another medical professional had done so while the therapist was present. Further, the therapist, a mental health professional, was not acting in her professional capacity when the issue of abuse presented itself. The investigator's focus was, "Did you file a report?" It was necessary to inform the investigator that a report had been filed by another professional with the simultaneous knowledge of my client. Moreover, the law does not require that two reports be made under those circumstances. The Board decided to close the investigation without filing an accusation against the professional.

The Penal Code imposing a duty to report on professionals does not make a distinction as to what role the professional is in at the time (i.e., therapist, mother, or friend). A reasonable interpretation of the penal law is that a "mandated reporter" does not have the duty to report when he is wearing a different hat (i.e., as a parent, friend, or neighbor).

It is essential that a written release of information from all clients participating in the particular therapy be received by the therapist before any discussion with an investigator. Instances of noncustodial parents filing complaints against therapists concerning treatment or an evaluation are not uncommon. It is important that the release be signed by the proper guardian of a minor client before information is turned over. When family therapy has been conducted, a release from all involved family members is necessary. Although the Board may issue an administrative subpoena for the materials that are the subject of the investigation, it forces recognition of the fact that the complaining party has no right to a release of the information.

INVESTIGATIVE SUBPOENAS: GOVERNMENT-SANCTIONED INVASION OF PRIVACY?

The ability to subpoena private records of individuals who may not even be aware of the investigation is a threat to everyone's fundamental right to privacy. The Board can, and has, obtained records on private individuals without their knowledge or permission. They do this by issuing investigative subpoenas. In one instance, the Board issued a subpoena for a minor's records when a noncustodial mother complained to the Board. The minor had previously been removed from the mother's custody by the State of California. The custodian of the minor was never contacted to ascertain whether the release of information was acceptable. Although therapists may refuse to release records sought by an investigative subpoena, many individuals do not know this.

THE BOARD AS A TOOL OF PLAINTIFF'S COUNSEL

Many times, a complaint is filed by a plaintiff who has filed a concurrent civil action. Plaintiffs' attorneys who are knowledgeable in this area understand that the initiation of an administrative investigation will increase the likelihood that a civil action will settle. This is because any finding against the licensee in the administrative matter can be used by the plaintiff in the civil action, under a doctrine known as *res judicata*. For instance, if the Board determines that the licensee has been grossly negligent in his/her treatment of the plaintiff, this can operate as a finding of misconduct in the civil action. The only remaining issue in the civil action would be damages.

COMPLAINTS INITIATED BY INVESTIGATORS

Complaints have also been initiated against therapists by Department of Consumer Affairs investigators, rather than by clients. Sometimes in the investigation of other treating professionals, the conduct of a subsequent therapist is brought into question by the investigator.

Many clients have complained that the Board has singled them out because of the modality of therapy they utilize, even though these modalities are accepted within the profession. I have heard statements that if a therapist says he practices "experiential psychotherapy," for instance, he is asking to have his license revoked by the Board. Other instances of similar statements involve Reichian therapy and psychodrama. There have also been situations in which graduate students have presented theses that were approved by the graduate school but were found unacceptable by the Board (e.g., limited physical examinations of minor clients).

COMPLAINTS BY NONCLIENTS

Complaints against therapists have also been lodged by other professionals, both mental-health and law-related individuals. In one instance, a therapist testified about a meeting she had with her own client's family members. The client had been accused of sexually molesting his daughters. The therapist met with these girls and they recanted their allegations at this informal meeting. The therapist subsequently testified about these recantations at her client's criminal trial. The criminal prosecutor attempted to exclude the therapist's testimony about her conversations with these other family members on the basis of therapist–client confidentiality. His contention was that the girls were also clients. The trial court allowed the therapist's testimony, which decision was upheld by the Court of Appeal. This did not stop the prosecutor, however, from initiating an administrative complaint against the therapist, based, in part, on this purported disclosure. The BBS filed an accusation against the therapist. After several years and a full administrative hearing, the administrative law judge's proposed decision was to dismiss the accusation. Although the Board initially nonadopted the decision, it finally decided to adopt the proposed decision as its own. Unfortunately, the therapist died before this final decision was issued by the Board.

Complaints can also be initiated when the Attorney General in charge of prosecuting the case contacts the press. In one instance, an Attorney General contacted the newspapers about an Accusation before it was even served on the therapist. The therapist actually read about the Accusation in the morning paper before having any knowledge about it. Although she had cooperated with the investigation, there was no subsequent contact by the Board to notify her that they would be filing an Accusation prior to the newspaper account. The contact with the press has been justified by the Attorney General's office as a further step in protecting the public. The reasoning is that if there are any other members of the public who have been harmed by this therapist, they would come out of the woodwork after seeing the inflammatory article. Once an Accusation is filed against a therapist it becomes a matter of public record. Of course, the complainants are usually identified only by initials in the Accusation, while the therapist's full name and address are on its face. Thus the identities of the complainants are protected, while the therapist's name and the details of the Accusation, whether true or not, are available to the public. Obviously, significant harm can be done to a professional's practice and reputation when the Attorney General's office contacts the press and/or the press publishes this information. The press's coverage of both civil and administrative actions is fairly common, especially if the case involves allegations of sexual misconduct.

INVESTIGATIVE REPORTS

The investigator's report is provided to the Board. If the decision is made to go forward with the case, the investigator's report is then forwarded on to an expert(s) for an opinion on the validity of the charges. The expert's opinion

then furnishes the basis for the Board's decision to file an accusation against
the professional. Government Code §11503 states in part: "[T]he accusation
shall be a written statement of charges which shall set forth in ordinary and
concise language the acts or omissions with which the respondent is charged,
to the end that the respondent will be able to prepare his defense." Thus, if the
investigation is poorly conducted the entire process becomes tainted by it.

While investigators often state that they make no recommendation to the
Board in their reports, it is obvious that the Board relies on and is persuaded
by the information as it is presented in the report. On numerous occasions, exculpatory information communicated by witnesses has not appeared in the reports prepared by the investigators. The only way to discover this information
is through a subsequent interview with a witness. The only time this is possible is when the witness is willing to discuss the matter informally. Most of the
time, adverse witnesses are not willing to discuss information voluntarily
prior to the administrative hearing. This is true even when the witnesses are
other professionals. Subsequent treating professionals of complainants, who
previously supplied information to the Board during the investigation, will
often refuse to discuss their statements with attorneys for the licensee. One
would think that if their accounts were justified and truthful they would not
hesitate to discuss their statements. The problem is that there is no way to
compel them to discuss anything with defense counsel before a settlement or
the final hearing.

The inherent bias of the investigative reports can be illustrated by a case in
which a supervisor was being accused of aiding and abetting an unlicensed
person to practice. The only intern who was interviewed was the one who was
also the subject of the investigation and so had a stake in telling the investigator that he had left the responsibility of completing the paperwork up to the
supervisor. Of course the investigator did not interview any other of the supervisor's interns. These other interns/psychological assistants ultimately testified at the administrative hearing that they were clearly told by this same supervisor that they were required to fill out all paperwork. Moreover, these
other interns and psychological assistants testified about the high quality of
supervision that they had received from the supervisor in question. The names
of these other interns were given to the investigator by the supervisor during
the investigation. The investigator did not, however, contact them. Their testimony was important to show that the custom and practice of the supervisor
were more than adequate and directly contradicted the statements of the only
"problem" intern. Although the Administrative Law judge's proposed decision was to dismiss the accusation, the BBS nonadopted the judge's decision.
Ultimately, the Board agreed to dismiss the accusation.

The failure to have a verbatim transcript of interviews makes it completely
unknown what the investigator initially communicated to the witnesses about

the complaint. One of the only ways of attacking the information in the report is by cross-examination of the witnesses and the investigator at the time of the administrative hearing.

DEPOSITIONS

Discovery is also limited in an administrative matter. Discovery is the gathering of information held by the opposing party in a case. Normally, in civil actions, a party can send out written questions, known as interrogatories, and can schedule depositions, which are statements given under oath.

The only time a deposition is allowed in an administrative matter is on a verified petition of either party. A verified petition is a statement under oath indicating, in part, why the testimony of the witness is material and why the witness is unable to attend or cannot be compelled to attend the hearing (Government Code §11511). The deposition consists of questions and answers taken under oath. Depositions are a recognized method of discovery in civil actions, as are interrogatories (written questions) and requests for admissions. The purpose is to ascertain the truth and to obtain adverse testimony under penalty of perjury. These safeguards are not available in the administrative context. As was previously discussed, the statements of witnesses are rarely obtained under oath. Of course, obtaining permission to take a deposition in these matters is another expense that the licensee must bear.

Most of the time, adverse witnesses will not voluntarily speak to a representative of the respondent. Without the tool of a deposition it is not possible to ascertain the knowledge of the witness or biases prior to the hearing. The information about the possible testimony is primarily contained in the investigator's report.

DOCUMENTARY EVIDENCE

It is also necessary to aggressively seek out the documentation that may be contained in the Attorney General's file about the case. Cases may take years to reach the hearing stage. Both parties may continue to obtain documents during the entire process. Moreover, there may be a change of attorneys handling the matter at the Attorney General's office. On some occasions, documents have been unintentionally withheld. On other occasions, documents such as a complainant's subsequent therapy notes have been intentionally withheld. Those notes were extremely relevant to issues in dispute, such as credibility and damage resulting from the purported wrongful conduct. At an administrative hearing, an Attorney General attempted to have a subsequent treating therapist testify about how damaged the complainant had been by the accused's conduct, but refused to release therapy notes for a portion of the treatment. The administrative judge ordered the production of the therapy notes if the subsequent therapist was to testify.

If it is discovered prior to the hearing that the Attorney General is withholding documents, the recourse is to file a petition to compel discovery in the superior court (Government Code §11507.7[a]). Obviously, this is another costly alternative for the licensee.

EXPERT WITNESSES

Experts for the Board are chosen by informal means and are usually recommended by another individual. They forward a resumé to the Board and an informal telephone interview is conducted of the potential expert. Experts are not chosen who necessarily have the same therapeutic approach as the professional under scrutiny. This often leads to a criticism of conduct that is a recognized therapeutic approach within the discipline used by the therapist under attack. I have seen an expert's report provided to the Board where the expert admits that he is totally unfamiliar with the therapeutic approach in question, but states that it is unacceptable under any circumstances. Many times, experts' reports are not qualified in any way, such as by statements indicating that they are based on the limited information provided. Most of the time an expert's report does not indicate he could only determine if a violation had occurred with additional information.

Although I have had the Board file an accusation against a therapist for diagnosing an individual that she has not personally seen (i.e., comments made about a husband in a court report when the only client seen by the therapist was the wife), the Board's experts have done the same thing. In one matter, a Board expert prepared a report stating that my client suffered from a "psychotic break with reality." He had never seen or met my client. He was relying on the investigator's report to make his diagnosis. Further, this diagnosis-in-absentia formed the basis for the Board to seek an order compelling a psychological examination of my client. The Board's expert psychiatrist who conducted an evaluation concluded there was no evidence of any current problems. He could not, of course, rule out any past conditions. The Board still filed an accusation against this therapist and later criticized its own evaluation because it was conducted by a psychiatrist and not a clinical psychologist. Ultimately, after several years, a settlement was reached with the Board, in large part because of the financial constraints of defending the action.

ADMINISTRATIVE HEARSAY

Another means by which due process is lacking in the context of administrative proceedings is the type of evidence that may be admitted in administrative hearings. According to Government Code §11513, hearsay may be admitted at the time of the hearing. The limitation on this evidence is that "[H]earsay evidence may be used for the purpose of supplementing or explaining other evidence but shall not be sufficient in itself to support a finding unless it would be admissible over objection in civil actions" (Government Code §11513 [c]). This is not the case in civil actions. In civil actions, hearsay is excluded except in limited circumstances. This means that the Board investigator may testify about what a witness told him during the interview. In some cases this obviates the necessity of the Board calling the witness because the investigator can testify to what was supposedly discussed between them during an investigation. This means that there may never be an opportunity to confront the "real" witness. Although the Board may not rely exclusively on hearsay testimony, the hearsay testimony of the investigator still makes its way into the record. This is the same record the Board is looking at when it nonadopts the administrative law judge's proposed decision.

SETTLEMENTS PRIOR TO HEARING

Prior to the hearing, a matter may be settled between the parties if the Board is willing to discuss settlement. Many times clients wish to discuss settling the case, not because of the perception of any wrongdoing but because of the cost of defending an action. There is generally no insurance coverage for an administrative action. This, of course, depends on the actual language of the insurance policies. There are some carriers now offering limited reimbursement insurance toward defense fees. Even a simple case can run into tens of thousands of dollars in preparing a defense and then participating in an administrative hearing. If any intervention of the superior court is needed the cost escalates. Moreover, if a complaint is filed against an individual awaiting the results of the oral examination, the Board can hold the results of the oral examination until the investigation is concluded or until any Accusation is carried to its ultimate conclusion. Thus, an intern can be deprived by the process of years of compensation as a fully licensed individual.

In attempting to settle matters with a Board, the disciplinary guidelines are instructive. According to the BBS, it "recognizes that these penalties and conditions of probation are merely guidelines and that mitigating or aggravating circumstances may necessitate deviations" (State of California Board of Behavioral Sciences "Disciplinary Guidelines," Revised 2/6/97). These guidelines are directed to the following violations: sexual misconduct with clients; commission of an act punishable as a sexually related crime; conviction of a crime substantially related to duties and functions of license; securing or attempting to secure a license by fraud; substance abuse impairing ability to function safely; use of drugs with clients; intentionally/recklessly causing harm to clients; commission of dishonest/fraudulent acts related to duties and functions of license; performing, offering to perform, permitting to perform beyond scope of license; gross negligence/incompetence; misrepresentation of license/qualifications; impersonating licensee/allowing impersonation; aiding and abetting unlicensed/unregistered activity; failure to maintain confidentiality; failure to disclose fees in advance; pay, accept, solicit fee for referrals; false/misleading advertising; improper supervision of trainee/intern; violations by registrants/applicants acquiring hours of experience; and discipline by another state or by California against a corresponding license.

DISCIPLINARY GUIDELINES

The maximum penalty for all these violations is revocation/denial of license and the minimum penalty is revocation stayed. This means that regardless of the charged offense the minimum penalty is revocation of the license with a stay of the revocation. While technically the license is revoked, the status of being revoked is held in abeyance or stayed, and the therapist can continue to practice. In addition to the condition of revocation, there are numerous other conditions that may be required by the Board to settle a matter. The standard probation conditions listed in the guidelines are as follows:

1. *Obey all laws* (this is a general requirement ensuring that the licensee continues to obey all laws).
2. *File quarterly reports* (comprehensive reports prepared by a supervisor of a licensee. The reports are to focus on monitoring and rehabilitation efforts, including a recording of all supervision sessions and a brief summary of the treatment of all the licensee's current clients.)
3. *Comply with program monitoring* (can be either, by the Board-approved supervisor, and/or by a monitor with the Department of Consumer Affairs).
4. *Conduct interviews with the Board* (the Board may require an interview at any time, and the licensee must comply with the request. The interview may be conducted by the Board or by its agents, for example, investigators).

5. *Toll probation if respondent moves out of state* (if a licensee does move out of state, then the Board must be informed, and any remaining period of probation will be put on hold).
6. *Prohibition of supervision of unlicensed persons.*
7. *Violation of any of the above-referenced terms of probation.*
8. *Completion of probation.*

There are optional conditions of probation as well, which are: a time period of suspended practice, a psychological evaluation by a Board-chosen evaluator as a condition to continued practice, supervision of respondent's practice, individual psychotherapy, continuing education, taking and passing the current licensure examination as a condition precedent to continued practice, community service, drug and/or alcohol abuse counseling/detoxification program, restricted practice (e.g., no female patients, restricted setting), notification to clients of the terms and conditions of probation, passing a special oral competency examination on sexual misconduct as a condition for continuing practice, reimbursement to the Board of the costs of investigation and prosecution, and financial restitution to the victim.

In the lesser charged offenses (other than sexual misconduct), there is generally no requirement for suspension from practice. Time periods of suspension can range from thirty days on up. The greater the period of suspension, the greater the likelihood that a therapist in private practice will lose all of his or her clientele. Obviously, it becomes difficult to explain an absence of greater than a few weeks' duration. There is also an ethical issue about abandonment if alternative treatment sources are not presented to clients under these circumstances. There is usually a request for supervision versus individual therapy, although on occasion both are sought by the Board. The Board of Psychology emphasizes the imposition of the full licensing exam, whereas the BBS focuses more on an exam tailored to the issues in the case. The danger in any "special" exam is that it is harder to challenge the fairness in the content and/or administration. On the other hand, the current licensing examination may be more arduous, particularly where someone has been practicing for a long period of time.

With California's budget crisis, the reimbursement condition to the Board is usually a term of probation. In general, the only time restitution to the "victim" is ordered is in cases involving alleged insurance fraud. Other hidden costs to the licensee are the entire expense of the supervisor, exams, evaluations, and individual therapy.

The power held by the enforcement coordinator in negotiating settlements is immense. This is the individual who preliminarily decides what type of penalty should be imposed in each case. Negotiations concerning settlement are conducted with a deputy Attorney General, who, in turn, converses with the enforcement coordinator. Ultimately, the stipulation for settlement has to be approved by the Board.

Penalty is the appropriate term in this context. Although the focus of the Board should be to protect the public, as stated in the governing laws, more often than not the conditions required to settle amount to more of a punitive action than any type of protective measure.

In my experience the Board is virtually never willing to discuss settlement in cases involving therapist/client sex between a male therapist and a female client. The Board is usually willing to discuss settling a matter in which the conduct is less involved than intercourse or in which the therapist is a female and the client is of either sex. The Board is not interested in any mitigating factor in these matters, such as genuine affection for the client or a single act of misconduct. The only option for a therapist when a client contends that they have had sexual intercourse is for the therapist to try the matter. As of 1994, if an administrative law judge finds that a therapist has engaged in sexual contact with a patient or former patient, the judge has to order revocation of the license. The judge no longer has discretion to order a lesser penalty, even if the facts of the case call out for it (Business and Professions Code §4982.26). Moreover, licensees used to be able to petition for reinstatement of their license after one year. This time period has been extended to three years in some cases (Business and Professions Code §4982.2). A petition for reinstatement is also up to the discretion of the Board, and most of the time involves a "mini-trial" of the original charges, even though this is expressly prohibited in the laws governing this procedure.

The Board is more amenable to discussing settlement when the allegations in the accusation are several years old and/or the licensee has taken substantial steps toward mitigation. However, the Board usually argues that the only reason the individual participated in rehabilitation efforts was because of the pending investigation. Recently, several therapists have been contacted about conduct that allegedly occurred twenty years ago. Some of the mitigating factors identified by the Board include restitution to the victim, the fact that there is only one victim, and substantive rehabilitation efforts prior to the commencement of the investigation. Many times these matters take years to resolve themselves, so that rehabilitation efforts should be taken even after the beginning of the investigation. The importance of seeking supervision and/or individual therapy, even after the commencement of an investigation, is that these providers can testify on behalf of the licensee at any administrative trial. The longer the pendency of the case, the more weight this testimony should carry in terms of fitness to practice, and so forth. Rehabilitation efforts can include seeking individual and/or group therapy. The licensee can also retain a supervisor for his or her practice during the pendency of the administrative hearing, and/or participate in alcohol/drug programs and continuing education.

The agreement to any of these conditions of probation should not be entered into lightly. In one case, I had a client who agreed to participate in an oral examination as a condition precedent to continued practice. This was one of the conditions of the settlement that was reached prior to the administrative trial. The Accusation contained charges of having a dual relationship with a client (i.e., student and client) and of being sexually inappropriate (i.e., using "seductive" language during sessions). At the time of the oral examination, the examiners had a copy of the investigative file in front of them and proceeded to question my client about the allegations contained in the accusation for a majority of the examination time. Obviously, this was not the administration of the oral examination that is normally given to individuals attempting to gain licensure. This also could not be considered the purported special competency examination in sexual issues that the disciplinary guidelines set forth. Further, and more important, it amounted to the conduct of a hearing without the benefit of counsel.

At the time of the oral examination, the licensee denied the charges of sexual misconduct. This was consistent with the truth, and our position during the entire pendency of the case. The panel of three examiners, by a majority vote, decided to fail the licensee, based, in part, on his "denial" of the purported charges. This licensee had been practicing for over ten years. After correspondence with the Board and the retaking of an appropriately conducted examination, the licensee passed the oral examination and is now completing the remainder of the agreed-to terms of probation. Of course, the Board in response to my letter indicated that the first examination was not conducted in violation of any regulations. This is because there are no regulations about these types of examinations, which are left to the Board's discretion. Obviously, the first examination was violative of the notion of reasonableness and due process. This type of questionable conduct may be subject to scrutiny by the Superior Court.

LAST-MINUTE AMENDMENTS ALLOWED

The Accusation can be amended by the Board up to the time the matter is submitted for decision to the administrative law judge (Government Code §11507). Although the respondent is supposed to be given a reasonable opportunity to prepare a defense to these charges, if they are "substantially similar" to the existing charges, then amendments may be allowed, even on the last day of the administrative hearing. For example, if the testimony at the hearing differs factually from the Accusation, the Accusation pleading can simply be amended to conform to the testimony. On the other hand, significant prejudice to the professional can occur when new complaints are allowed to be added to the accusation. This most commonly occurs in cases of purported sexual misconduct with multiple victims. New alleged victims may come out of the woodwork shortly before the hearing.

CHANGING STANDARDS IN THE PROFESSION: DUAL RELATIONSHIPS

The Board also attempts to prosecute violations that are not based on the recognized standard of care in the profession at the time of the alleged misconduct. This is a frequent occurrence. In one accusation, the therapist allegedly had a dual relationship with a client in the early to mid-1980s. It consisted of a therapeutic relationship with a client and, during a short period of time, the client as a student in a graduate class. The reason this client had sought therapy was to fulfill a requirement of the graduate school, which required that students have a certain number of personal therapy hours. The Board's expert was prepared to testify that this dual relationship constituted gross negligence. The decision was made to settle with the Board, with terms including a probationary period with supervision, a psychological evaluation, and continuing education.

In other cases, Board experts have testified that a dual relationship is defined as having any type of relationship with a client other than a therapeutic one (i.e., business). The proscription against dual relationships comes about because they allegedly take advantage of the client and without the therapeutic relationship, the therapist would not be in a position to manipulate the client to gain an undue advantage. The obvious dual relationship is when the therapist has a sexual relationship with a client.

The concept of a dual relationship, however, has changed over time. In the early 1980s, the recognition of dual relationships was just developing, as it continues to do today. Many graduate schools still require that students participate in some type of therapy, either individual or group. There is still a current practice among certain psychoanalytic schools to allow instructors to see students in psychoanalysis. The American Psychological Association has reexamined its proscription against therapists trading or bartering goods for services. Moreover, another expert witness for the Board, who was adamantly opposed to any type of dual relationship with clients, indicated that she had accepted gifts from clients. She qualified her conduct by indicating that she only accepted "small" gifts. The question then becomes what constitutes a "small" gift—is it the monetary value or the importance that the client attaches to the item?

The significance is that the Board is moving forward to revoke a practitioner's license in areas that are still being defined by the profession itself. While a practitioner is safe with the knowledge that sex with a current client is wrong, any relationship with a former client may still be the subject matter of a Board inquiry. At what point does a dual relationship become "gross negligence"? The danger is in who defines the answers to these questions. What about a psychoanalytic institute that requires its students to participate in a long-term course of psychoanalysis? If the instructors are well-regarded psychoanalysts, can students begin a course of psychoanalysis if they aren't yet in that instructor's class? What about the probability that they may be in the psychoanalyst's class at some point? Shouldn't the size of the community impact the determination of acceptability?

It is still quite common in civil professional negligence actions to have a subsequent treating therapist in a dual relationship. This occurs in actions where a client brings a malpractice action against a prior treating therapist. One of the witnesses usually called by the plaintiff-client is his current treating therapist. Of course, the client is still in therapy because this is an item of damage in his civil action. Also, by continuing in therapy, he now has someone who will corroborate his story as well as someone who can testify as to how damaged he is now as a result of purported negligent conduct by the defendant-therapist. Typically, subsequent therapists do not attempt to discover the truth of the statements that their new clients are making but take those statements at face value.

The duality occurs when these subsequent treating therapists testify at the civil trial that the prior therapist breached the standard of care in the community by mistreating the client in question. Not only is testimony elicited about their subsequent treatment of the client, but now they are testifying about whether the prior treater committed malpractice. On the one hand, they are testifying as an advocate of the injured client, while on the other hand, they are supposedly occupying an unbiased position as an expert witness on the standard of care issue.

In a Board action, the Board's expert on the issue of gross negligence testified that to testify on both the issue of the client's condition and whether the respondent's conduct constituted gross negligence would constitute an inappropriate dual relationship. This testimony was then used to prevent the complainant's subsequent treating therapist from testifying about the appropriateness of the respondent's conduct.

The Board of Psychology has taken an active position in prosecuting what it perceives as dual relationships. In one matter, a therapist had seen a client in an initial session. During this initial session, the therapist determined that this client would most appropriately be handled by a transfer to another therapist. Within the first fifteen minutes, the issue of the transfer was discussed and referrals given to the client. The balance of the session was spent in small talk concerning the client's employment and general matters. The next contact the therapist had with the client was two weeks later, when it was determined by telephone that the client had established contact with another therapist and had been in therapy with that individual for the two weeks. At that time, the therapist inquired whether the client would like to volunteer her time by utilizing her employment skills in the therapist's college-level course. She made a short seven-minute presentation to the students in the course. She subsequently made another short presentation to a group of this therapist's mentally impaired clients. The respondent-therapist then provided her with some tapes on relaxation to aid her in her presentations, which she picked up at the therapist's office. Although she attempted to present personal problems at this last visit to his office, the respondent-therapist refused to address these issues and referred her back to discuss them with her therapist.

The Board contended that the respondent-therapist had an ongoing therapeutic relationship with this client from the initial referral session to the last "meeting" at his office when she picked up the audiotapes almost two months later. This was in spite of the fact that this client had been in ongoing therapy with another therapist and was being followed by a psychiatrist as well.

Further, the Board contended that the respondent-therapist had committed sexual misconduct or had certainly "manipulated" the client. They based this assertion on the fact that the respondent-therapist had the client perform a belly dance at the presentations. The Board contended that this form of dance was sexual in nature, and, therefore, requesting the performance of it constituted sexual misconduct.

The reality of the situation was that the client was a professional belly dancer. She performed many times in public and was employed to belly dance at hotels and had done so for several years. She had been through extensive training as a belly dancer and belonged to professional belly dancing organizations.

Ultimately, the Board adopted the administrative law judge's decision dismissing the accusation. The case was pending for over two years and ultimately cost approximately $20,000 for defense. No cost can be placed on the stress experienced by the therapist and his family. The investigation against the therapist was initiated by a Department of Consumers investigator because this same belly dancer had filed a complaint against another therapist, contending that they had a sexual affair during the course of her therapy. During the investigation of the therapist who allegedly sexually assaulted the belly dancer, it was discovered that she had performed for students of this subsequent therapist. The investigator initiated the complaint based on this discovery.

THE BOARD'S UNIQUE DEFINITION OF OWNERSHIP

The regulation stating that a psychological assistant shall have no proprietary interest" in the supervisor's business has been interpreted by the Board as including more than a simple ownership interest in the supervisor's business (i.e., a partnership) (Title 16 *Regulations relating to the Practice of Psychology*, §1391.8[b], hereinafter "regulations"). The determination of what constitutes a "proprietary interest" rests within the Board's discretion. In one matter involving an intern, the Board was contending that the signature by an intern on a contract for office cleaning services was evidence of a proprietary interest. The intern had signed the contract because the supervisor was not physically available when the contract was presented for signature. Based on the fact that the intern was losing money during the pendency of this case (the difference between the compensation as an intern versus a licensed MFT), the intern opted to settle the case so he could begin to practice in a fully licensed capacity. Other cases of alleged "proprietary interest" include interns who have signed lease agreements or have placed their names on bank accounts.

Many times the Board attempts to undermine the supervisor as well as the intern and/or psychological assistant during an investigation. While a supervisor may be the individual under investigation, an intern may be contacted under the auspices that the investigation is really about him, or vice versa. The investigation attempts to discover any discrepancies between statements of the supervisor and the intern on any issue. Often, the interns suffer the most from such investigations. While everyone is responsible for being informed about the letter of the law, on occasion supervisors have not forwarded the appropriate paperwork to the Board. Sometimes the accounts will not be set up appropriately, with the intern having access to the monies. Again, this is regarded as having a proprietary interest in the business. The manner in which the books and/or accounts are set up is often on the recommendation of an accountant who may not be familiar with the regulations. The issue of treating interns and psychological assistants as independent contractors rather than employees is a common one. Unfortunately, these technical problems can be the basis for the imposition of a penalty.

The intern or psychological assistant is held to the same standard as the supervisor. Thus, while these employees rely on their supervisor's experience, or lack of it, the Board does not make a distinction. The Board's position is often harsher in dealing with the interns, as opposed to the supervisor. The rationale is that they want to send a message out to other interns. Moreover, interns have a greater stake in resolving these matters as expeditiously as possible because the Board will not issue their license until the complaint is resolved, either by settlement or hearing.

SEX EQUALS REVOCATION

Another important aspect of the therapist–client contact is the issue of sexual relations. Testimony has been elicited from Board experts that a therapist should never engage in sexual relations with a client at any time. The axiom most often given is "once a client, always a client." The law only imposes a two-year hiatus between termination of therapy and the commencement of a sexual relationship (Civil Code §43.93).[2] This law is of recent vintage, and became effective in or about January 1988. Prior to that time, some experts believed that a personal relationship was acceptable after a six-month hiatus. An earlier historical opinion indicated that as long as therapy was terminated or perhaps the client was referred to another therapist, then a personal/sexual relationship could begin. Arguments have been made in the administrative context that these code sections do not apply because the time limitations placed on the conduct by the legislature are simply arbitrary and do not parallel the standard of care in the profession. Another means of getting around the legislation is in the interpretation by the Board of laws and regulations in ways different from the clear intent of the legislature.

In most cases where a client files a complaint alleging that she has had a sexual relationship with a therapist, the Board will not negotiate a settlement that involves anything less than revocation of the license. This is true in cases involving male therapists and female clients where intercourse has allegedly occurred between them. When the contact is something less than intercourse, such as fondling, and/or kissing, the Board will most likely negotiate a settlement. The degree of the alleged offensive conduct usually affects the terms of probation that the Board would be willing to accept. Not all of the sexual misconduct cases involve a male therapist and a female client, although this scenario is certainly the most common. Some cases involve instances where the therapist is female and the client is male, while others involve situations in which the therapist and the client are the same sex.

The most common scenario, however, invokes the most punitive response from the Board. This is partly true because the cases involving the uncommon scenarios allow a better view of the manipulation and sexualization by the client to be accepted as an argument. The Board is least punitive in matters involving claims of sexual misconduct on the part of female therapists toward female clients.

If the Board is not willing to accept less than a revocation in cases involving sexual intercourse between male therapists and female clients, the option is to try these cases and then seek court intervention if and when the Board nonadopts a favorable ruling from an administrative law judge. Of course, any court intervention is an added expense to the therapist. If the matter involves a one-time occurrence of sexual misconduct together with all of the other mitigating circumstances, an administrative law judge would probably have imposed a penalty of something less than outright revocation of the license in past cases. As of January 1994, however, judges no longer have the discretion to impose any lesser penalty than revocation if there is a finding of sexual contact with a client or former client (Business and Professions Code §4982.26).

Rather than focusing on the imposition of punishment, the Board should be concentrating on the danger to the public posed by the licensee's continued practice. This, however, is not the case. Minimal effort is spent in attempting to fashion a set of conditions designed to protect the public in cases involving sexual intercourse. It is much easier simply to revoke an individual's license when faced with these allegations because to fashion terms of probation would not remove the risk entirely. The Board, however, should have a duty to balance the competing interests. Most of the time, these allegations arise against a practitioner who has been licensed for over ten years. A past executive director for the BBS previously testified that these individuals may not have the same level of competence as those licensed after that time. Although some of these cases occur because of insufficient training or supervision, many involve two adults who become emotionally involved over the course of time. There should be a distinction made between predatory conduct and involvement based on emotional commitment.

A therapist interested in negotiating with the Board and attempting to show that his conduct was not "predatory" in nature should seek both individual therapy and supervision from other well-respected practitioners. Marital counseling should also be considered if the therapist is experiencing difficulties. The option of an independent mental examination by a recognized forensic expert should be explored as a part of the defense arsenal. The focus should be on showing that the public is safe in treatment with the therapist.

While financial mitigation is mentioned in the disciplinary guidelines, this is rarely given weight. Financial mitigation occurs when a therapist pays the complainant money. The Board's position in the past has been to discount these payments because they were made by the insurance company for the therapist. There is no consideration given to the fact that the settlement has to be consented to by the therapist and many times means that the therapist may not be able to obtain insurance in the future. Of course settlements affect all aspects of practice, including hospital privileges, and so on.

Therapists frequently think that by paying the complainant a settlement this forecloses the possibility of their being reported to the Board. Certain provisions of the business and professions code, however, prohibit the conditioning of settlements on a lack of cooperation with the licensing authorities. Moreover, there are laws that mandate reporting of these settlements by insurance carriers and attorneys to the Boards (see Business and Professions Code §§800 *et. seq.*). There are also provisions requiring that a therapist report that he has settled a matter with a complainant. These provisions are governed by the amount of the settlement, regardless of how or why the lawsuit or threat of an action was instituted by the client. For instance, if a psychologist settles a matter involving a fee dispute for over $3,000, this settlement may have to be reported to the Board. For marriage and family therapists, the amount is $13,000 (Business and Professions §801). The duty to report is governed by the amount paid, not by the nature of the purported claim. In one matter where the client received monetary payments from a therapist and signed a release of all claims, she still reported the therapist to the Board. A settlement cannot be conditioned on the client not reporting the therapist to the Board. Further, if the therapist pays a settlement and does not make the requisite report to the Board, she can be subject to sanction for the failure to report as well. Attorneys can also be fined and jailed for attempting to circumvent these laws, for instance, by calling a payment to the client a refund of fees and not reporting the "settlement" to the Board.

BIG BROTHER IS WATCHING

Not only is there a requirement that a civil settlement be reported to the Board, a settlement must also be reported to the federal entity known as the National Practitioner Data Bank. The avowed purpose of the federal information bank is to improve the quality of care available to the public by restricting the ability of incompetent practitioners from simply moving to a new state.

The National Data Bank collects information on adverse actions taken against a health care practitioner by Boards, health care entities (i.e., clinical privileges), professional societies, and civil courts. There is a large fine ($10,000) for failing to report a monetary settlement made in a malpractice action. The information collected by the National Data Bank is available, with certain limitations, to hospitals, state boards, professional societies, and plaintiffs' attorneys (National Practitioner Data Bank *Guidebook*, U.S. Department of Health and Human Services). All of the entities are required to file reports as delineated in the guidelines. According to the National Data Bank, if an individual licensee settles a malpractice claim without the benefit of his malpractice carrier (the licensee pays the claimant directly), the licensee must report himself.

What if the complainant refuses to cooperate with the Board at the time of the hearing? The Board can simply subpoena the complaining client to testify. It can also introduce the investigator's testimony of its conversations with the complaining client. In some instances, if the Board cannot get the client to cooperate with the ultimate hearing, it will look for other means of attacking the practitioner. An example would be if the practitioner has had any criminal convictions since receiving a license.

IS REINSTATEMENT SIMPLY A DREAM?

It should be noted that when a license is revoked by the Board, this revocation is effective for a minimum of three years in certain cases (Business and Professions Code §4982.2). The period for reinstatement by petition was previously one year, but the statutes were amended in 1994. After this period, the respondent may petition the Board for reinstatement. By way of this petition, the respondent may provide either oral or written arguments to the Board as to why she should be granted reinstatement of her license (Government Code §11522). Even if the Board allows the reinstatement of the license, it can impose conditions on this reinstatement. In rare cases, the Board has permitted, after a period of several years, reinstatement of the license of licensees who have had sexual intercourse with a client. If the initial petition seeking reinstatement is denied, the respondent may continue to petition for reinstatement or seek judicial review of the Board's decision to deny it. Again, the individual would have to show that the Board abused its discretion in refusing to reinstate the license.

The Board of Psychology has devised several factors it considers in its decision regarding a petition, as follows:

1. The nature and severity of the act(s) or crime(s) under consideration as grounds for denial
2. Evidence of any act(s) committed subsequent to the act(s) or crime (s) under consideration as grounds for denial, which also could be considered as grounds for denial under §480 of the Code
3. The time that has elapsed since commission of the act(s) or crimes (s) referred to in subdivision (1) or (2)

4. The extent to which the applicant has complied with any terms of parole, probation, restitution, or any other sanctions lawfully imposed against him

5. Evidence, if any, of rehabilitation submitted by the applicant (Title 16 *California Administrative Code* §1395).

Other Boards have similar guidelines.

RECOVERY OF COSTS OF INVESTIGATION AND PROSECUTION

In January 1991, a law was enacted that provides that the Board may recover the "actual and reasonable costs of the investigation and prosecution of the case" (Business and Professions Code §4990.17). A similar law was also passed affecting psychologists. This section affects MFTs, educational psychologists, and social workers. Although Boards had been requesting costs during settlement negotiations, this recent legislation puts therapists at an even greater disadvantage. Moreover, it is one more reason for the Board to nonadopt a proposed decision by an administrative law judge and impose its own penalty, including a monetary one.

The Board may recover all costs of investigation and attorneys' fees in prosecuting a case from the licensee at the time of a hearing. Even more outrageous is the fact that the *only* proof necessary for an administrative law judge to fix these costs is the certification by the Board's executive officer. This means that it is very difficult to challenge the costs requested by the Board.

The coercive nature of this section comes into play in settlement negotiations. Although the Code section only allows recovery at the conclusion of a hearing, the Board regularly demands thousands of dollars in payment from the licensee at the time of a settlement. If the amount is not agreed to, the licensee runs the risk of having these costs imposed upon him by the administrative law judge. Ultimately, the Board may impose these costs when it nonadopts the administrative law judge's decision. Obviously, if the Board goes through a hearing, the costs and attorneys' fees requested will be much greater. So the licensee is faced with paying for two attorneys—his own and that of the Board's, if he ultimately loses.

A provision in the law states, "the board shall not increase the amount of any assessed costs specified in the proposed decision." This means that if the Board nonadopts an administrative law judge's decision, it cannot increase the assessed costs *only if* they are shown in the proposed decision. Thus, it is necessary to request that the administrative law judge rule on the imposition of costs one way or the other. One should ask for a ruling on costs even if the judge recommends dismissal, to ensure that the Board can't increase costs after it nonadopts the proposed decision. The inference from the language in the law is that if there is no reference in the proposed decision to costs then the Board can modify that issue. This would occur when the proposed decision recommends the dismissal of the accusation without the mention of costs. There are also contingencies stated for when these costs are imposed and not paid by the licensee in a timely manner.

Of course there is no provision for the recovery of any type of costs from the Board by the licensee should the licensee successfully defend against the accusation. Thus, thousands of dollars can be spent in a successful defense with no prospect of recovery. This differs from civil actions where the "prevailing party" and not just the state agency may recover costs. The civil process operates to foster the prosecution and/or resolution of legitimate claims. The danger is that with budget cuts being made and the conditions imposed on the manner in which funds can be spent in California, the Board has an even greater incentive to nonadopt favorable decisions. Nonadoption allows the Board to impose a greater penalty on the licensee.

The danger in this type of law can be seen by the move of the Boards to demand costs not provided for in the legislation as part of a settlement. For instance, the Boards are now negotiating the payment for their review of quarterly reports, which reports are a required condition of the probation process. These cannot be considered as part of either the investigation or prosecution of a case. Thus, they are asking for costs not even provided for by the statute during settlement negotiations.

DIFFERENCES BETWEEN THE DEFENSE
IN CIVIL AND ADMINISTRATIVE MATTERS

In civil matters, the tools of discovery are available to obtain all relevant information about the complainant. Normally, all education, employment, medical, and personal journals are obtained during the discovery phase in a civil action. Further, depositions can be taken and written interrogatories and requests for admissions can be obtained to form a comprehensive understanding of the complainant. If the plaintiff's claim alleges that she suffered from emotional distress, an independent mental examination can be demanded by the defendant. This independent mental examination can be conducted by a professional chosen by the defense. Interviewing the plaintiff and administering psychological tests are part of a standard examination. Much information can be gained in this manner about the psychological profile of the plaintiff. These are all unavailable in the administrative context.

As a consequence, the defense is approached differently in civil and administrative matters even when the claim is the same. In civil matters, the defense is approached as follows: that the conduct did not occur; if the conduct did occur, it was not below the standard of care; if the conduct did occur and it is clearly below the standard of care, there was no damage resulting to the client as a result; and procedural arguments, such as the fact that the plaintiff waited too long to bring the action.

The defense that the conduct did not occur is much more difficult to show in the administrative context. In the civil context, the information gained during discovery can be used to show several inferences, such as: the plaintiff is motivated by money, the plaintiff is prone to distort reality, the plaintiff experienced transference with the therapist and the conduct complained of was experienced by the plaintiff at an earlier time but experienced again with the therapist.

In terms of motivation, if the complainant in the administrative case has not brought a civil action, there exists no argument that he is motivated by money. The argument still remains that he may be motivated by revenge, that he feels rejected by the therapist and so reports.

As to the defense of distorting reality, less information is available in administrative cases to show this propensity. It is best established by drawing testimony from several sources that the plaintiff has misperceived other professionals' treatment. This can be accomplished by taking the depositions of the plaintiff's treating professionals to ascertain what complaints were presented by the plaintiff, and whether they were based in reality in the other professional's opinion. An example would be a plaintiff who has a history of somatic complaints or one who has sued several professionals. In sexual misconduct cases, the plaintiffs have often historically made complaints about people being abusive toward them. In one case, I was able to establish that a young woman had complained that every significant male figure in her life had been sexually abusive toward her (i.e., father, brother, cousin, general practitioner, and psychologist). The interesting information was that she had reported inconsistent stories about each one of these individuals to the numerous treating professionals she was currently seeing, so that her credibility was seriously questioned by her own attorney by the time of trial. The bottom line was that she could not literally keep her stories straight. Without all her medical/psychological records and the depositions of many treating therapists and other professionals, we would not have uncovered the truth about the plaintiff's fabrication. This same truth would never have been established in the administrative context because of the unavailability of the information.

The less time a therapist has treated a client the less information she will have about him at the time of the administrative hearing. If the Board has not adequately investigated the complainant, it is the licensed professional who is at a disadvantage.

The same holds true for the defense of transference. For instance, a client may complain that he was abandoned by a therapist. It may be that the therapist acted appropriately, but the client experiences the therapist's taking a vacation as abandonment. In one case, the therapist knew the client had terminated the therapeutic relationship only because there was a letter from an attorney informing him of that at the time he returned home from a one-week vacation. The attorney subsequently dismissed this action. The more information available, the greater the likelihood that patterns may begin to emerge that would support an inference that the alleged conduct did not really take place.

As to the defense that the conduct was not below the standard of care, there is a greater level of proof at the administrative level. The administrative issue is whether the professional's conduct constitutes gross negligence, which is obviously more than mere negligence. Of course, there are other issues that may be focused on as violations that do not necessarily give rise to a civil cause of action. For instance, improper advertising may occur by a professional without any damage to individuals. This could still be grounds for an administrative claim.

The issue of damage to the complainant is not the criterion to determine if the professional's actions are grossly negligent. In the civil context, there can be no monetary damages without some damage being suffered by the plaintiff. In the administrative context, however, a professional can be found to be grossly negligent without a grave amount of damage being suffered by the complainant. This is because the focus is on the conduct. The prosecution always wants to show just how damaged the complainant was by the professional's conduct as a means of arguing that a greater penalty should be imposed on the therapist.

In one matter, the Attorney General's office refused to agree to a stipulation that all alleged sexual misconduct set forth in the accusation was true. If they had been agreeable to doing this, then the only issue to be determined at the administrative hearing would have been what penalty to impose. They refused to do so because they admittedly wanted to march each and every complainant through to testify at the hearing to all the egregious things that the therapist had allegedly done. Obviously, this was only to present an emotional appeal to the administrative law judge, so that he would impose a harsher penalty.

Generally, administrative law judges are more interested in mitigating factors than is the Board. This is evident by the proposed decisions received from the judges, even in cases involving sexual misconduct. While the administrative law judges have proposed something less than revocation in previous matters involving therapist/client sex, the Board nonadopted in these situations. Under these circumstances, the administrative law judges imposed penalties such as revocation stayed with a given number of days when the professional may not practice (e.g., 180 days), supervised practice, psychological examination, and continuing education.

The overriding focus in these matters should be the danger to the public posed by the professional. This is not the focus in civil proceedings. Defense tactics used in administrative matters, therefore, include such tools as an independent mental examination of the professional in question, witnesses to the character of the professional, testimony by the professional's private therapist, testimony by the professional's supervisor, and at times by the spouse of the licensee. As to an independent mental examination, the defense retains a forensic expert to conduct an examination of the licensee to determine, for instance, whether there is a propensity toward perpetration. In contrast, the examination is conducted of the plaintiff rather than the therapist in civil actions. In the civil context, the defendant's mental state is not discoverable through this means.

It is hoped that the independent mental examination will conclude that the therapist does not fit the profile of a "predator." This is particularly significant in sexual misconduct cases. Other personality traits can be utilized to infer that the therapist will not repeat the offensive conduct. Administrative law judges are also receptive to other mitigating factors: the date since the last wrongful act, whether the therapist has sought therapy and/or supervision, the number of victims, restitution, and, in particular, the demeanor of the therapist (i.e., whether the professional sincerely regrets the acts and/or acknowledges wrongdoing).

In terms of the supervision/therapy, the Board tends to discount therapy and supervision if they were sought after the accusation was filed. This is not justified given the fact that often several years have elapsed between the filing of the accusation and the hearing. Participation in these things shows a commitment to improve oneself.

Generally, if sexual misconduct occurred between a therapist and client over a long period of time or there are multiple victims, the Board will not negotiate anything less than a full revocation. Even if the therapist decides to surrender the license, the Board can continue with the hearing and take testimony against the therapist. Simply surrendering the license does not divest the Board of jurisdiction. Why would the Board go forward with a hearing when the therapist has conceded defeat? The reason is to make a record of the misconduct. Should the therapist ever attempt to seek relicensure and/or a different type of license, there will be a record of the wrongdoing and a decision revoking the license.

In all other cases, except the multiple or lengthy sexual misconduct cases, the Board is usually willing to stipulate to some type of settlement. In my experience, male therapists receive less favorable settlement offers than do their female counterparts. This is especially true in matters involving any type of alleged sexual misconduct.

FUTURE TRENDS

Several new matters have involved the investigation of therapists because of a criminal history, ranging from drunk driving convictions to sex-related offenses. In one case, the investigation was dropped, in part because the complainant refused to cooperate with the investigation after a change of heart. The investigator continued to pursue the licensee based on two past convictions of lewd conduct and/or public nuisance. Not only is the Board focusing on convictions occurring after licensure, but they are also focusing on arrests, not necessarily convictions, which were not disclosed on the applications for licensure. How is the Board now able to discover these undisclosed charges? All licensees are now required to provide a set of fingerprints to the Board as part of the application process. Although potential licensees have at times forgotten to disclose arrests that may have been made years ago, these will become an issue later if the Board discovers them through this process. This is true even if the arrest never amounted to a conviction.

The licensing laws do indicate that one of the grounds constituting unprofessional conduct is the "conviction of a crime substantially related to the qualifications, functions, or duties of a licensee or registrant." (Business and Professions Code §4982).

The issue then becomes what is substantially related to the functions of a marriage and family therapist or as a mental health professional. Crimes that have been considered related are tax evasion by a physician and child molest of his minor client by a psychiatrist (see *Windham v. Board of Medical Quality Assurance* [1980] 104 Cal.App.3d 461; *Bernstein v. Board of Medical Examiners* [1962] 204 Cal. App.2d 378). The risk to the professional becomes greater if there is evidence of repeated offenses. The role of an independent evaluator becomes important in these matters to help establish that the type of crime does not bear on the professional's ability to perform as a therapist.

A statute making it a misdemeanor to "sexually exploit" a client was enacted in 1989 (Business and Professions Code §729). This statute is broadly worded to include a prohibition against sexual intercourse, sodomy, oral copulation, or "sexual contact." Sexual contact is defined by Penal Code §729 as coming into physical contact with the skin of another, regardless of whether the individuals are clothed at the time. Additionally, "intimate part" refers to the sexual organs, groin, buttocks, anus, or breast of a female (Penal Code §243.4[d]). Thus, a hug by a fully clothed therapist of a fully clothed client could constitute sexual exploitation under the terms of the statute, subjecting a therapist to a fine and imprisonment. The offense applies to former as well as current patients, if the relationship was terminated for the primary purpose of pursuing the sexual relationship. The consent of the patient is not a defense (Business and Professions Code §729). Although this section was enacted into law in 1989, criminal prosecution of therapists under this section is rare. This section does, however, affect the manner in which cases are presented by the defense. It must always be remembered that any admission of sexual contact with a patient could expose the client to criminal prosecution. Clearly, Boards are extremely concerned about *any* kind of physical contact between the therapist and a client. Further, any therapist who hugs clients or is involved in any type of physical contact with clients is at risk.

Professionals on probation have been similarly harassed based on things like deceptive advertising. In one case, a marriage and family therapist was contacted by the Board because he had written a letter of recommendation for a client who was seeking employment with the Department of Consumer Affairs. The letter was signed with the designation of "Ph.D." The Board took the position that a marriage and family therapist could not utilize this designation because the university from which the professional had obtained the degree was not accredited by an acceptable accrediting agency. Interestingly, over eight years earlier, the California Court of Appeal had held that the BBS was enjoined from taking this position. In *College of Psychological and Social Studies v. Board of Behavioral Science Examiners* (1974) 41 Cal.App.3d 367, the court stated that the use of a Ph.D. degree from an unaccredited school was not improper advertising in regard to persons licensed or entitled to be licensed as marriage and family counselors. So the pursuit of this untenable position approximately eight years later amounts to little more than harassment of a professional on probation.

Another recent trend in investigations is to pursue therapists for failing to report child abuse. In my experience these investigations never have any sound basis. In one case, a therapist was accused of not filing a report of suspected abuse. The fact was that the child did not disclose sufficient facts to the therapist during initial outpatient sessions. Once the child was hospitalized, she disclosed further details that warranted the filing of a child abuse report. The therapist had only briefly treated the child before the hospitalization. A report was ultimately filed by hospital staff. The Board subsequently closed its investigation.

There have been several recent investigations about therapists' failure to provide the booklet "Professional Therapy Never Includes Sex." A failure to provide this booklet constitutes unprofessional conduct, which is grounds for revoking a license. According to Business and Professions Code §728, enacted in 1987, this booklet *must* be given to a patient when the therapist becomes aware that the patient either had sexual intercourse or "sexual contact" with a prior treating professional. Even if the subsequent therapist may feel that the reported sexual contact is not an accurate perception of events and that providing the booklet may be countertherapeutic, the booklet must be provided to and discussed with the client.

The language in the booklet is incredibly broad. For instance, a 46 "warning sign" may be "telling sexual jokes or stories," "making eyes at," or giving seductive looks to the client; "discussing the therapist's sex life or relationships; or sitting too close or lying next to the client" (*Professional Therapy Never Includes Sex*). These same "warning signs" can also be seen as appropriate therapeutic interventions, (i.e., limited self-disclosure, or limited physical contact with a client). The booklet illustrates conduct that the Board sees as inappropriate. The danger is that a patient's misinterpretation of a therapist's conduct could lead to false allegations of misconduct (e.g., compliments given to the client to encourage an improved self-concept are viewed by the client as seductive in nature). In the past, the Board has pursued therapists for using "foul language" during sessions. In one matter, the client complained that the therapist utilized four-letter words in therapy, which he found offensive. The therapist's position was that the intentional use of such language was a form of therapeutic intervention (i.e., it was designed to elicit a response that could then be dealt with in therapy). The Board has also pursued therapists for purportedly using satanic rituals during therapy.

The punitive nature of the Board's actions can be demonstrated by the pursuit of matters that are many years old. As was mentioned at the beginning of this chapter, investigations had been conducted of twenty-year-old allegations. Currently, the Board may investigate matters that are seven years old. This means that the therapists have been practicing for many years without any other complaints. What public good does it serve to investigate these old complaints? In other instances, the investigation of cases drags on for years. In one case, the investigation had been conducted over an eight-year period. During this time, the investigators would periodically contact both past and current clients of the therapist. Of course, each time they began contacting clients they would completely disrupt the practice. The statute of limitations has drastically limited the pursuit of old accusations by the Boards.

There has been in increase in the number of board investigations of therapists involved in custody disputes. These investigations are being conducted against therapists that are treating therapists of family law litigants, as well as therapists retained as court appointed evaluators. Many of these matters are being followed through with Accusations against professionals on issues such as breach of confidentiality (providing an opinion without a release of information from each spouse seen in couples' counseling), dual relationships (acting as a treating therapist but providing a forensic opinion on custody), forming opinions of individuals that they have not seen in therapy, and using out-dated psychometric evaluative measures. Based on the volative nature of family law proceedings, mental health professionals should be acutely aware of their role in the proceedings and of safe-guarding their own license.

CONCLUSION

The purpose of this chapter is to raise questions about the laws that have been drafted under the auspices of protecting the public. Do they guarantee a professional's fundamental right to due process? Can simple changes to the laws be made to ensure on a basic level that taking away someone's livelihood is legitimate? Clearly, safeguards need to be instituted that would offer some guarantee of fairness to the administrative process. Fairness in this context will only strengthen our system of justice as a whole.

NOTES

1. All references are to the California Business and Professions Code, and the Government Code (Matthew Bender & Co., Inc. 2004). Other states and provinces have similar codes.
2. Editor's Note: As of 2006 the Standard is no sex with client's family members or friends of clients, students, supervisees, and employees forever.

10

The Highest Risk Cases for Clinicians Who Work with Children

High-Conflict Divorce/Custody Cases

Steven Frankel

A visit to the Internet Web sites of either of California's nonphysician mental health professional licensing boards (Board of Psychology [BOP], located at www.psychboard.ca.gov/; or Board of Behavioral Sciences [BBS], located at www.bbs.ca.gov/) provides a broad variety of interesting and helpful information. Since licensing boards are consumer protection agencies, there is a wealth of information available on the Web sites for consumers. For example, each Board has a web page for consumers to file complaints about licensed professionals regulated by the Boards.

Of particular note is that the first substantive question on each of those forms is whether the complaint concerns professional services for children involved in divorce/custody disputes. This is because complaints about professionals who work with children in the divorce/custody context seem to be the most frequent type of complaint filed. The high frequency of these complaints reflects the intensity of the feelings that parents have about custody/visitation and the vulnerability of mental health professionals as targets for those feelings.

This chapter is devoted to the protection of those professionals and the services they provide to children and families. The services addressed in the chapter are those provided by licensed mental health professionals and their supervisees in private practice or in agencies. Relevant services include mental health assessment/treatment (the chapter does not speak to problems encountered by mental health professionals when working in schools or school-related industries that may be governed by California's Education Code).

I begin with two critically important professional attitudes and then proceed through the legal and ethical principles for clinical work with children, applying those principles to the high conflict divorce/custody situation, with suggestions for prudent practice and caveats about decisions that are particu-larly imprudent (the "deadly sins"). Finally, I have included on the CD-ROM accompanying this book a set of documents: the first two might be included as part of "informed consent" for the treatment of minors (anyone under eighteen, in California) one document for the parent(s) and the other for the child(ren). The last document is the "Caregiver's Affidavit."

IMPORTANT ATTITUDES FOR PROFESSIONALS

In my view, the provision of a safe and secure treatment context—essential to all mental health care—is critical for professionals who treat children. In addi-tion to understanding the legal and professional/ethical issues below, there are two attitudes that can be of immeasurable service to the interests of both pro-fessionals and children/families in the pursuit of treatment security and safety:

1. Symptom focus: Treatment should focus on helping the child cope with symptoms, especially symptoms that may reflect the stress of being in a dissolving/dissolved family. As I will more fully discuss below, pro-fessionals for whom treatment takes on an advocacy nature, perhaps supporting contact with one parent over the other and/or viewing one parent as "bad" and the other as "good" (absent, of course, findings of abuse/neglect by one or the other), are at increased risk for treatment failure, for harm to children and for legal/administrative problems. Such professionals tend to make recommendations for custody/visitation and may use language such as "best interest of the child." They may write letters for one of the parties to use in a custody/visitation conflict, some-times including comments about the other party, that are not based on evaluation and professional contact that fall within the standard of care. Not only do activities such as these dramatically increase the risk of board complaints and/or malpractice suits, the professionals are very unlikely to fare well in either type of action.
2. Willingness to "let go": It is helpful when professionals appreciate whatever time/space is available to assist the child and be willing to "let go" when that time comes to an end, rather than struggling to prolong professional contact in the face of opposition by either parent. Profes-sionals who, whether due to countertransference, overdriven strivings to rescue children, arrogance and/or narcissism, or even accurately per-ceiving that they are in unique positions to help children, tend to resist a parent's efforts to terminate treatment (unless serial engagement and disruption of treatment has been a pattern for that particular parent, in which case the presiding judge might well be so informed), tend to fare

poorly, and expose the child to scenarios in which someone presenting as an ally acts as if s/he has enough power to take on a very powerful parent, only to fail miserably at the hands of that parent. Such scenarios cannot help but be countertherapeutic for children. As I see it, the prudent clinician (who cares about self and patients) appreciates the time available to work with children, has the grace to consider which professional(s) might be good referrals when that time comes to an end, and commits to facilitating transfer with dignity and respect for the needs of children for further care.

FIRST PROBLEM AREA: AUTHORIZATION TO TREAT MINOR CHILDREN IN CALIFORNIA

Prudent Policy: *Require two signatures.*

Many of the problems encountered by professionals who treat children might be avoided through the adoption of a policy that requires the signatures of both parents prior to initiating treatment. In fact, the failure to obtain both signatures can lead to such serious problems that it qualifies as a "deadly sin."

First, while either parent in intact families (you remember intact families, right?) can authorize health care for a minor child,[1] and while either parent with some form of legal (not physical) custody—joint[2] or sole[3]—in a nonintact family may authorize care (unless a judge's order specifically states otherwise), many California courts are reported to expect both joint legal custodians to sign authorizations.

Second, having both parents sign authorizations to assess or treat their minor children tends to decrease the stress and strain that develops when a parent who has neither authorized nor perhaps even been informed about the services suddenly contacts (or has an attorney contact) the professional with unsettling questions about how services are being provided without their knowledge or authorization.

Third, the policy of requiring two signatures helps professionals understand and manage the possible "alienation" of children from one parent by the other. The overwhelming number of parents in high conflict cases tend to see custody/visitation decisions as a zero-sum game, in which one's gain is the other's loss. Thus, among the agendas of parents who bring children for treatment (most of which include a concern for the well-being of children) is a desire to ally with treating professionals in order to increase their chances of winning rather than losing. Given that it is not at all unusual for a parent who seeks treatment for a minor child to (directly or indirectly) devalue the other parent (for many sets of parents, the devaluation is mutual), professionals must be wary of alliances that may form between them and the authorizing parent, lest they become part of an alienating and polarizing process that can only make matters worse for everyone.

Fourth, having both parents sign authorizations supports the goals of communicating the same things to both parties and of utilizing the channels of communication with parents to articulate and implement a firm policy of avoiding contact with either of their attorneys. As attorneys are bound to zealously represent the interests of their clients, any contact with either party's attorney will provide an occasion for that attorney to move the professional to a view that supports his/her client's interests. Thus, it is more than prudent for professionals to avoid contact with either party's attorney—such contact is a "deadly sin"—one that may easily result in more harm than good.

Prudent Policy: *When only one parent (or neither parent) is available, use the "Caregiver's Affidavit"*

There may be occasions when professionals decide to provide services for children with only one parent's authorizing signature, as when a parent is unavailable (missing, incarcerated, disinterested, deceased, and the like), or where the person bringing a child for treatment does not have legal standing to authorize professional services (that is, the person is neither the natural/adoptive parent nor the child's appointed guardian or conservator). There is no doubt but that these situations may present risks for professionals in the event that a parent who did not authorize services enters the picture, but the California Family Code has provided a means for professionals to minimize legal risk (although the risk of some harassment by the newly-arriving parent continues to exist).

The Caregiver's Affidavit[4] recognizes that there are many children in California who are not raised by natural/adoptive parents, but by people who are part of a broad extended family/kinship/friendship network—people who often do not have legal standing to authorize care for children. Thus, the Code indicates that a "qualified" relative includes: "a spouse, parent, stepparent, brother, sister, stepbrother, stepsister, half-brother, half-sister, uncle, aunt, niece, nephew, first cousin, or any person denoted by the prefix 'grand' or 'great,' or the spouse of any of the persons specified in this definition, even after the marriage has been terminated by death or dissolution."[5]

The Code also provides an incentive for professionals to provide care for such children by offering them protection from three forms of legal action: criminal actions, civil (e.g., malpractice) actions, and administrative (licensing board) actions.

In addition, these protections for professionals apply even if the caregiver's statements are actually false, as when, for example, the caregiver actually knows that the natural/adoptive parent would not authorize or support care for a child. In essence, as long as a professional does not *know* that the information provided by the child's caregiver is untrue, that professional may rely on a Caregiver's Affidavit to provide services without fear of criminal, civil, or administrative liability. The specific language reads as follows: "No person who acts in good faith reliance upon a caregiver's authorization affidavit to provide medical or dental care, without actual knowledge of facts contrary to those stated on the affidavit, is subject to criminal liability or to civil liability to any person, or is subject to professional disciplinary action, for such reliance if the applicable portions of the form are completed."[6] (A sample Caregiver's Affidavit is on the CD-ROM.)

> *Prudent Policy: Even with a Court Order signed by a judge, have parents execute the Caregiver's Affidavit, because there are times where a judge may use ambiguous language—over which the parents may argue—and, there are occasions when a custodial parent will present a Court Order that has been superceded by a newer Court Order. (You don't need to be there.)*

> *Prudent Policy: Know which minors have legal standing to authorize their own care, without parental knowledge or consent.*

California law provides for certain minors to authorize their own care, without parental knowledge or consent. Such minors would have to sign any releases of information that may be needed over the course of care, even if a parent knew of and supported their care. In fact, parents of these minors could not access their children's mental health records or obtain verbal reports from professionals concerning their children's treatment without authorization by the minor. Parents also could not be held financially responsible for care when authorized by the minor under the relevant statutes.

Importantly, some of the statutes authorizing minors to consent for care also encourage professionals to contact and include parents in treatment. These are specifically noted below. There are also some statutes that provide for minors to seek medical/dental care without parental consent/approval. Unless those statutes or annotations of cases involving them specify mental health care as well, I have not included them here.

Minors who can authorize their own care fall into the following categories:

I. Emancipated minors[7] (who are still considered minors for purposes of California's child abuse reporting statutes). There are three subtypes of emancipated minors:
   A. A judge finds that emancipation is in the minor's best interest, the minor is *at least fourteen years old*, willingly living apart from

parent(s)/guardian(s), with parental/guardian approval/acquiescence, is managing his/her own financial affairs and his/her income is not from criminal activity; or

B. The minor is legally married in California; or

C. The minor is on active duty with the armed forces of the United States.

II. A minor who is *at least twelve years old* may consent to outpatient mental health treatment if:[8]

A. "The minor, in the opinion of the attending professional person, is mature enough to participate intelligently in the outpatient services. . . ."[9]

B. "The minor (1) would present a danger of serious physical or mental harm to self or to others without the mental health treatment or counseling or residential shelter services, or (2) is the alleged victim of incest or child abuse."[10]

However, "the mental health treatment or counseling of a minor authorized by this section shall include involvement of the minor's parent or guardian unless, in the opinion of the professional person who is treating or counseling the minor, the involvement would be inappropriate. The professional person who is treating or counseling the minor shall state in the client record whether and when the person attempted to contact the minor's parent or guardian, and whether the attempt to contact was successful or unsuccessful, or the reason why, in the professional person's opinion, it would be inappropriate to contact the minor's parent or guardian."[11]

III. Minors *at least twelve years old* may consent to chemical dependency-related treatment,[12] but the authorizing statute only applies to services provided pursuant to a county or state contract. *The statute also states* that "[t]he treatment plan of a minor authorized by this section shall include the involvement of the minor's parent or guardian, if appropriate, as determined by the professional person or treatment facility treating the minor. The professional person providing medical care or counseling to a minor shall state in the minor's treatment record whether and when the professional person attempted to contact the minor's parent or guardian, and whether the attempt to contact the parent or guardian was successful or unsuccessful, or the reason why, in the opinion of the professional person, it would not be appropriate to contact the minor's parent or guardian."[13] And, to emphasize the importance of family involvement, the statute states: "Notwithstanding any other provision of law, in cases where a parent or legal guardian has sought the medical care and counseling for a drug- or alcohol-related problem of a minor child, the physician shall disclose medical information concerning the care to the minor's parent or legal guardian upon his or her request, even if the minor child does not consent to disclosure, without liability for the disclosure."[14]

SECOND PROBLEM AREA: ACCESS TO WRITTEN/VERBAL ASSESSMENT AND/OR TREATMENT RECORDS OF MINORS

Prudent Policy: Because high conflict families often succeed in having mental health assessment/treatment records of minor children admitted into evidence in court, often over the objections of the mental health professionals and of children as well, information should be maintained and shared in ways that minimize harm to children.

Prudent Policy: Since the Health Insurance Portability and Privacy Act (HIPAA)[15] is in its early implementation stages, the unavailability of a "right" for a patient to view a professional's "psychotherapy notes" is difficult to apply in California. Professionals are wise to act as if patients (and parents of minor patients) can and will be able to gain access to psychotherapy notes).[16, 17]

In California, minors generally do not have legal standing to authorize treatment, to release records, or to inspect records.[18] Those prerogatives are held by their parents.[19] However, professionals may withhold records/information if they make a good faith determination that disclosure would have a detrimental effect on their professional relationship with the patient or "on the patient's physical safety or psychological well-being."[20]

California law places great value on a child being able to benefit from relationships with both parents. Thus, even a parent who does not have sole or joint legal custody (a "noncustodial" parent) cannot be denied access to records/information solely because she or he does not have legal custody.[21] However, if one of the determinations listed above is made in good faith (jeopardy to the professional's relationship with the patient or danger to physical/psychological well-being), access can be denied to the noncustodial parent.

An illustration might help in reaching a determination in a case like this: assume you get a telephone call from someone who properly identifies himself/herself as the noncustodial parent of one of your patients. The person tells you that just because she or he is noncustodial doesn't mean she or he doesn't love and care about the child and that the call is out of interest and concern. She or he just wants to find out how the child is doing. Your response will depend on whether, in your good faith judgment, the provision of information will result either in damage to your professional relationship with the child and/or in increased risk of physical or psychological abuse to the child.

California law also provides for disclosures necessary to effect involuntary commitment of minors who are deemed to be dangerous to themselves or others or gravely disabled,[22] and for disclosures in legal proceedings when a child under the age of sixteen has been the victim of a crime.[23]

> **Prudent Policy:** *Professionals should always discuss the particular applications of rules of confidentiality and access to records/information with all parties to a case as early as possible in the provision of assessment/treatment services. Such a policy is consistent with the codes of ethics of psychologists, social workers, and marriage and family counselors,[24] and also minimizes the likelihood of violating the most fundamental axiom of risk management: the "law of no surprises."[25]*

Generally, professionals should be prepared to discuss information with parents and to provide records, although information should be presented in a light that is most helpful to and protective of the child.

THIRD PROBLEM AREA: WHO HOLDS "THE PRIVILEGE" FOR MINORS?

> **Prudent Policy:** *Professionals should assert the psychotherapist-patient privilege on behalf of minor patients who do not authorize disclosure of confidential information into the legal system. Professionals are best advised to respond to subpoenas for information about minor patients by requesting that a judge decide whether they should provide oral or written testimony/evidence as well as the specific information they should disclose.*

Let's assume that Johnny is an eight-year old child of Jim and Jean, who are in the midst of a painful divorce and battling for custody of Johnny as well as visitation. Let's also assume that Johnny doesn't have an attorney to represent him, that Jim and Jean have their own attorneys, and that Johnny is in a treatment relationship with a licensed mental health professional on a private practice basis or through an agency. Let's also assume that there have not been allegations of abuse made about either parent by either parent.

Let's assume, further, that Jean, who has been bringing Johnny to his weekly sessions, feels that Johnny's therapist sees her as helpful and sees the relationship between Jean and Johnny as very good, while seeing problems with Johnny's relationship with Jim (let's not worry about how Jean got this impression—let's just assume she has it). Let's also assume that Jim would agree that the therapist is less supportive of his relationship with Johnny than Jean's. Finally, let's assume that Johnny would rather be left out of all of the legal struggles his parents are having and just meet with his therapist to talk over what is on his mind.

Given these facts, it may well be that Jean would like Johnny's therapist to provide oral testimony, along with a letter and supporting records to the court regarding Johnny's treatment, while Jim would prefer to block this evidence from being admitted into the legal proceedings. It may also be that Jean's attorney sends Johnny's therapist a subpoena to produce records and to testify in court. Does Johnny get a vote here? Does his vote count?

In legal terms, we are concerned here with who "holds the privilege" (the psychotherapist-patient privilege)[26] regarding disclosures of information about Johnny's treatment into the legal arena. Asserting privilege means that the holder of the privilege refuses to allow such information to be entered into the legal process, while waiving privilege means that the holder agrees to allow the information to come in. In essence, privilege refers to the portion of confidentiality (the umbrella concept that refers to the expectation that communications made to a professional will be kept private) that involves the legal arena.

The issue of who holds a minor's privilege has been highly problematic because the California courts and the legislature have spoken definitively only for dependency court cases,[27] but neither case law nor the legislature has spoken to the issue of who holds the privilege for children in family court, where much of the parental conflict considered in this chapter plays out. Will family courts hold that children like Johnny can assert/waive their own privilege, when deemed (by the court) to be of sufficient age/maturity? Will those who are too young/immature have counsel appointed, who might then hold the privilege (judges are free to appoint counsel for children in family court)? We don't know as yet, because neither the legislature nor the courts have addressed the issue. Thus, the most prudent policy that professionals can adopt is to assert privilege on behalf of their minor patients and have the matter decided by a judge.

What this means on a day-to-day basis is that professionals who treat minor children in the context of high conflict divorce/custody situations should be clear with both parents and children that they would prefer to keep the children's treatment out of the conflict but, if this is not possible, would prefer to appear before a judge, whose orders would be followed. Then, if served with a subpoena for records and/or testimony, the attorney who served the subpoena wouldn't be surprised when asked to have the matter scheduled before a judge.

FOURTH PROBLEM AREA: MANAGING DEMANDS BY ONE PARENT THAT TREATMENT BE TERMINATED

Prudent Policy: Keeping in mind the second important attitude (see above, p. 174) about "letting go," it's helpful for professionals to be prepared to transfer responsibility for treatment when one parent indicates displeasure rather than to assert any legal or ethical bases for remaining involved, other things equal.

The "other things equal" refers to the need to discriminate between a parent whose repetitive pattern is to demand that treatment terminate, no matter who the professional is or how treatment is structured (if the parent is a frequent fault-finder, it may be helpful to inform the judge of the pattern), as opposed to a parent who happens to have a problem with a particular professional. Often, this may be more of a continuum than two discreet categories, but when a parent who is not a frequent fault-finder begins to complain, professionals should keep in mind that children suffer when a professional plants his/her feet solidly on the ground and refuses to step away from a case, given that the parent may well escalate to a point at which interruption of treatment is the only alternative to dramatically increasing symptoms for the children.

FIFTH PROBLEM AREA: REQUESTS BY ONE PARENT (OR HIS/HER ATTORNEY) FOR LETTERS/TESTIMONY WITH OPINIONS ABOUT THAT PARENT'S RELATIONSHIP WITH THE CHILD OR ABOUT THE PROFESSIONAL'S VIEW OF WHICH CUSTODY/VISITATION ARRANGEMENTS MIGHT BE IN A CHILD'S "BEST INTERESTS."

Prudent Policy: Politely refuse to write any letters of this kind, refuse to make recommendations about custody/visitation arrangements and please (!) refrain from using the phrase: "best interests of the child."

A major problem area for professionals who treat children arises when one of the parents (most often the one bringing the child to sessions) requests a letter describing their parenting of the child and their relationship with the child, to be used by that parent's attorney in the conflict over custody. Such a request may be made at the time an intact family falls apart as well as when the custody conflict was already underway at the time the child was brought for treatment.

This type of a request signals a change in the alignment of the family members and the professional—a change that is both clinically and legally/ethically important. No longer is the parent simply bringing the child for help with his/her symptoms or adjustment to the family strain; the parent is now making an active request of the professional. The request seeks to align the professional with the requesting parent, resulting in a likely reaction by the non-requesting parent. That reaction most often takes one of the following forms: (1) the nonrequesting parent becomes critical of the professional, sees the professional as siding with the requesting parent, and acts in ways ranging from threatening to the professional to threatening to the child's treatment; (2) the non-requesting parent seeks an independent relationship with an alternative professional to obtain a letter to counteract the one requested first; (3) the nonrequesting professional seeks to provide more information to the professional in an attempt to modify the opinions the professional might express in order to make the requesting parent look worse; (4) the nonrequesting parent may attempt to stop the professional from preparing the letter with any of a variety of legal tactics. Any of these alternatives places the professional under considerable strain and can't help but impact the child's treatment, most often negatively; and (5) the nonrequesting parent may attempt to terminate the child's treatment altogether.

A second aspect of this problem is that any letter that a professional might prepare is clearly for the use of the requesting parent to gain an advantage in the custody conflict. As such, the nonrequesting parent will frame the letter as an attempt to support the requesting parent's efforts to prevail in the custody conflict and will further frame the letter as reflective of an ethical/professional problem, thereby discrediting the professional. This issue becomes clearer when we look at the difference between a treater's role and a custody evaluator's role.

Custody evaluators perform formal forensic evaluations with a judge's order, pursuant to California Evidence Code §730—the section of the code that describes the judicial appointment of an expert to perform an assessment and report to the court. So-called "730 Evaluations" are to be objective assessments of the forces operating in the lives of children, with collateral data (that is, information gained from many sources, including teachers, therapists, friends, day care centers, pediatricians, and the like), leading to recommendations regarding the legal elements that are considered by judges in deciding which custody/visitation arrangements are in the "best interests of the child."

Frequently, clinicians develop their own views of which parent seems to do better with the child, which parent has the harder time, which parent-child contexts seem to be associated with increases in symptoms, and which contexts are associated with symptom improvement. However, without a formal, structured forensic evaluation, treating professionals are often too close to the child and too limited in their view of the entire set of forces acting on a child to present a view that is objective. Thus, when treating professionals make recommendations about custody/visitation, and especially when they use the phrase "best interests of the child," they assume a role that is inconsistent with their role as treater. This is a dual relationship with the child, and the duality is highly risky for both child and professional.

The first and most obvious manifestation of the risk of this particular form of dual relationship can be seen in the civil suits and board complaints filed by aggrieved parents, who raise issues such as whether there was informed consent for the treating professional to perform a custody evaluation, whether that professional has had adequate training and experience to perform a custody evaluation, and whether the professional's recommendations adequately address the legal elements of "best interest of the child."[28]

The second, and related manifestation lies in the development of a standard of care in the mental health professions that such dual relationships are improper. For example, as of July, 2001, the AAMFT revised its ethics code as follows: Section 3.14. *"New Explicit Duty:* " To avoid a conflict of interests, marriage and family *therapists who treat minors or adults involved in custody or visitation actions may not also perform forensic evaluations for custody, residence, or visitation* of the minor. The marriage and family therapist who treats the minor may provide the court or mental health professional performing the evaluation with information about the minor from the marriage and family therapist's perspective as a treating marriage and family therapist, so long as the marriage and family therapist does not violate confidentiality." (Emphasis in the original.)

Since professional society ethics codes articulate standards of care for the professions, and since extreme departures from a standard of care form the basis for the form of unprofessional conduct known as "gross negligence,"[29] professionals should be very careful to refrain from making recommendations for custody/visitation and should especially be careful to avoid using the phrase "best interest of the child."

However, descriptions of symptoms and the patterns within which they occur remain the domain of treating professionals. Thus, it is still quite helpful, appropriate, and important for treating professionals to make correlational observations (e.g., the child's symptoms increase under these circumstances and decrease under those) and treatment recommendations that bear on symptoms (e.g., more time with parent A to work on a particular symptom in a particular way, and so forth). Such a recommendation would be consistent with the treater's role, even though it might have custody/visitation implications.

SIXTH PROBLEM AREA: SHARING INFORMATION WITH MINOR'S COUNSEL VS. SHARING INFORMATION WITH CUSTODY EVALUATORS

Prudent Policy: While you have a duty to share any information requested by minor's counsel, you should use discretion when released to speak to a custody evaluator.

All dependents of the court and some children whose families are struggling with custody/visitation issues in family court will have court-appointed attorneys to represent their interests. Under the law, you have an absolute duty to speak with minor's counsel and to share any written or verbal information requested as to the status of a child, his or her progress in treatment, and any other relevant information requested.[30]

Such is not the case, however, regarding a court-appointed custody evaluator. While parents will have signed releases, protecting you from liability for disclosing otherwise confidential/privileged information to a custody evaluator, a release does not establish a duty to disclose—simply a freedom to do so without exposure to liability.

The decision as to what, if anything, to disclose to a custody evaluator might well be based on how you view the degree of advocacy in your professional relationship with any given child. Where professionals are closer to the "treater of symptoms" end of the continuum, disclosure to a custody evaluator is helpful to all. The professional would disclose what symptoms the child has, how the symptoms manifest, what the patterning of the symptoms looks like, what skills the child is being taught to cope with the symptoms, and how the child is doing in terms of mastering the symptoms. Such treaters are likely to be represented sympathetically by custody evaluators.

However, when a professional is more toward the advocacy end of the continuum, such that s/he wishes to share "the real story" about the parents—which is "good" and which is "bad"—that professional might well be described by the evaluator as a part of the problem as much as the solution. Professionals might well reflect on their position along the "treater-advocate" continuum when deciding whether/how to share information with a custody evaluator.

SEVENTH PROBLEM AREA:
HOW TO INTEGRATE THE CONSIDERATIONS OUTLINED ABOVE INTO AN "INFORMED CONSENT" PRESENTATION

I have prepared a set of documents that you might find helpful to review with parents and children at the outset of treatment. These documents weave together the legal, ethical, and professional issues I have outlined above into what I hope is a positive and coherent statement about boundaries, limits, roles, privacy, and expectations for all. There is nothing sacred about the documents, especially the one for children. That one must be approached only in ways that work for any given child—framed in the child's language, presented consistent with the child's capacity to understand and integrate the material, and at a pace that neither bores nor overwhelms the child. You are thus encouraged to modify the documents as you see fit and to integrate them with other informed consent materials that describe the various reactions families have to mental health care during divorce/custody conflicts, other possible treatment approaches, and the kinds of outcomes that may be associated with not having children in treatment at all, to the degree that these are known and understood.

To all who have read this chapter, I wish you the best in the work that you take on. This work reflects a great responsibility, as our children are our future.

Note: On the CD-ROM provided with this book please find:

1. Treating Children in High Conflict
2. Caregiver's Authorization Affidavit

NOTES

1. California Family Code §§ 6902, 6903; and see G. Rick and L. Tebbe. (2002). Treating psychologists in child custody matters: principles for prudent practice. California *Board of Psychology Update*, 2–4.

2. California Family Code §3003.

3. California Family Code §3006; and see Benitez, B. (2001). Consent for the treatment of minors with divorced parents. *The California Therapist*, 13(6), 33–34.

4. California Family Code §6550 *et seq.* and see Benitez. (2002). Consent for the treatment of minors: Caregiver Authorization. *The California Therapist*, 13(3), 16–18.

5. California Family Code §6552, at (i)(2).

6. Ibid.

7. California Family Code §7050.

8. California Family Code §6924.

9. Ibid.

10. Ibid.

11. Ibid.

12. California Family Code §6929.

13. Ibid.

14. Ibid. and see, for example, B. Benitez. (2002). Treatment of minors without parent consent (including alcohol/drug and pregnancy). *The California Therapist*, 14(3), 26–28.

15. 45 CFR 160 *et seq.*

16. In its pamphlet, *Implementing the Federal Health Privacy Rule in California*, the California Healthcare Foundation indicates that "[t]he interplay between the Federal Privacy Rule and California law is complex in this area. . . . We have attempted

to analyze this complicated interaction of state and federal law with an eye toward giving a patient the most access to their own health information, but advise providers to exercise caution in denying patients' access to their own information based on endangerment." (2002), 44n160.

17. The report adds: "Health Information for Minors: The Federal Privacy Rule will not change how the health information of minors is treated. Under both the Patient Access to Medical Records Act and the Federal Privacy Rule, generally it is the parent (not the minor) who has the right of access to the minor's health information. Both laws make an exception, however, when the information relates to medical treatment for which the minor is authorized by law to consent. . . . In these situations, the minor, not the parent, has the right of access to the related health information." Ibid., 37.

18. California Health & Safety Code §123110(a) states that minors who have legal standing to authorize care also have standing to inspect records, but their parents do not, absent their consent, under California Health & Safety Code §123115(a)(2).

19. California Health and Safety Code §123110(a).

20. California Health and Safety Code §123115(a)(2).

21. California Family Code §3025.

22. California Welfare and Institutions Code §5585.50.

23. California Evidence Code §1027.

24. *Ethical Principles of Psychologists and Code of Professional Conduct*, American Psychological Association. Washington, D.C. (2003); *Code of Ethics*, American Association of Marriage and Family Counselors, Washington, D.C. (2002); *Code of Ethics*, National Association of Social Workers, Washington, D.C. (1999).

25. See, for example, S. Behnke, J. Preis, and R. Bates. (1998). *The essentials of California mental health Law.* New York: Norton, 26; Z. Pelchat. (2002). Minor's privilege: Florida follows California, *California Therapist,* 14(1), 25, 27.

26. California Evidence Code §1010-1027: Psychotherapist-Patient Privilege.

27. California Welfare and Institutions Code §317(f) was amended in 2001 to read: "(f) Either the child or the counsel for the child, with the informed consent of the child if the child is found by the court to be of sufficient age and maturity to so consent, may invoke the psychotherapist-client privilege, physician-patient privilege, and clergyman-penitent privilege; and if the child invokes the privilege, counsel may not waive it, but if counsel invokes the privilege, the child may waive it. Counsel shall be holder of these privileges if the child is found by the court not to be of sufficient age and maturity to so consent. For the sole purpose of fulfilling his or her obligation to provide legal representation of the child, counsel for a child shall have access to all records with regard to the child maintained by a health care facility, as defined in Section 1545 of the Penal Code, health care providers, as defined in Section 6146 of the Business and Professions Code, a physician and surgeon or other health practitioner as defined in Section 11165.8 of the Penal Code or a child care custodian, as defined in Section 11165.7 of the Penal Code. Notwithstanding any other law, counsel shall be given access to all records relevant to the case which are maintained by state or local public agencies. All information requested from a child protective agency regarding a child who is in protective custody, or from a child's guardian ad litem, shall be provided to the child's counsel within 30 days of the request."

Regarding the courts: In 1990, Daniel C. H., a nine-year-old boy who was a dependent of the court, was allowed to assert the psychotherapist-patient privilege by a California court when his father, who had been found by the court to have abused him, subpoenaed his psychologist to produce records and testify. In its review of laws bearing on the holder of the privilege, the court noted that the holder is, first, the patient, then the guardian or conservator of a patient (guardians/conservators are appointed by courts; parents are not, by definition, guardians of their children), or the personal representative of a deceased patient. Daniel C. H. was a living patient who had no appointed guardian. Since Daniel was a dependent of the court and since the legislature has determined that children who are dependents of the court, when deemed to be of sufficient age/maturity, can assert or waive the privilege (and when too young or immature, will have it asserted/waived by their appointed counsel), it's reasonable to assume that the matter is resolved for dependents of the court. See *In re Daniel C. H.* (1990) 220 Cal. App. 3d 814.

28. The "best interest of the child" is defined in California Family Code §3011, and includes consideration of the following elements: (1) child's health, safety, and welfare; (2) parents' histories of abuse; (3) nature and amount of contact between the child and both parents; and (4) parents' use of illegal/controlled substances.

29. California Business and Professions Code §§2936/2960 (psychologists), 4992.3 (LCSWs) and 4982 (MFTs).

30. See, for example, B. Benitez. (2001). The role of minor's counsel in family court proceedings. *The California therapist*, 13(5), 12–13.

11

Ethical Risks in Child Custody

Where Is the Wizard of Oz When You Need Him?[1]

Ira R. Gorman

Like Dorothy, mental health professionals in the field of child-custody are at times caught in a tornado of events. In her quest to return home, Dorothy encountered her share of trauma—the Wicked Witch of the West, flying monkeys, lions, tigers, and bears. She was fortunate. Providing her consultation, nurturance, and guidance were a host of willing and able supporters—an intelligent scarecrow, a courageous lion, a compassionate tinman, an endearing good witch, and the Wizard himself. She did not have to confront ethics committees, licensing boards, combative attorneys, litigious clients, and impatient judges. Mental health professionals must often find their way home alone without a well-marked yellow brick road. This chapter will provide some of those markers to help the professional circumvent dangerous obstacles along the road home.

Data compiled by the American Psychological Association demonstrates that between the years 1997 and 1999, 10 to 16 percent of ethics complaints were against custody evaluators (APA Ethics Committee 1998, 1999, 2000). Comparing this to 33 percent in 2001 (APA Ethics Committee, 2002) reveals that the risks to custody evaluators for ethical complaints have increased exponentially.

Combine this with the frequency of licensure complaints, threats of malpractice, umbrage of angry and violent clients, and posturing of attorneys causes one to yearn nostalgically for the days of fee-for-service psychotherapy.

Having handled approximately 2,500 child-custody matters over the last quarter century, and reviewed hundreds of child custody reports with common, but high risk, practices, I hope to aid the custody evaluator in escaping this emotional maelstrom.

Although the court offers psychologists quasi-judicial immunity when they are appointed to complete a custody study (*Gootee v. Lightner*, 274 Cal. Rptr. 697; Howard *v. Drapkin*, 222 Cal. App. 4th 459, 462; *Laborde v. Aronson*, 92 Cal. App. 4th 459, 462; *Silberg v. Anderson* 1990, 50 Cal. 3d, 205, 21), this legal protection is not offered to consultants or therapists who unwittingly find themselves involved in the litigation process. It also does not protect the professional from licensure or ethics complaints.

Common errors that can have wide-ranging consequences will be discussed in this chapter. The child-custody evaluator is subject not only to the "Ethical Principles of Psychologists and Code of Conduct 2002," but among other codes, the "Record Keeping Guidelines" (APA, 1993), "Guidelines for Child Custody Evaluations" (APA, 1994), "Specialty Guidelines for Forensic Psychologists" (APA, 1991), and "Standards for Educational and Psychological Tests" (APA, 1999).

CLARIFYING ROLES

Evaluators as Mediators

In the child-custody discipline, the mental health professional fills several roles: *court appointed* evaluator; therapist; special master; mediator; consultant to the attorney; and consultant to a party.

It is incumbent upon the mental health professional to understand his/her role and not deviate from that position. The child-custody evaluator, who must render an unbiased report and perform his/her tasks with neutrality, often assumes multiple and conflicting roles, jeopardizing the benefit of the evaluation for the court, endangering the family and risking incurring an ethics complaint.

APA Ethics Code 3.05 states:

> A multiple relationship occurs when a psychologist is in a professional role with a person and (1) at the same time is in another role with the same person. . . .
>
> A psychologist refrains from entering into a multiple relationship if the multiple relationship could reasonably be expected to impair the psychologist's objectivity, competence, or effectiveness in performing his or her functions as a psychologist, or otherwise risks exploitation or harm to the person with whom the professional relationship exists.

Shifts in roles may occur with the best of intentions, yet, may nevertheless be departures from the standard of care. For example, a mental health professional may begin as the court appointed child custody evaluator, but during the course of the evaluation, the parents may want the expert to help them informally resolve their custody issues rather than go through litigation. The parents may want the evaluator to help them negotiate a parenting plan. In this scenario, the evaluator agrees, because he/she understands the benefits of the parents working together (Saposnek, 1983). The parents meet with the evaluator for several sessions, but then distrust and anger between the parents mount and mediation breaks down.

What should the evaluator do? He/she was appointed by the court to render an opinion regarding the best interests of the children. The court and the attorneys expect a report as ordered. In the scenario, if the expert resumes his role as the evaluator, is he practicing unethically? The mental heath professional's role has shifted from evaluator, to mediator, and now to evaluator. Should it?

Mediation and evaluation are distinct roles, each with unique procedures and role expectations (Ackerman, 1995; Gardner, 1989). Clients are encouraged in mediation to shift from their polar positions. They are asked to overlook their concerns about the other parent's foibles in order to agree to a parenting plan. In an evaluation, parents generally apprise the evaluator of their concerns about the other parent, sometimes vehemently. In an evaluation, parents often hide their true intent in the interest of obtaining the maximum amount of custody time. In mediation, parents are requested to honestly express their custody preference.

Evaluators and mediators also differ in procedure, style, and purpose. The evaluator is expected to be impartial; the mediator is expected to be an active participant and to periodically take sides. The evaluator is required to be dispassionate and neutral,[2] neither suggesting nor attempting to influence the evaluation process. In contrast, the mediator is likely to use his/her personality to gain the cooperation and trust of the parties with one major goal in mind: to reach a mutually acceptable agreement.

The evaluator is rendering an expert opinion and is not determinably influenced by the parties' preferences. The mediator listens to the parties to find areas of compromise and help negotiate a contract based on their preferences. The evaluator is interested in rendering an expert opinion regarding the best interests of the children, while the mediator may subjugate his judgment if the parties can reach an agreement based on the principle that if the parties' agree, this is in the "best interests" of the children. Obtaining all relevant data, including family history and multiple data sources, is a requirement for the evaluator but not the mediator.

Other ethical problems are raised by this hypothetical situation. Is it reasonable to assume that the mediation sessions, much like counseling sessions, are privileged and hence subject to the psychotherapist-patient protection? Mediation has more in common with psychotherapy than evaluation. Like therapy, mediation is attempting to benefit the parents and children by working within the therapeutic relationship. The evaluator is attempting to benefit the court, and only indirectly, the family.

In *Mediation: A Comprehensive Guide to Resolving Conflict Without Litigation* (Folberg and Taylor, 1984), the authors write:

> [T]here is general agreement that the success of mediation is dependent upon an expectation of privacy and confidentiality. If the participants do not trust that the mediation is private and that the revelations will be held in confidence by the mediator, they may be reserved in revealing relevant information and hesitant to disclose potential accommodations that may appear to compromise earlier positions. (364)

Another basis that J. Folberg and A. Taylor offer for keeping statements made during mediation out of the courts is that offers of settlement and statements and evidence of conduct during negotiations for settlement are generally inadmissible. It would follow that mediation to facilitate the settlement should be protected.

In the hypothetical scenario, the evaluator was initially ordered to render a report. What should the evaluator do with the information obtained in the mediation sessions? Since the mediation was discontinued, are the limited resolutions that the parents agreed to now void? Should their proposals be incorporated into the custody report even though the parties believed that they were negotiating under different presumptions?

Does the evaluator lose his quasi-judicial immunity if he is no longer serving as an evaluator when performing mediation? Must informed consent be revisited during the mediation process?

These and other ethical dilemmas create almost insurmountable peril for the mental health professional.

The ethical risks escalate with what appears on the surface to be an accommodation to help the parents work out their own custody plan.

The child-custody evaluator should resist the temptation to informally assist the parties mediate their custody issues. If the parents believe that they can agree and work out their differences, they may attempt mediation or counseling with a professional appointed by the court or stipulated to by the attorneys and parties for that purpose. This procedure permits the evaluator to remain in his/her original role and avoid the risk of entering into a different relationship that raises ethical questions.

Evaluators as Therapists

"Once the evaluator, always the evaluator" should be the canon of the professional. Requests for therapy, much like requests for mediation, should be declined and left to others.

The implications of APA Ethics Code Section 3.05 are clear: evaluators should not assume the role of a therapist to one of the parties during or subsequent to an evaluation.

The evaluator who advises one of the parties during an assessment has shifted to a counselor or social worker. Providing counsel, instruction, or even advice during the evaluation creates bias, or at least the appearance of bias. Even if the evaluator believes he/she continues to be neutral, the impression has been cast.

Consider the ethical dilemma when the evaluator prematurely formulates a custody plan and begins to implement the plan by making suggestions and recommendations prior to the completion of the evaluation. Is the expert who offers counsel actually serving as a therapist rather than as a neutral, objective, detached evaluator?

For example, I was asked to review a report of an evaluation of a hyperactive three-year-old boy and his parents. The custody evaluator, during a home visit, made several suggestions to the mother on ways to make her home child-proof. The evaluator suggested that she clean up the garage and install safety latches on the bathroom cabinets to ensure the child's safety. The motivation of the evaluator was well-intended. However, by providing advice and instruction, the evaluator compromised his role. The mother followed the evaluator's suggestions, and their relationship shifted. She tried to please the evaluator by following his advice, and he was pleased by her efforts. Was he also influenced by her responsiveness? Was he invested in her success because she complied with his suggestions?

Child safety is an assessment issue and offers invaluable information relevant to a parent's competence. In the scenario, the mother's failure to offer a safe environment—especially with the awareness that the evaluator was viewing her home as part of a custody study—suggests poor judgment, lack of awareness of detail, and possibly neglect. If the evaluator were sufficiently concerned for the safety of the child, then a report to a child protective agency would be appropriate, not advice to the parent. Recommendations for remediation should be reserved for the final report.

In another case, an evaluator assessed a family in a child-custody matter. The mental health professional recommended early on that the mother join a support group for victims of domestic violence. The evaluator shared with the mother her own experience of being a victim of spousal abuse and the benefits of a support group. The mother subsequently thanked the evaluator in a letter. In that letter, the mother inundated the evaluator with complaints about the father's history of violence. The mother also expressed how she appreciated the evaluator's help and sensitivity and how much she had learned from other victims in her domestic violence group.

Unfortunately, the mother fabricated and exaggerated the incidents of domestic violence to malign the father and to obtain custody of her child. The evaluator was flattered by the mother's effusiveness. Did the evaluator also become biased? In this scenario, the evaluator should have waited to make recommendations in the final report. The evaluator's file came to the court's attention. The mother's letter became part of the court record, leaving the child-custody evaluator fumbling to explain whether she prematurely formulated her opinion.

The court saw through the mother's facade of victimization and stated that he did not believe any violence had occurred. The court awarded custody to the father. The evaluator should not have made recommendations prior to the completion of the evaluation. The time for recommendations is at the completion of the study, not in the beginning or middle of an evaluation. Did the evaluator formulate her opinion that the father was the perpetrator of domestic violence prior to the completion of the evaluation? Might the evaluator's own experience with domestic violence have affected her objectivity? Should the evaluator have declined the case at the outset because of potential bias, since the evaluator may also have departed from APA Ethics Code 2.06—Personal Problems and Conflicts.

Issues are already complex in child-custody matters. Evaluators should not further complicate the already daunting task. As indicated, once appointed as a custody evaluator, this role should continue and not be supplanted by another. To avoid risk, the mental health professional should heed APA Ethics Code Section 3.05 and avoid simultaneous assumption of roles. The neutral stance of the evaluator should continue into the courtroom as well.

Evaluators as Consultants

A child-custody professional, once appointed as the family evaluator, should remain in that role unless the court relives him/her of that duty or the professional requests to be released from further responsibility. It is not uncommon for an evaluator to be subpoenaed or asked to testify by one of the attorneys after a report is released or, as frequently occurs, asked to reevaluate the parties following a period of adjustment to a custody plan.

Often an evaluator makes the mistake of assuming that with the completion of the report, he/she has finished the job. So the evaluator thinks nothing of conferring and assisting that parent's attorney. How can this evaluator testify neutrally when he has made it his cause to help the recommended parent win the case? How can the evaluator be neutral if he has a vested interest in the outcome? A better approach would be to let the chips fall where they may, to testify upon the report only, to decline to meet unilaterally with either attorney, and instead request a joint attorney meeting or a joint conference call.

Therapists as Evaluators

The child-custody evaluator is the only mental health professional who should recommend a custody plan. The evaluator is the only professional who has critically interviewed both parents and children. He/she is the only professional who has observed the children with each parent, performed collateral interviews, and/or tested family members with the goal of providing a neutral report.

Therapists, even a therapist for the child, have not approached the family from a neutral, fact-finding vantage point (see Greenberg and Gould, 2001, for a discussion of this point). In therapy, the parents and the children are distressed. The therapist's role is to help solve a problem. His/her neutrality as a dispassionate "expert" is compromised by emotional involvement with the family. S. A. Greenberg and D. W. Shuman (1997) have described the conflicting roles and role expectations of therapists and evaluators. In a later publication, D. W. Shuman et al. (1998) recommend that therapists should be excluded from the courtroom.

Should the therapist be required by subpoena or court order to appear at trial, he/she is advised to heed Section II – 7 of "Guidelines for Child Custody Evaluations in Divorce Proceedings":

> A psychologist asked to testify regarding a therapy client who is involved in a child custody case is aware of the limitations and possible biases inherent in such a role and the possible impact on the ongoing therapeutic relationship. Although the court may require the psychologist to testify as a fact witness regarding factual information he or she became aware of in a professional relationship with a client, that psychologist should generally decline the role of an expert witness who gives a professional opinion regarding custody and visitation issues.

The therapist for the child may have information about the child's preferences and insight into the parents' problems, yet, has not taken an evaluator's disinterested perspective. Preference of a child does not always equate with "best interest."

To practice ethically, it is advisable to discourage the parties and/or attorneys from soliciting expert opinions from the therapist. Should the court request an opinion, the therapist should alert the court to the limitations and should respectfully decline to tender a custody or visitation opinion or recommendation.

In a case for which I served as an expert for the Board of Psychology, a psychologist lost his perspective and unfortunately also lost his license. The doctor treated a man and woman in marital therapy but subsequently offered a recommendation supporting the mother's effort for custody. Years after the parties discontinued their marital counseling, the woman contacted the therapist and explained how her former husband's sexual problems have manifested and feared that he might sexually abuse their teenage daughter. The distressed mother sought the therapist's assistance. She needed a letter from the psychologist outlining the father's sexual perversions (which the mother willingly provided), and the doctor's opinion why she was the better parent to have custody and why the father should have restricted visitation.

The therapist, in his interest to accommodate, complied. When the father read his former therapist's recommendation, he reacted by filing a complaint with the licensing board. The psychologist may have been helpful to the mother but not to himself. He lost his license for deviating from the standard of care by violating confidentiality (APA Ethics Code 4.02, Maintaining Confidentiality) among other code sections. He provided a custody recommendation and accepted the veracity of the mother's description of her former husband's sexual problems.

The psychologist should have clarified the limits of his role as the couple's marital counselor. It goes without saying that he should have declined to provide recommendations regarding custody, which clearly exceeded his role as a therapist. He violated the confidentiality of his client.

CLARIFYING PROCEDURES

A psychologist should also be clear about procedures. APA Ethics Code 3.10 (c) and (d) state:

> When psychological services are court ordered or otherwise mandated, psychologists inform the individual of the nature of the anticipated services, including whether the services are court ordered or mandated and limits of confidentiality, before proceeding and Psychologists appropriately document written or oral consent, permission and assent.

The "Guidelines for Child Custody Evaluations in Divorce Proceedings" (III 8/9) direct the evaluator to obtain informed consent from all adult participants and inform the participants about the limits of confidentiality and the disclosure of information. The "Specialty Guidelines for Forensic Psychologists" (Section IV E; V-B) also advise the professional to clarify the purpose of any evaluation, the nature of the procedures, the intended use of any product of their services, and the identity of the party who has employed the evaluator, as well as the limits of confidentiality.

On the CD-ROM accompanying this book, I provide an informed consent and disclosure form that describes the factors relevant to informed consent in a child custody evaluation.

Initial lack of specificity of procedures can only lead to confusion, anger, and retaliation when a disgruntled parent turns his/her anger to the person held responsible for the court's adverse custody decision. Adopting a disclosure form should obviate myriad complaints. Such a form may be a safeguard for defending psychologists against complaints by a litigious parent.

Failure to document informed consent may also lead to an ethics complaint. Written documentation is preferable to oral documentation. My informed consent and disclosure form includes categories discussing custody procedures, confidentiality, testimony, depositions, and payment.

Evaluations differ, depending upon the referral question. At times, the evaluator may test the parents, stepparents, and children; at other times, interviews suffice. A home visit may be necessary such as when allegations concern neglect; at other times, a visit would be superfluous. Words or phrases such as "may," "under some conditions," "if applicable," assist the parents in understanding that custody procedures may vary and that each evaluation is not just a cookie cutter approach to assessment.

State and local court rules guide evaluators to determine who is permitted to receive a copy of the child custody report. Each jurisdiction has information regarding release of reports to pro per clients. The evaluator is urged to review the local and state guidelines as well as the family code for his/her particular state and adapt the informed consent and disclosure form accordingly.

As noted in the informed consent (disclosure), it is important to cautiously approach information that may be either private or illegal. Before an evaluator reviews tape recordings of phone conversations, including those between a parent and a child, approval may need to be obtained from the court and/or both parties and attorneys to determine if the phone calls are approved for review. Transcripts should be made available and provided to all attorneys. Phone transactions, diaries, and journals also may be private and not authorized for review.

As denoted in the informed consent (disclosure) form, to dispel any appearance of bias, the evaluator should avoid unilateral contact with attorneys (including the attorney for the child) regarding substantive issues. The evaluator should request that all documentation submitted for his/her review be provided to all counsel, including counsel for the child if applicable. Questions about bias can be averted by requesting that the parties share all information initially with counsel before submission to the psychologist.

Withholding of Records

Collecting money for a child-custody evaluation is the challenge. When payment has not been received, the child-custody expert is reluctant to release a report, after spending sometimes twenty or more hours on an evaluation. But failure to release a report may anger judges and attorneys. Clients who are responsible for paying for the evaluation may resent having to spend several thousand additional dollars after already paying his/her own attorney and sometimes the attorney for the spouse. Court costs, spousal support, and child support further burden the client.

Obviously, well-documented financial procedures avoid or minimize conflict when payment for services later becomes a problem. Obtaining payment before the evaluation begins is always wise, but not always possible. In the consent/disclosure form several sections suggest how to handle situations likely to lead to conflict. Clients generally become angry when asked to pay for missed appointments, for costs exceeding early estimates, and for preparation for testimony. The evaluator needs to be aware that following the release of the report, the chances of collection decrease dramatically.

But if the report has not been written, it cannot be released. The attorneys requesting the report cannot subpoena that which has not been created. Awaiting payment for the report before writing the document or obtaining a cashier's check upon its release should resolve most problems.

Nevertheless, despite the evaluator's attempt to be clear and to document payment, clients with intent to not pay intend to not pay. Small claims court may be the final remedy. Malpractice attorneys advise mental health professionals to forgive the bill because angry clients frequently seek redress. Remember that child custody combatants are the 10 percent who have not resolved the custody issues by alternate means (Melton, Petrila, Polythress, and Slobogin, 1987). They are litigation savvy. Defending against an ethics complaint, board action, or lawsuit requires the mental health professional to spend countless hours responding to complaints and attending depositions. The evaluator needs to weigh the risks.

If payment is pursued, it is advisable to wait until the statute of limitations has expired for tortious action. The evaluator will then only have to contend with an ethics complaint or a board complaint and not a malpractice suit. Boards are generally hesitant to enter into fee dispute resolution, which helps the mental health professional. But clients may restate their complaints in other than fee disputes (such as bias or inadequate practices), to obtain the attention of the licensing board (Thatcher, P., personal communication, January 4, 2004).

Ethics committee members and licensing board reviewers are guided by the standard of care for their profession. Ethics code sections are often ambiguous. The mental health professional is often at the mercy of the expert reviewer. The standard of care is identified at an early stage by the expert who performs the review and renders an opinion to the ethics committee or to the licensing board. Since not all experts are equally versed in ethics, forensic practices, and child-custody procedures, it is always best for the custody evaluator to interpret code sections in the direction of circumspection and caution.

The 2002 APA Ethics Code Section 6.03 (Withholding Records for Nonpayment) is a good example of a code section where the mental health professional is dependent upon an interpretation of the code.

> Psychologists may not withhold records under their control that are requested and needed for the client's/patient's emergency treatment solely because payment has not been received.

Since the child-custody report would be used for a legal purpose, and not for emergency treatment, one would assume that the custody evaluator would be protected and not be subject to this section. Treatment, especially emergency treatment, is not the crux of a forensic report. One would therefore assume that the child-custody evaluator would be safe should he/she elect to not release the report until payment is received. What if one of the recommendations to the court is that treatment be ordered? How might this be interpreted by an expert reviewer? Is the psychologist withholding records that are requested and needed for treatment?

The "Record Keeping Guidelines" add another twist: "Psychologists do not withhold records that are needed for valid health care purposes solely because the client has not paid for prior services." What are valid health care purposes? A forensic report and records for valid heath care purposes appear to be distinct. But are they when treatment is recommended in the report? (Section 5, Disclosure of Record Keeping Procedures)

The 1992 Ethics Code is similar to the 2002 version in the section regarding withholding records for nonpayment:

> Psychologists may not withhold records under their control that are requested and imminently needed for a patient's or client's treatment solely because payment has not been received, except as otherwise provided by law.

In a public forum, one of the State of California Board of Psychology experts broadly interpreted "treatment" to apply to child custody evaluations. M. B. Canter et al., (1994) interpreted this section that child custody evaluations are exempt, but were this to be construed globally as the California expert opined, the psychologist might have to defend himself against an ethics complaint. The board's expert stated that he would find a mental health professional who withheld a custody report solely for lack of payment to be unethical.

Competence to Perform Child Custody Evaluations

To be an expert in child custody requires knowledge gained from a lifetime of learning. The evaluator, at times, must address issues such as child and adult psychopathology, family dynamics, substance abuse, sexual and child abuse, domestic violence, child development, personality disorders, psychopathy, dynamics of divorce, and cultural factors. As experienced evaluators know, each of these categories involves subcategories requiring additional specific knowledge. Mental health professionals who perform psychological testing are expected to understand both nomethetic and idiographic tests and proper test interpretation.

How does one acquire the knowledge base to meet APA's Code Section 2.01 (Boundaries of Competence): "Psychologists provide services, teach, and conduct research with populations and in areas only within boundaries of their competence, based on their education, training, supervised experience, consultation, study, or professional experience."

The trier of fact depends upon the expert's judgment and reasoning ability and his/her special expertise. In addition to the obvious ethical risks, families place hope that their evaluator will be fair and competent.

The 2002 APA Ethics Code permits psychologists to provide services in areas "closely related to one's prior training or experience to ensure that services are not denied if they make a reasonable effort to obtain the competence required by using relevant research, training, consultation, or study." (2.01d)

A similar provision is described in the "Guidelines for Child Custody Evaluations in Divorce Proceedings" (1994):

> In the course of conducting child custody evaluations, allegations of child abuse, neglect, family violence, or other issues may occur that are not necessarily within the scope of a particular evaluator's expertise. If this is so, the psychologist seeks additional consultation, supervision, and/or specialized knowledge, training, or experience in child abuse, neglect, and family violence to address these complex issues. (II-C)

Ethics committees as well as licensing boards are comprised of well-meaning professionals. To paraphrase an Orwellian precept: Not all experts are created equal. Some are more equal than others.

For example, a colleague was the subject of a complaint to his licensing board that he was functioning outside his boundary of competence. He accepted a referral from the court to perform a child-custody evaluation in which sexual abuse was alleged. The Board of Psychology's expert provided his opinion that the evaluator deviated from the standard of care because his background did not include conducting sexual abuse evaluations. The psychologist had related experience with adults who had been physically abused and sexually abused as children, but this was not discussed in the review by the expert.

After spending thousands of dollars on attorneys, and experiencing overwhelming stress, my colleague was allowed to retain his license. I pointed out to the Board that the psychologist utilized a psychiatric consultant who was an expert in child sexual abuse. The consultant primarily conducted the interviews with the child. APA Ethics Code Section 2.01 and the "Guidelines for Child Custody Evaluators" permit evaluators to conduct evaluations in related areas with consultation, which is exactly the procedure the psychologist followed.

Despite my colleague's reprieval, a valuable lesson can be learned. The mental health professional should refer out aspects of the evaluation that lie outside of his/her expertise or obtain consultation during the evaluation process. Note that the consent/disclosure form informs parents that the evaluator may seek consultation as needed. The most prudent and safest course of action is to decline appointments for assessments outside one's areas of expertise or risk reproval.

Psychological Testing

Psychological testing is a minefield of risk. Mental health professionals often fail to consider K. Heilbrun's (1992) precautions and use tests that have poor reliability, are not relevant to the legal issue, or are a psychological construct underlying the legal issue. Tests are utilized that are not generalizable to the examinee and the purpose, have inadequate manuals, are not listed in test compilations such as the *Mental Measurements Yearbook*, and are not administered in a standardized manner.

With low internal consistency, an obtained score may have great variability from one testing session to another. Tests may have been developed on mothers, yet have limited research with fathers or stepparents (e.g., the Parenting Stress Index [Abidin, 1995]). Nevertheless, parents are being compared in child-custody evaluations with such measurements. Testing an individual from a minority culture may be a problem with many of the instruments used in child-custody evaluations (e.g., the ASPECT [Ackerman and Schoendorf, 1992] and the Personality Assessment Inventory [Morey, 1991]).

Empirically sophisticated assessment tools have not caught up with the clinical demand. Tests such as the Minnesota Multiphasic Personality Inventory-2 (Butcher et al., 2001) and the Millon Clinical Multiaxial Inventory-III (Millon, 1997) measure constructs that may underlie "parenting," but are not child-custody instruments. In this void, A. B. Caldwell (2002) combined several MMPI-2 scales to formulate a theory of parenting. Sufficient research is currently not available to support Caldwell's conceptualization.

Most tests utilized in child custody have not been standardized on the child custody population. Even the Parent Child Relationship Inventory (Gerard, 1994), which touts itself as a child-custody tool, does not provide directions in the manual how single parent families differ from intact families (Heinze and Grisso, 1996), an important consideration for the child custody evaluator. The Bricklin instruments (Bricklin 1984, 1990), the most used tools with children (Ackerman and Ackerman, 1997), have generally received negative reviews (Brodzinsky, 1993). Much of what occurs in child-custody evaluations is art, not science. Studies are available for matters such as attachment (Ainsworth, 1979; Solomon and George, 1999), divorce (Maccoby and Mnookin, 1992), child development (Amato and Gilbreth, 1999; Lamb and Kelly, 2001), and high conflict families (Johnston et al., 1989; Peterson and Zill, 1986). But the procedures to obtain information are clinically based—primarily interview and observation, rather than testing. Because of the paucity of well-standardized instruments, the mental health professional should explain in the report the limitations of the instruments used. A footnote explaining to the reader (whether it be the court, attorneys, or a mental health professional) the limitations of the test would permit proper weight to be assigned the instrument in the report.

This recommendation is not only good practice but is also in accord with the American Psychological Association Code of Ethics Section 9.02:

> [P]sychologists use assessment instruments whose validity and reliability have been established for use with members of the population tested. When such validity or reliability has not been established, psychologists describe the strengths and limitations of test results and interpretations.

Convergent Validity

Tests should not be used in isolation as if they are the gold standard for child-custody determinations. Even the best instruments have limited predictive validity. Psychological tests provide hypotheses (Gould, 1998). Without convergent validity from interviews or collateral sources, the results of any particular psychological test may be misleading. Psychologists should not accept the results of a personality test unless they are independently corroborated.

The APA Committee on Professional Standards cautions psychologists against using computer narratives in absence of data to validate their accuracy (Butcher et al., 2000).

The PAI (Morey, 1991), the MMPI-2 (Butcher et al, 2001), and the MCMI-III (Millon, 1997) have scales that generate hypotheses about substance abuse. The test results may suggest that the individual tested has an alcohol potential. Alcohol potential does not equate with alcohol abuse. Alcohol potential may occur because of a past history of alcohol abuse, or because of personality characteristics such as gregariousness. The individual may never manifest actual abuse. To use the MCMI-III as an example, a parent may elevate on the Alcohol Dependence or the Drug Dependence scales and may be endorsing traits based upon past history rather than current alcohol or drug abuse (Craig, 1999).

Background and current data would be required to diagnose a parent as having a substance abuse problem. Unless collateral sources support the condition, or admission to substance abuse occurs, reliance upon test results may stigmatize a parent and prejudice his/her chance for custody. Inserting a sentence into a custody report such as, "Mr. Jones has a potential for alcohol or drug abuse," based upon a statement contained in a computer narrative, without corroboration, might reasonably dissuade a judge from awarding custody to that parent.

Test questions are written in such a way that the average person understands the intent of the questions, yet someone mentally challenged may misinterpret the test questions and produce a distorted but otherwise interpretable profile.

I administered the PAI to a mildly mentally retarded adult who had a twelfth-grade reading level and had graduated high school. He was evaluated following the allegation of sexual molest. A preliminary reading test showed that he had a reading level beyond the requisite fourth grade as described in the manual.

The validity scales of the PAI confirmed that the test accurately reflected his personality. The results of the test suggested that this individual was a "drug addict." How was this possible? He lived a sheltered life with his mother as his caretaker. He was reclusive. Although he took walks, he rarely left the home, and had little opportunity to either buy or use drugs. The answer to the quagmire was within the items of the test. In reviewing the questions, he endorsed such items as, "Sometimes I use drugs to feel better," and, "I've tried just about every type of drug." Reviewing the test at the item level clarified the obvious. The client confused illegal drugs with prescription medication. The test results were skewed. By reviewing the individual items of the elevated scale, the misdiagnosis of this individual was avoided.

Although global personality tests are most powerful at the scale configuration level, one should always review the endorsed items on elevated scales to ensure accurate interpretation.

Proper Test Interpretation

Mental health professionals who rely upon others to test, or over rely on computer narratives, are cautioned to not insert the printed narrative computer report into a custody report without explanation, as if this were a blank place in a photo album. Test results must be understood and integrated into the report. The conscientious practitioner should always review the manual and utilize the manual and interpretive texts and research articles to fully understand the strengths and weaknesses of the scales and subscales and to accurately interpret a particular subscale.

The Need for Affection scale (Hy2)[3] of the MMPI-2 is often interpreted as a "need for affection," based on its name alone. The evaluator whose report was reviewed explained how this parent required affection and turned to her child to meet her unfulfilled need.

R. L. Greene (2000) discusses the correlates associated with this subscale. The individual who scores high on the Need for Affection Scale believes that others can be relied upon and trusted. He/she is optimistic and believes that others have their best interest in mind. The high scoring Hy2 individual does not question other's motives. Often he/she is depressed, fatigued, and not in good physical health. It might be better to consider this scale to measure the construct of naiveté rather than need for affection. This is an example of, "a rose by any other name is not a rose." The name of the scale or subscale in this situation does not accurately denote the construct, and if interpreted literally would misinform the reader.

As another example, the Hostility Scale (Ho) has been found to be a measure of cynicism rather than hostility or anger. J. R. Graham et al. (1999) indicated that in an outpatient population, that the Ho Scale seemed to be more related to general maladjustment and distress than to anger.

The recommendation is to not accept the name of a scale as equivalent to its interpretation, but to instead rely upon its empirical correlates. Mental health professionals should also not solely rely upon the computer interpretation of a scale as if the narrative represents the individual tested. In computer narratives, an individual who obtains an elevation on Scale K is often described as "lacking in insight." Yet, child-custody parents elevate from ½ to 1.25 T scores above 50 (Baer and Miller, 2002; Bathurst et al., 1997; Caldwell, 2002). The most pragmatic interpretation of child-custody parents who obtain an elevated K scale is that they are trying to put their best foot forward, not that they lack insight. Child-custody parents who typically elevate on the validity scales are saying they want to obtain custody of their child. To acknowledge psychological problems on a paper and pencil test might defeat their purpose of winning the custody battle. One could make a case that parents who do not elevate on the Faking Good validity scale are the ones lacking in insight, and parents who place themselves into a positive light are actually showing good judgment under the circumstances.

Psychiatrists or marriage counselors who perform child-custody evaluations, but lack the knowledge base for testing often employ psychologists to test and rely upon the psychologist's report. It is crucial that the child-custody evaluator confer with the psychologist/psychometrician and not rely solely upon the individual's delineation. Often, evaluators in haste omit this face-to-face consultation and incorporate the psychometric findings into their custody study without discussion with the tester. Without conferring, how can the evaluator fully understand the implications of the test results or the limitations of the test findings? The quality of the final product is diminished. The risk of harm caused by misinterpretation and misapplication of the test results is enhanced.

The consultant psychologist may risk deviating from APA Code of Ethics Code 3.04:

> Psychologists take reasonable steps to avoid harming their clients/patients, students, supervisees, research participants, organizational clients, and others with whom they work, and to minimize harm where it is foreseeable and unavoidable.

Situational Factors

With the marital separation wounds still fresh, and the intensity of parents' anger and depression acute, clients often turn their emotions into competition and jockey for position in their quest to become the primary custodial parent. In the midst of this chaos, probably the worst time to test or interview parents, courts order child-custody evaluations.

Courts and attorneys set due dates for custody reports sometimes within months of the marital separation. In this time of angst, anger between spouses may elevate and be reflected in the interviews and testing. Depression may be acute following the loss of the spouse and the failure of the marriage. Removal from the family home, truncation of visitation with one's children, and deterioration in lifestyle add to a parent's felt pain.

Evaluators with an eye on the impending court date may confuse test elevations due to situational factors with psychopathology. It is important for evaluators to not only look at clinical elevations as indices of psychopathology but to consider situational factors as causative.

Anger, depression, anxiety, and distractibility may skew test findings. Even the test-taking situation may need to be factored into the evaluator's conclusions.

A parent may reasonably be upset following an interview with the custody evaluator, especially if the other parent is present. The parent may be angry, frustrated, depressed, or anxious following a probing, uncovering interview. This would not be an opportune time to administer tests.

In addition to affective interference, cognitive factors may also confound test results. Individuals in a highly aroused state may be easily confused. Lack of concentration and distractibility may prevent careful reading of items. Items may be endorsed on a personality test that might have been influence by the preceding interview and the parent's emotional state, and fail to represent the parent's actual personality trait.

In custody evaluations, as traits are more important to assess than states, it is incumbent upon the evaluator to heed the risk that traits may occluded by an individual's state of mind.

In addition to the stress surrounding the divorce, and the conditions of the evaluation protocol, evaluators need to take into consideration how other external factors might affect the client's test performance.

Performance also might be affected by use of prescription medication. It is important to counsel examinees in preparation for the evaluation to modulate their medication to permit the most propitious testing environment. Clients should be advised to bring their reading glasses. And tests should be administered after a client is sated.

I have had the unfortunate experience of watching a colleague be interrogated on the witness stand because of inadequately considering the impact of test setting and situational variables. The mother was administered the MMPI-2 (a long and laborious test of 567 questions) in the waiting room of the psychologist's office. The examinee was frequently interrupted by a series of intrusive visitors—a delivery person, other clients, raucous children, someone lost and needing directions.

The mother was unable to concentrate, failed to carefully read several questions, was frustrated with the test-taking setting, and left the test incomplete but scorable. Afraid to express her dismay, she was late for her appointments. The evaluator interpreted the client as being resistant, passive-aggressive, and made comments in his report consistent with this interpretation. He supported the father for custody.

The mother ultimately lost her child. Incensed and seeking redress, she filed an ethics complaint. The board reviewed the complaint and agreed with the mother that the psychologist deviated from Standard 3.04 and indeed caused harm to his client.

If the luxury of a private testing room is not possible, than the examiner needs to arrange his/her schedule to permit the examinee to have a quiet, distraction-free environment for the testing.

Proper Test Instruments

APA Ethics Code 9.08 directs psychologists not to use obsolete tests. "Psychologists do not base such decisions or recommendations on tests and measures that are obsolete and not useful for the current purpose."

This rule creates a conundrum. As updated versions of tests utilized in child custody become available, the mental health professional is faced with a dilemma. Research on updated tests may not be readily available. By the time a test is updated, texts and peer reviewed articles on the test are not accessible. The mental health professional choosing a test is then placed in a quandary: risk practicing unethically by using an obsolete test or use a test that has limited research.

The Millon Clinical Multiaxial Inventory was updated in 1994 to coincide with the publication of the DSM-IV. The MCMI-III replaced the MCMI-II (previously published in 1987). Ninety items were changed—more than half of the 175 test questions. In addition, the number of items per scale were reduced by half. In essence, the MCMI-III is a new instrument. It takes several years for sufficient research to catch up so that one may comfortably rely upon an updated test.

What should the clinician do in the interim? Rely on an instrument that may be considered obsolete or use a newer version not necessarily supported by the data?

The solution lies in Ethics Code Section 9.02 (a):

> Psychologists administer, adapt, score, interpret, or use assessment techniques, interview, tests, or instruments in a manner and for purposes that are appropriate in light of the research on or evidence of the usefulness and proper application of the techniques.

The mental health professional should clarify his procedures. A footnote in the report would suffice. Until sufficient research is available to justify utilization of the newer instrument, the mental health professional should clarify the reason for using an older version of the test.

On the other hand, if a test is obsolete and not useful for the current purpose, then it is necessary to use the updated test. Continuing to use the MMPI rather than the MMPI-2 will likely lead to a licensure complaint.

Intelligence tests are the exception. Updated tests must be used as soon as they are available. As the population becomes more intelligent (Kanaya et al., 2003), administering older versions of intellectual instruments based on old norms produces distorted test results. An individual may be misclassified if he/she is administered an obsolete intelligence test. This error in test usage would place the mental health professional at high risk for an ethical violation.

CONCLUSION

On her way to Emerald City, Dorothy had to confront her share of dangers—the Wicked Witch of the West, flying monkeys, the threat of lions, tigers, and bears. Psychologists face licensing boards, ethics committees, demanding attorneys, impatient judges, irate clients, and alienated children. And we don't have a Wizard of Oz to help us at the end of our path. Dorothy had help—an intelligent scarecrow, a courageous lion, and a supportive tinman. Dorothy also had Glenda the good witch on her side, and let's not forget her ruby slippers. Luckily, she also had the Wizard of Oz when she needed him. Unlike Dorothy, the child-custody evaluator does not have such helpful companions.

The mental health professional who enters into forensic practice, especially child custody litigation, leaves behind the more casual, client-friendly, therapist-trusting treatment setting for an atmosphere of hostility, distrust, machination and grief.

The evaluator must be aware, as Dorothy exclaimed in the Wizard of Oz, "Toto, I have a feeling we're not in Kansas anymore!" The courtroom bears little semblance to the comfort of the couch. Ruby slippers are ineffective on this meandering labyrinth.

As described in this chapter, mental health professionals must approach the litigious environment of child-custody assessment with caution, circumspection, and care. I have alerted the reader to some of the potential dangers in the areas of role clarity, custody procedures, competence, and psychological testing. Hopefully, with the landmarks provided, both the apprentice and journeyman may practice more artfully. By being vigilant to the risks, the mental health professional can practice at the highest level of professionalism and avoid malpractice and ethics complaints.

NOTES

1. The chapter is copyright © 2004 Ira Gorman, Ph.D., Family Conciliation Services, 930 West 17th Street, Suite D, Santa Ana, California 92706, 714-542-4144. All rights reserved. Items from the PAI are reproduced by special permission of the Publisher, Psychological Assessment Resources, Inc., 16204 North Florida Avenue, Lutz, Florida 33549 from the Personality Assessment Inventory by Leslie C. Morey, Ph.D., copyright 1991. Further reproduction is prohibited without permission of the Publisher.

2. Guidelines for Child Custody Evaluations in Divorce Proceedings II-4.

3. Because the Harris-Lingoes subcales have relatively few items, reliability may be low. One should therefore not interpret the subscale without the parent scale also being elevated (Butcher et al., 2001).

12

The Two Ewing Cases and *Tarasoff*[1]

David G. Jensen

On July 16, 2004 and July 27, 2004 moderate earthquakes rocked the otherwise staid world of psychotherapy in California. On July 16, 2004 the Court of Appeal, Second District, issued an opinion in the case of *Ewing v. Goldstein, Ph.D.* (2004) 120 Cal. App. 4th 807 ("Ewing I"), and on July 27, 2004 the same appellate court issued an opinion in the case of *Ewing v. Northridge Hospital Medical Center* (2004) 120 Cal. App. 4th 1289 ("Ewing II"). By abandoning the literal reading of California Civil Code section 43.92, Ewing I and Ewing II have sent shockwaves throughout California's legal and therapeutic communities. Understanding these cases begins with a working knowledge of the factual and procedural backgrounds of them.

THE FACTUAL UNDERPINNINGS OF EWING I AND EWING II

The facts stated herein are taken from the facts as reported in Ewing I and Ewing II; however, these cases may not recount the facts as they will be testified to at trial. This does not mean that someone is not telling the truth, or has not told the truth. For tactical reasons occurring *before* trial, attorneys will argue certain facts or avoid bringing up certain facts to try and effectuate some desired outcome, that is, an early dismissal of the lawsuit. Consequently, at trial, individuals may testify to facts not included here.

Ewing I and Ewing II grew out of a tragic murder-suicide that occurred in the Los Angeles area on June 23, 2001. On that day, Geno Colello ("Colello"), a former member of the Los Angeles Police Department, shot and killed Keith Ewing ("Ewing"), the new boyfriend of Colello's former girlfriend, Diana Williams ("Williams").[2] The murder occurred as Ewing was washing his car in the driveway of his home.[3] Colello then turned the gun on himself and committed suicide.[4] It seems, however, that Colello's life had been unraveling for years.

In 1997, Colello began receiving counseling from David Goldstein, Ph.D. ("Goldstein") for work-related emotional problems and problems concerning Williams.[5] In early 2001, Colello became increasingly depressed and despondent over the termination of his seventeen-year relationship with Williams.[6] His feelings escalated in June of 2001 when he learned that she was romantically involved with another man.[7]

Goldstein last saw Colello for treatment on June 19, 2001, but he spoke with Colello via the telephone on June 20, 2001 and again on June 21, 2001.[8] During the June 21 conversation, Goldstein asked Colello if he was suicidal and Colello admitted to thinking about suicide.[9] Goldstein discussed voluntary hospitalization with Colello, (presumably to avert a suicide) and Goldstein obtained permission from Colello to speak with Colello's father, Victor Colello.[10]

At dinner that evening, Colello asked Victor Colello for a gun so that Colello could shoot himself, but Victor Colello refused to give him one.[11] Colello then said that his alternative was to get a gun and go kill Williams' new boyfriend and then himself.[12] Some type of altercation ensued between Colello and his father, and Colello ended up punching his father in the face.[13] Victor Colello then called Goldstein and reported what Colello had said about harming Williams' new boyfriend,[14] although, at trial, it is expected that Goldstein will deny that Victor Colello told him that Colello had threatened Ewing. Goldstein urged Victor Colello to take Colello to Northridge Hospital Medical Center ("Northridge"), where Goldstein arranged for him to obtain psychiatric care;[15] again, presumably to prevent a suicide.

At Northridge, Art Capilla ("Capilla"), a licensed clinical social worker, assessed Colello.[16] During the assessment, Colello's father told Capilla about the threat Colello made concerning Williams' new boyfriend,[17] although Capilla will likely deny that Victor Colello told him that Colello had threatened Ewing. Capilla was initially going to have Colello involuntarily committed, presumably for being a threat to self, but fearful of the effect such an action would have on his career as a policeman, Colello agreed to voluntarily enter Northridge on June 21, 2001.[18] He then came under the care of Dr. Gary Levinson ("Levinson"), a staff psychiatrist.[19] Levinson did not believe that Colello was suicidal and, over Goldstein's remonstrations, on June 22, 2001 he discharged Colello from Northridge.[20]

No one ever warned Ewing that Colello was dangerous to him, and, tragically, on June 23, 2001, one day after being discharged from Northridge, Colello murdered Ewing and then took his own life.[21]

In February 2002, the Ewing family filed a wrongful death action for professional negligence against Goldstein, which resulted in Ewing I, and a wrongful death action for professional negligence against Northridge, which resulted in Ewing II. The Ewing family also filed suit against the Colellos and Dr. Levinson. This tragic tale of despondency, lost love, and rage is certainly heart rending for all those impacted by it. But, the unique factors of this tragedy have spawned legal ramifications that affect California psychotherapists and their *Tarasoff* obligations.

EWING I AND EWING II AND CALIFORNIA CIVIL CODE SECTION 43.92.

In Ewing I,[22] at the trial court level and in harmony with the literal reading of California Civil Code section 43.92, Goldstein contended that he could not be held liable for failing to warn Ewing and the police about the danger that Colello posed to Ewing because Colello (patient) had not directly disclosed to Goldstein (psychotherapist) his intention to harm Ewing. The Ewing family countered Goldstein's argument by claiming that by virtue of Colello's statements to Goldstein, Colello's interactions with Goldstein, *and* the information Victor Colello allegedly communicated to Goldstein about the threat of harm that Colello posed to Ewing, Goldstein was aware of the threat of harm that Colello posed to Ewing. Consequently, Goldstein should have warned Ewing about such a threat.

The Ewing family's contention runs countercurrent to the express, literal language of California Civil Code Section 43.92, which generally immunizes psychotherapists for failing to warn of, protect against, or predict a patient's violent behavior except in cases where the "patient has communicated to the psychotherapist a serious threat of physical violence against a reasonably identifiable victim or victims" and the therapist fails to make reasonable attempts to notify the intended victim and law enforcement. The trial court sided with Goldstein because Colello did not tell Goldstein *personally* that he intended to harm Ewing and it dismissed the case, a decision that was subsequently appealed by the Ewing family to the Court of Appeal, Second District.

In Ewing I, the Court of Appeal, Second District examined the question of whether a communication from a patient's family member, made for the purpose of advancing the patient's therapy, is a "patient communication" within the meaning of Civil Code section 43.92. The Court of Appeal, Second District, in Ewing I, and then again in Ewing II, said yes, communications from family members are patient communications within the meaning of Civil Code section 43.92. With Ewing I, the literal reading of section 43.92 was turned on its head.

Why would the Court of Appeal, Second District rule this way? After all, the decision creates enormous confidentiality problems for psychotherapists, who do not even acknowledge the identities of their clients to third parties, including family members, without written authorization. The Court of Appeal, Second District in Ewing I arrived at its conclusion for four reasons:

1. California law requires confidentiality to give way to disclosures of otherwise confidential information to protect third parties from physical harm.[23]
2. California law protects as privileged communications any communications between patients and third parties that are made in furtherance of the patient's therapy.[24]
3. There is no good reason why a threat that a parent shares with his or her child's therapist about the risk of grave bodily injury the patient poses to another should not be considered a patient communication in determining whether the therapist's duty to warn is triggered under 43.92.[25]
4. A narrow, literal reading of 43.92 leads to the possibility of murder or grave bodily injury occurring when such violence could have been prevented had the therapist warned the intended victim and law enforcement.[26]

Goldstein and Northridge appealed to the California Supreme Court to overrule Ewing I and Ewing II, but on November 10, 2004 the California Supreme Court declined to review the cases. Consequently, Ewing I and Ewing II have become part of California's legal landscape. These cases raise five questions for consideration.

DOES PATIENT JUST MEAN PATIENT?

The term "patient" in Civil Code section 43.92, post Ewing I and Ewing II, does not literally mean just a therapist's actual patients, but the term also includes "family members of patients."[27] Therefore, a communication from a patient's "family member" to the patient's therapist, made for the purpose of advancing the patient's therapy, may create a duty upon the therapist to warn an intended victim of the patient's threatened violent behavior.

This expansive interpretation of the term "patient" in section 43.92 has two wrinkles. The first being that Ewing I and Ewing II expressly limit this rule to "family members" or to the patient's "immediate family." But, what exactly is a family? Does the court mean a family in the Leave It To Beaver sense, or in the Mrs. Doubtfire sense? Must there be an intact marriage with a mother and a father living under the same roof? What if there has been a divorce? What if "mom" and "dad" were never married and have never lived together? Can a second cousin be a family member? What about domestic partners? Ewing I and Ewing II do not answer these questions, which is unfortunate because the lack of a definition for the key concept of "family" only creates more questions with which to wrestle.

We believe that the emphasis on family members is misplaced anyway because the information conveyed, that is, the threat, is more crucial than the family relationship. A boyfriend or girlfriend, a college roommate, or a best friend may have more accurate information about a patient's mental state than a member of the patient's family.

Moreover, what about communicating with third parties who are not family members? This is a thorny issue for therapists because of their obligation to maintain confidentiality. In a footnote to Ewing I, the Court of Appeal, Second District declined to consider the question of what occurs when a third party who is not a member of the patient's "immediate family" is involved in the patient's therapy and that third party discloses a threat made by the patient to the patient's therapist.[28] Consequently, we are left to postulate about what should be done in such a situation.

Since the threat is more important than the family relationship, the analysis set forth herein should be followed, although this is an issue on which there is no definitive answer. One of the problems stemming from Ewing I and Ewing II is that it opens the door to possible liability if a therapist fails to act on a threat from a credible third party and the patient then harms the intended victim. The family of the victim will certainly want to hold the therapist liable for failing to warn, and Ewing I and Ewing II give such family more ammunition for doing so. Hence, we believe that threats from credible third parties, in addition to threats from family members, may also give rise to a duty to warn. By credible, we mean someone who knows that the therapist is treating the patient and that is providing information to the therapist that is consistent with the therapist's knowledge of the patient. This rationale comports more closely with the state's goal of preventing murder or grave bodily injury than a rule that does not allow for such contact.

But, what happened to patient confidentiality? The Court of Appeal, Second District was not unmindful of a patient's right to confidentiality and the need to maintain confidentiality in therapy. In Ewing II, the court opined that assurances of confidentiality are important for three reasons: (1) to avoid the stigma that results from seeking mental health care; (2) to effectuate counseling; and, (3) to facilitate trust between the patient and the therapist.[29] However, it remains the public policy of the state to limit confidentiality in order to protect individuals from physical harm.[30] Although our recommendation takes another chunk out of the wall of confidentiality, any lawyer that defends therapists will tell you that it is easier to defend a breach of confidentially action than a wrongful death action. And, in reality, choosing between the two does not necessarily lead to liability. There is room for a therapist to successfully navigate both options by acting competently under the circumstances.

Although therapists should not be acknowledging the identities of their clients to third parties, in a situation where a patient is dangerous to himself or herself, or dangerous to the person or property of others, the law permits the therapist, under section 1024 of the Evidence Code, to contact whomever is necessary to prevent the threatened danger from occurring. Patient suicides or patient homicides rarely "come out of the blue," like lightning on a sunny day. Therapists generally have a context, in light of the treatment relationship, for gauging whether a particular patient is potentially suicidal or even potentially homicidal. This context is best developed through conducting thorough assessments, reviewing previous treatment records, taking thorough patient histories, and rendering good clinical work. This context will be the impetus for the need to communicate with family members or credible third parties.

The second wrinkle is that hearing a threat, whether from a patient, a family member, or even a credible third party, does not necessarily mean that a *Tarasoff* obligation has been created. The operative word is the word "may." Just because a patient, a family member of a patient, or a credible third party calls and tells a therapist that his or her patient has threatened to kill someone or harm someone does not mean that a *Tarasoff* obligation has been created. Further analysis is required.

THE KINDLING AND THE SPARK: WHEN DO I HAVE A DUTY TO WARN?

Ewing I and Ewing II require threats of patients—again, whether from the patient, a family member of a patient, or, we believe, even a credible third party—to be analyzed in light of what the therapist already knows about his or her patient. A therapist will have a duty to warn if the information communicated to the therapist by the patient, a family member of the patient, or a credible third party leads the therapist to believe that his or her patient poses a serious risk of grave bodily injury to another.[31] A good metaphor for this concept is the kindling and the spark, with the kindling being what you already know about your patient and the spark being the information that is communicated to you by the patient, a family member of your patient, or a credible third party.

For instance, you may already know that your patient has a previous history of violence, or that your patient has never harmed anyone; you may know that your patient has an inability to control his or her anger, or that your patient never loses his cool; you may know that your patient has command hallucinations and he does or does not do what the voices inside his head are telling him to do; you may know that your patient is abusing alcohol or drugs and that while under the influence of such substances he or she has become violent before, or you may know that your patient has never abused alcohol or drugs; or, you may know that your patient is impulsive and violent, or impulsive but not violent. What you know about your patient, or what you should know about your patient, based on your review of the patient's records, your assessments, and your clinical work, constitutes the kindling, but kindling without a spark is just small pieces of wood.

Kindling ignited by a spark, however, can turn into a destructive fire. What you are told by your patient, a family member of your patient, or a credible third party about your patient is the spark, which may or may not ignite the kindling. The law requires you to analyze the information communicated to you by your patient, the family member of your patient, or a credible third party in light of your knowledge of your patient. Does the information communicated lead you to believe that your patient is dangerous to another? Does the spark ignite the kindling?

For instance, suppose the mother of your male client calls and tells you that your client has just said that he is going to kill his girlfriend because she wrecked his new car. Although there is a threat, or a spark to complete the metaphor, the threat alone does not mean that you have a *Tarasoff* obligation. What you have to do is ask yourself the next question: does the threat cause you, as the therapist, to believe that your client is going to harm the girlfriend? If, after hearing the threat, you *determine* or *believe* that your client is dangerous to the girlfriend, you would then make reasonable efforts to notify the intended victim and law enforcement; conversely, if you did *not determine* or *believe* that your client is going to harm his girlfriend, then you would not have to make such attempts at notification. The key, however, is having reasons that you can articulate for your belief. Why do you believe he is dangerous? Is it because your patient has hurt women who have betrayed him? Is it because you know he values his car more than life itself and has threatened to harm anyone who even scratches it?

On the other hand, why do you believe he is not dangerous? Is it because he's made similar threats in the past and never carried out any of them? Is it because there is no history of violence? Whatever the rationale, it should be documented in the patient file.

But what if I judge wrongly? What if I determine that a patient is not dangerous to a third party and then that patient harms the third party? Although this looks like a situation where the therapist would be liable, in reality he or she may not be. In *Tarasoff*, the California Supreme Court recognized that it is difficult to forecast violence. Hence, the court stated:

> [O]bviously, we do not require that the therapist, in making that determination, render a perfect performance; the therapist need only exercise that reasonable degree of skill, knowledge, and care ordinarily possessed and exercised by members of [that professional specialty] under similar circumstances. Within the broad range of reasonable practice and treatment in which professional opinion and judgment may differ, the therapist is free to exercise his or her own best judgment without liability; proof, aided by hindsight, that he or she judged wrongly is insufficient to establish negligence.[32]

The key to avoiding liability is having good reasons for the decisions you make. We cannot stress enough that such reasons should come from your review of prior treatment records, that is, you have a duty to obtain the treatment records of a patient with a history of violence;[33] your assessments and findings; and, your interactions with your patients.

What about so-called conditional threats? A conditional threat is one in which the patient says "I am going to kill X if . . .," or "I might kill X if. . . ." Ewing I opines that even conditional threats can trigger a duty to warn,[34] assuming the therapist *believes* the patient is dangerous to the intended victim. The condition appears to be irrelevant. A therapist may believe that a patient is dangerous to another even though the threat was made conditionally. Since the therapist will likely have no knowledge about whether the condition occurs, it seems prudent to warn the intended victim *if* the therapist believes his or her patient is dangerous to another.

What if, in the previous example, the mother had told the therapist that she *believes* her son is dangerous to the girlfriend, but the son had never actually threatened the girlfriend? The Court of Appeal in Ewing I pointed out that a belief, unaccompanied by a statement of a threat, would not give rise to liability under section 43.92. There must be an actual threat for section 43.92 to be triggered. Hence, the mother's mere belief would not give rise to a duty to warn under section 43.92.[35]

WHAT IS GRAVE BODILY INJURY?

A therapist has a duty to warn an intended victim when information is communicated to the therapist that leads the therapist to believe that his or her patient poses a serious risk of physical violence. The concepts of serious physical violence and grave bodily injury are synonymous. But, what exactly is grave bodily injury? Fortunately, Ewing I clarifies this concept. A threat to take another's life, if believed by the therapist, is sufficient to trigger the therapist's duty to warn, but the duty to warn can also be triggered if the patient "intends to commit an act or acts of grave bodily injury short of murder, but akin to "mayhem" or "serious bodily injury."[36]

Mayhem includes such things as depriving a human being of a member of his or her body; disabling, disfiguring, or rendering a part of his or her body useless; cutting or disabling the tongue; putting out an eye; or, slitting the nose, ear, or lip.[37] So, if your patient threatens to cut off his girlfriend's ear, and you believe him, you would have a duty to warn the girlfriend even though the patient's intent was not to kill the girlfriend.

Serious bodily injury means a serious impairment of physical condition, including, but not limited to: loss of consciousness; concussion; bone fracture; protracted loss or impairment of function of any bodily member or organ; a wound requiring extensive suturing; and serious disfigurement.[38] So, if your patient threatens to beat up his girlfriend, and you believe him, since the attack could cause loss of consciousness or concussion, you would have a duty to warn the girlfriend even though the patient's intent was not to kill the girlfriend.

Gently slapping or pinching a victim is not mayhem or grave or serious bodily injury.[39] Neither is grabbing and kissing.[40]

IS EXPERT TESTIMONY REQUIRED?

Expert testimony is not required to establish liability for a psychotherapist's failure to warn under section 43.92; rather, the mind-set of a therapist about whether a particular patient is dangerous or not dangerous can be evaluated by resorting to common knowledge without the aid of an expert witness.[41]

The key question is whether the therapist actually believes that his or her patient poses a serious risk of inflicting grave bodily injury.[42] In Ewing II, the Court of Appeal, Second District concluded, "it is not beyond the layperson's ken to understand that a patient's threat to take another's life, if believed, is serious."[43] Basically, the court is saying that it does not take any specialized knowledge or insight into the human psyche to make these kinds of determinations. Laypeople can understand whether and why a therapist believed his or her patient was dangerous without the need of expert testimony.

CAN A PATIENT BE DANGEROUS WITHOUT EVER THREATENING SOMEONE?

Suppose you have a patient that has a history of beating his children, although the last of his children has long ago left the home, whenever he has a problem with his boss at work. In session this patient has just disclosed that his boss has written him up again and is threatening to fire him for poor performance. You also know that he has recently remarried, and that he now has a thirteen-year-old stepdaughter living with him. As you are listening to your patient, the thought that the stepdaughter is going to be beaten enters your mind, like an unwelcome visitor, and you believe that your patient is going to harm the girl. You may even inquire about the girl's safety and your patient may deny that he will harm her, but you still have this gnawing belief that the girl is not safe. In essence, you have made a determination that your patient is dangerous to another, although the patient never said a word about harming her, and, in fact, denied that he would hurt her. Under these facts, do you have a *Tarasoff* obligation? Yes!

But, let's change the facts of the hypothetical a bit to further illustrate the concept. Same facts as above except that you believe that your patient is not now a threat to his stepdaughter because he has made tremendous progress in therapy. He is not the threat to his children that he was ten years ago. Do you still have an obligation under *Tarasoff*, the case, to do reasonable things to protect the girl? No! In light of your clinical work, you have determined that he does not pose a danger to her. The difference in the two outcomes is your knowledge of your patient.

Under *Tarasoff*, when a therapist *determines* that a patient poses a serious danger of violence to others, the therapist bears a duty to exercise reasonable care to protect the foreseeable victim from such danger.[44] The key word is "determines." A therapist can determine that a patient is dangerous to others in one of two ways: (1) the patient may tell the therapist directly that he or she intends to harm someone and the therapist then believes that such patient will harm such individual; or (2) the therapist may determine that a patient is dangerous to another from the therapist's knowledge of the patient's history or propensities and the patient's present situation.[45] These are very different determinations, and they are treated differently under *Tarasoff*. It is a mistake to think that section 43.92 has replaced *Tarasoff* in all instances; rather, it is more accurate to think of *Tarasoff* as having two faces. One face is concerned with actual threats of patients, which are then governed by *Tarasoff* and section 43.92; the other face is concerned with determinations that therapists make about their patients in the absence of actual threats, with such determinations then being governed just by *Tarasoff*.

Ewing I distinguishes between *Tarasoff*, the case, and section 43.92, the statute, by saying that the "resulting statutory provision, section 43.92, was not intended to overrule *Tarasoff* or *Hedlund*, but rather to limit the psychotherapist's liability for failure to warn to those circumstances where the patient has communicated an actual threat of violence against an identified victim."[46]

Moreover, Ewing I also states that section 43.92 "refers only to a patient's communication to his or her psychotherapist."[47] Section 43.92 was created by the state legislature to limit liability when patients threaten others. The legislative history of section 43.92 is clear, however, that it was not enacted to replace *Tarasoff*.[48] Consequently, section 43.92 functions as an immunity statute in situations where patients threaten to harm others. But, we have just seen that a patient can be dangerous to others without ever making a threat. This second way of being dangerous is not covered by section 43.92 because section 43.92 only deals with threats communicated to therapists by patients, or post-Ewing I and II to threats communicated to therapists by family members of patients or even credible third parties. *Tarasoff* has two faces, and because it has two faces there are two rules that must be followed. Those two rules are:

- If a patient threatens to kill or harm a third party, the patient has made an actual threat, which then allows the therapist to tap into the immunity afforded by section 43.92 of the Civil Code, which requires therapists to make reasonable attempts to contact law enforcement and the intended victim. If the therapist does these things, and his or her patient harms the third party, the therapist is immunized from liability.
- If, in the absence of a threat, the therapist determines that a patient is dangerous to another, under *Tarasoff*, but not under section 43.92, the therapist must do reasonable things to protect such person from harm, including notifying the police, warning the victim, warning others likely to apprise the victim, arranging for the patient to be hospitalized, or really do anything that is *reasonable* under the circumstances to protect the intended victim.

For a schematic outline of this information, please see "The Two Faces of *Tarasoff*" diagram that follows.

The Two Faces of Tarasoff

Pursuant to Tarasoff, when a therapist determines that his or her patient presents a serious danger of violence to another, such therapist incurs an obligation to use reasonable care to protect the intended victim from such danger.

If your client communicates intent to physically harm a reasonably identifiable victim, meaning that your client intends to kill or cause grave bodily injury to such individual, ask yourself the following question:

Do I believe that my patient will harm this person?

- **If you believe** that your patient will harm the person, to capitalize on the immunity afforded by section 43.92 of the Civil Code, make reasonable efforts to contact law enforcement and the intended victim and then document in the patient file your reasoning and your attempts at notification.

- **If you do not believe** that your patient will harm the person, document your reasoning in the patient file.

If you believe that your patient is dangerous to another, although the patient has not expressed intent to physically harm the person, you must take reasonable precautions to protect the safety of such person, which may include notifying the police, notifying the intended victim or someone likely to apprise the intended victim, arranging for the patient to be hospitalized, or anything else that you deem reasonable under the circumstances.

WHAT HAPPENED TO GOLDSTEIN?

The Court of Appeal's decision in Ewing I does not mean that Goldstein did anything wrong or that he has lost the case. The decision in Ewing I simply means that the case can proceed to trial, where a jury will decide whether Goldstein had a duty to warn Ewing because Goldstein believed Colello intended to kill or cause serious physical harm to Ewing. In making such a determination, the jury will take into account all of the relevant evidence, including the threat to kill that Victor Colello allegedly communicated to Goldstein. Alternatively, the case may settle out of court and we will never know what a jury would have decided in this case.

[Author's Note: The author was notified in July 2005 that Ewing I settled out of court for an undisclosed amount of money; however, as of September 2005, Ewing II was still proceeding to trial.]

Although both *Ewing* cases in this article refer to a duty to warn, the rule of law from *Tarasoff* originally set forth a duty to protect, which may, depending on the facts of the particular case, involve warning foreseeable victims and/or the police; however, the duty to protect, in many cases, could also be met by hospitalizing a patient dangerous to others. Moreover, legislation in California (AB 733 (2006)) has clarified that psychotherapists have a duty to protect, not necessarily a duty to warn. Because these are complex issues, please consult with your own legal counsel regarding them.

NOTES

1. Jensen, David. 2005. The Two Ewing Cases and *Tarasoff. The Therapist* 17, no. 2, 31–37. The journal is a publication of the California Association of Marriage and Family Therapists, headquartered in San Diego, California. The information contained in this chapter is intended to provide guidelines for addressing legal dilemmas. It is not intended to address every situation that could potentially arise, nor is it intended to be a substitute for independent legal advice or consultation. When using such information as a guide, be aware that laws, regulations, and technical standards change over time, and thus one should verify and update any references or information contained herein.
2. Ewing I, p. 811.
3. Ewing II, p. 1293.
4. Ewing II, p. 1294.
5. Ewing I, p. 811.
6. Ewing I, P. 811 and Ewing II, p. 1294.
7. Ewing I, p. 811.
8. Ewing II, p. 1294.
9. Ewing I, p. 811.
10. Ewing I, p. 811.
11. Ewing II, p. 1294.
12. Ewing I, p. 811.
13. Ewing II, p. 1294.
14. Ewing I, p. 812.
15. Ewing I, p. 812.
16. Ewing II, p. 1294.
17. Ewing II, p. 1294.
18. Ewing II, p. 1294.
19. Ewing I, p. 812.
20. Ewing I, p. 812.
21. Ewing I, p. 812.
22. In Ewing II, Northridge made a similar argument.

23. Ewing I, p. 817.
24. Ewing I, p. 818.
25. Ewing I, p. 819.
26. Ewing I, p. 819.
27. Ewing I, p. 813; Ewing II, p. 1296.
28. Ewing I, FN 10, p. 819.
29. Ewing II, FN 5, p. 1299.
30. Ewing I, p. 816.
31. Ewing I, p. 821.
32. *Tarasoff v. Regents of University of California* (1976) 17 Cal. 3d 425, 438.
33. *Jablonski v. United States* (1983) 712 F. 2d 391, 397.
34. Ewing I, FN 13, p. 821.
35. Ewing I, FN 12, p. 820.
36. Ewing I, p. 821.
37. Ewing, p. 821.
38. Ewing I, p. 821.
39. Ewing I, p. 821.
40. *Barry v. Turek* (1990) 218 CA 3d 1241, 1246.
41. Ewing II, p. 1303.
42. Ewing II, p. 1302.
43. Ewing II, p. 1302.
44. *Tarasoff v. Regents of University of California* (1976) 17 Cal. 3d 425, 431, 439.
45. *Jablonski v. United States* (1983) 712 F. 2d 391, 398.
46. Ewing I, p. 816.
47. Ewing I, p. 814.
48. Assembly Committee on Judiciary, AB 1133, May 14, 1985.

13

Guidelines for Compliance with Federal HIPAA Laws for Mental Health Practitioners[1]

OVERVIEW

All mental health practitioners are now required to be in compliance with the federal Health Information Portability and Accountability Act (HIPAA). Willful noncompliance is punishable by fines up to $250,000 and ten years imprisonment! A widespread false rumor has it that if you are a solo practitioner accepting only cash for services and not storing or transmitting client information electronically that you do not have to comply with HIPAA. This is simply not true for reasons I will explain—*you must comply now* or risk federal punishment as well as licensing board discipline and/or malpractice charges for practicing below the standard of care!

WHAT TO DO NOW

1. Take some time to go over this chapter thoughtfully so you know what HIPAA is about and so that you are clear what your basic obligations are. At this point in time we are in a transition and compliance period and no one understands all of the fine points or their implications for the future. Content yourself to have an overview and to put basic procedures in place as soon as possible.

2. Begin two new file folders for yourself—one on **HIPAA Compliance Information** that will include this document and any articles or other information you come across to be saved for future reference. The second folder will contain **HIPAA Compliance** documentation that will include various signed and dated statements of policies and procedures

you have adopted that document clearly how you are in compliance with the new federal laws.

3. Develop the essential forms you will use for compliance. The forms you need to get started are on the Web sites of all of our professional organizations. Start downloading forms and adapting them to your practice. (For Web sites, see footnote above.)

4. Prepare your basic privacy policy statement and go over it personally with each client; have them sign at the bottom indicating that they have: (1) gone over it with you; (2) asked whatever questions they have; (3) have been informed about who your Privacy Officer is for questions and requests (probably yourself); and (4) have been informed about their patient rights.

5. Good News! At long last federal legislation recognizes the *absolute privacy* of our Psychotherapy Notes—they are "for the exclusive use of the treating professional who created them. "No one, including the client, has a right to access them! They are *your* notes, *your* personal property, created for *your exclusive use and protection* and are not subject to release by subpoena or any other form of coercion—with a few very rare and very extreme exceptions to be explained later.[2]

You *must* create two separate file folders for each and every client beginning the date of your compliance which should have been 2003— this is federal law! All past storage folders should be labeled "Non-HIPAA Compliant."[3]

The first client file folder contains **Protected Health Information (PHI)**—this is the basic client record as we have always known it that can be released with the client's permission and inspected by the client. In the PHI folder you will have the client face sheet, basic intake information, diagnosis and treatment plan, informed consents, billing and insurance information, periodic case review summaries, medication information, a basic release of treatment information signed and dated, and, when the case closes, a dated termination summary on top (that includes the client's birth date) so it is easy to see *when* the case was closed so that the file can be purged (sample on the CD-ROM). [Case law holds that psychotherapy records must be maintained ten years from the date of termination or from when the client becomes an adult.]

The second client file folder must be clearly labeled "**Psychotherapy Notes**" and must be kept in a separate locked file cabinet accessible only by you—it's the law! This folder will contain what we have always called "process notes" of all client contacts along with other personal materials provided by the client or generated by the therapist describing interactions with the client as well as notes on case consultations.

I recommend putting all **documents generated by third parties** (e.g., test reports, letters from other health care providers, and prior treatment records) in the Psychotherapy Notes folder since by law you do not have the right to release these documents to anyone. Putting them here keeps them safe from accidental release. If they are later required, you can consult an attorney on their appropriate release.

The last three pages of this document contain six-per-page labels which you can copy or print onto Avery labels. Every patient file folder should have a label on the front. One label is for storage files making clear that they are not HIPAA compliant and giving instructions how to handle the materials in the folder. Another label is for the Client Record and another for Psychotherapy Notes—each with proper instructions. These labels are devised to keep you, and anyone else who ever has occasion to handle your files, straight on how to manage each folder.

If you work in a clinic or agency the administration may require—for its accreditation purposes—a note on every client contact other than simply the financial information. Your Psychotherapy Notes **do not** belong in the Client Clinic Record because they are your property for your exclusive use only! I recommend minimal compliance with the agency's administrative needs. For example, simply a log entry with nondescript statements that contain little or no personal information or use of some general form (samples on the CD-ROM) that provides only mental status information and/or assessments of legal concerns such as suicide, homicide, and/or abuse but no other information regarding the personal content of the session.

6. Put an "**Account of Disclosures**" form in each and every folder (sample on the CD-ROM) on which you must record each and every piece of information you ever release from the folder.

A new patient right under HIPAA is that the patient has the right to request a copy of this disclosure sheet of released information at any time. Patients have the right to know *what* PHI you have provided, *to whom* and *when* you provided it, and *the purpose* for which it was provided. This is because under HIPAA once they have signed a general release for your files their PHI information can automatically be released whenever appropriate to people involved in **TPO**—Treatment, **P**ayment, or health care **O**perations until and unless the client revokes it.

Note: Even though no one has the right to access your Psychotherapy Notes file folders, automatically put an Account of Disclosures sheet in those folders anyway in case, <u>with the special client Release for Psychotherapy Notes</u> form (on the CD-ROM), *you should ever choose* to release any of it. A general release form is insufficient, this is an entirely new form that specifies a number of new details such as why the information is being released and when it will be returned to you or shredded! As always, release of information that includes more than one person require each person's signature.

HIPAA requires that when seeking consultation from another provider for treatment purposes we may disclose PHI without additional authorization, but that a special authorization is required for disclosure of psychotherapy notes to a consultant. However, HIPAA does not supersede ethical and legal standards that allow us (in fact, mandate us) to use any information for consultation we need *without* client permission so long as it is carefully disguised.

7. HIPAA requires that you must train each and every employee and every other person who handles any of your patient business. You must go over your Privacy Policy Statement with every such person, explaining that deliberate or even accidental failure to comply may result in federal penalties and loss of his or her job—that you and they could face major law suit if any slips are made. Impress upon them the importance of taking HIPAA seriously. You might give a copy of this document to your employees and others.

As a part of your training of staff and outside others who handle patient names and dates, prepare a brief form for them to sign certifying: (1) that on a certain date you conducted a personal training session with them going over your policies; (2) that you gave them a copy of this (or some other) document explaining what HIPAA is and how people must comply; (3) that you or someone you have appointed is the Privacy Officer who is available for further information and questions; and that (4) in your training session any questions they had were answered and discussed. Do this when hiring new employees or contracting with outside entities.

8. **The Electronic Transaction and Security Rules**

Congress has been concerned that uniform standards for transmission of electronic health care information and that stringent security standards for the maintenance and storage of electronic information be established nationwide and that all health care providers be in compliance.

The **Transaction Rule** addresses the technical aspects of electronic health care requiring the use of standardized formats whenever information is sent or received. For example, each insurance company you transact business with will provide you with appropriate software to maintain these standards.

The **Security Rule** seeks to assure the security of client information. For example, each health care provider must address certain administrative, physical and technical procedures such as access to files and computers and the means by which electronic data is securely maintained and stored. You must systematically consider a series of possibilities and how you intend to address them in your practice. Further, you must make a written record of the security considerations that affect your practice. How to go about assessing your security issues, documenting your HIPAA compliance, and periodically reviewing and updating your policies will be discussed later.

HIPAA COMPLIANCE IS NOT ONLY MANDATED BY FEDERAL LAW, BUT, MORE IMPORTANTLY, AS A NATION WE NEED TO BE ASSURED OF THE PRIVACY AND SECURITY OF OUR PERSONAL HEALTH CARE INFORMATION. AS PRACTITIONERS, WE MUST DO OUR PART IN ESTABLISHING PRIVACY AND SECURITY FOR OUR CLIENTS AND FOR OURSELVES IN THIS ADVANCING TECHNOLOGICAL ERA. YES, GETTING IN COMPLIANCE IS INITIALLY TEDIOUS, BUT IN THE LONG RUN IT BECOMES A MUCH-NEEDED MATTER OF ROUTINE THAT IS IMPORTANT FOR US TO COMPLY WITH!

THE BIG PICTURE: WHAT HIPAA IS ALL ABOUT AND WHY WE NEED HIPAA[4]

General Information

1. **The Health Insurance Portability and Accountability Act (HIPAA)** was the result of a bill sponsored by Senators Nancy Kassebaum and Ted Kennedy, which was signed into law in August 1996 demanding compliance by 2003.
2. The "portability" part of the act was designed to protect Americans who were previously ill from losing their health insurance when they changed jobs or residences.
3. The "privacy" intent of the law was to streamline the national health care system through the adoption of consistent standards for transmitting uniform electronic health care claims. In order to make this work, it also became necessary to adopt standards for securing the storage of that information and for protecting an individual's privacy. When the rules are in place, it is believed that the health care industry will have a standardized way of transmitting electronic claims with increased privacy and security protection for the electronic dissemination of health care information.
4. Do not think you can evade HIPAA compliance because you only transmit information by fax or phone or only receive cash payments. Faxes sent to many private parties, insurance companies and most other large agencies are received by computers (quite unbeknownst to you) and your

client's private information becomes electronically stored—automatically making you a "covered entity" even without your consent or knowledge. The same is true for voice mails you leave on electronic systems which either have computerized voice recognition systems or some form of data entry that immediately involves you. Even receiving a third party check that has been computer generated immediately makes you a covered entity. Even if you only accept cash payments and do not fill out insurance forms, when your client submits your bill for reimbursement, information generated by you will then be transmitted and/or stored electronically. One piece of information created by you, if electronically transmitted or stored anywhere by anyone mandates HIPAA compliance for you—whether you were responsible for that trigger or not!

5. Start collecting now all articles and forms regarding HIPAA from your insurance company and professional organization. New rules are appearing daily and will continue to do so. You must keep up to date! Put them in a new "**HIPAA Information**" folder.

GOVERNMENT ENFORCEMENT AND PENALTIES

Formal compliance with the HIPAA requirements is a necessity because there are real and significant penalties for non-compliance. If a health care provider refuses to become informed or deliberately fails to take appropriate action, the consequences of failing to comply with HIPAA include:

- Administrative action taken by the HHS Office.
- Civil Penalties of not more than $100 for each violation with the total amount during a calendar year not to exceed $25,000.
- Fines of up to $250,000, imprisonment for up to ten years, or both for knowingly violating "wrongful disclosure of individually identifiable health information."

THE THREE HIPAA RULES: (1) PRIVACY; (2) SECURITY; AND (3) TRANSACTIONS

1. The **privacy rule** focuses on the application of effective policies, procedures and business service agreements to control the access and use of patient information.
2. The **security rule** addresses the provider/organization's physical infrastructure such as access to offices, files and computers to assure secure and private communication and maintenance of confidential patient information.

3. The **transaction rule** sets up standard formatting for electronic transactions and at present requires the use of ICD-9 and CPT-4 codes so DSM IV may become obsolete.[5] For those who transmit claims electronically, practice management software or an outside party such as a health care clearinghouse will be needed to handle the conversion of data to meet the requirements.

1. The Privacy Rule

What to Do to Achieve Compliance with HIPAA Now

- **To get started create two new file folders, one on "HIPAA Compliance Information" and one on "HIPAA Compliance Documentation."** In the first, collect on an on-going basis articles, Web downloads, handouts, and the like that will aid you in the event of questions—how to think, whom to contact, sources of information. In the second—which you might keep in your confidential patient file so no one has access to it but you—keep copies of the forms that you use, signed employee training forms, any complaints, restrictions, revisions—in short, all documentations that you are doing things correctly if anyone should ever demand documentation of full compliance. Any person who suspects you may not be in compliance (i.e., a disgruntled patient) can, in principle, have you investigated by a HIPAA compliance officer. Safeguard your HIPAA Compliance Documentation file so that *only you* have access to it!
- **Begin a check list** of items to be considered periodically and keep it in your "HIPAA Compliance" file.
- **Physically separate from the Patient Record portions of the file and begin a new "Psychotherapy Notes" file on all clients actively under your care. This is the Law!** These confidential psychotherapy files are by federal law being created exclusively for the use of the treating professional. They will include all notes on sessions and records of other contacts such as emails, faxes, telephone messages, cards, and so forth.
- **Note:** The above considerations also apply to all confidential psychotherapy materials that are computer stored. Only you can have access to the encryption and file passwords for Psychotherapy Notes.
- All files should be labeled as either Patient Record or Psychotherapy Notes and all inactive files should be put in storage clearly labeled as Non-HIPAA Compliant.
- **Note: Patients do not have the right to review their Psychotherapy Notes** but they can authorize you to release them. There are certain legal conditions in which your confidential Psychotherapy Notes can be opened so be sure your patient will not be surprised or enraged if she or

he ever reads them. While confidential Psychotherapy Notes now have an extra measure of federal protection, always assume that they are not totally immune from disclosure.

- **Note:** There are special rules under which a therapist may provide a timely *written* denial of access to patient PHI (HIPAA thirty days, California five working days,) provided that the denial is open to review by a third party mental health professional. Summaries of either PHI or Psychotherapy Notes may be provided to patients upon the professional discretion of the therapist. Be prepared to seek consultation on such issues—usually they entail the potential risk of harm to the patient.

- **Note:** Third parties do not have the right to review your psychotherapy notes nor to coerce patients to sign authorizations for their release. Psychotherapy Notes may not be released to other treating professionals without an authorization. Psychotherapy Notes can be disclosed without the patient's authorization when mandated by a court of law; for training, research and supervision (de-identified); when needed for oversight of the therapist who created them; when needed to avert imminent serious threat to health or safety of person or public (only to persons who can be expected to prevent or reduce that threat, including the person threatened); and to medical examiners or coroners for identification.

- **Note:** Documents received from another therapist should be kept in your confidential psychotherapy notes file and may not be re-disclosed except by authorization of the person who created them *and* the client.

- **New patient rights** are:(1) to receive notice of privacy policies; (2) to request to restrict the use and disclosure of PHI; (3) to access their own PHI; (4) to request amendments to PHI; and (5) to obtain an Accounting of Disclosures of their PHI.

- **Note:** Patients do not have the right to view information compiled for a civil, criminal, or administrative proceeding.

- **Minors:** HIPAA generally recognizes parents or legal guardians as personal representatives of their children for purposes of accessing PHI.

- **You must post in a conspicuous place in your office your privacy policies** and procedures along with a statement of who the Privacy Officer is who can answer questions and receive complaints and how this person can be reached.

- **You must train employees and all other persons who handle client data** so that they understand the privacy procedures. Have each employee sign and date a copy of the privacy procedures, stating in their handwriting that she/he has received a copy and that you have had a meeting with them to go over in detail the policies and procedures and to discuss any questions they have.

- **Document the training sessions** and file copies of signed statements of current and all new employees in your secured "HIPAA Compliance File."Your training must include a documented statement of sanctions, complaint processes and duty to mitigate concerns and infractions of privacy policies. Consider putting in writing how all employees must insure that emails, faxes, billing sheets, correspondence, and voice mails remain secured. *Retrain annually (think January) and document carefully.* Remember, full HIPAA compliance will become a national standard of care and you may be required at any time by a federal officer, court, or licensing board to document your full compliance.
- **Designate a Privacy Officer** to be responsible for seeing that privacy procedures are adopted and followed [in a small private practice the therapist may appoint him/herself the Privacy Officer].
- If you deal with insurance companies or managed care companies they are required to supply you with HIPAA compliant software and contracts. The same is true for contracts and transaction software for use of outside contracted agencies such as billing services, answering services and collection agencies. You must have in your "HIPAA Compliance" file documentation that all companies and agencies that you deal with have provided you with a HIPAA compliant contract.

To What Kind of Information does the Privacy Rule Apply?

In order to understand how the privacy rule treats health information, it is important to briefly review four definitions that are included in the rule:

1. **Health Information:** Any information, whether oral or recorded in any form, created or used by health care professionals or health care entities.
2. **Individually Identifiable Health Information:** A subset of Health Information that either identifies the individual or that can be used to identify the individual.
3. **Protected Health Information (PHI):** Individually identifiable health information becomes Protected Health Information (PHI) when it is maintained or transmitted in any form or medium. More specifically, PHI is information that relates to the past, present or future physical or mental health condition of an individual; the provision of health care to an individual; or the payment for the provision of health care to an individual; and that identifies the individual or could reasonably be used to identify the individual.
4. **Psychotherapy Notes:** HIPAA standards are designed to echo the *Jaffee v. Redmond* 1994 Supreme Court ruling regarding privacy of the

contents of psychotherapy. Notes recorded in any medium by a health care provider who is a mental health professional documenting or analyzing the contents of conversation during a private counseling session or a group, joint or family counseling session, and that are separated from the rest of the individual's medical record qualify as Psychotherapy Notes. (I am also including in my Psychotherapy Notes folder all communications from clients such as emails, cards, phone messages, and documents generated by other professionals.)

The definition in the privacy rule of psychotherapy notes specifically *excludes* information pertaining to medication prescriptions and monitoring, counseling session start and stop times, the modalities and frequencies of treatment furnished, results of clinical tests and any summary of the following items: diagnosis; functional status; the treatment plan; symptoms; prognosis; and progress to date. In the regulatory definition, one of the requirements for notes to qualify as "Psychotherapy Notes" is that they *must* be "separated from the rest of an individual's medical record." Due to the additional protection associated with Psychotherapy Notes, a conservative analysis is that psychotherapists have to segregate this information into different labeled file folders and ensure that increased procedural requirements for Psychotherapy Notes are met. The labels I use are on Web site for your convenience.

Once triggered (and you can't realistically avoid triggering), the privacy rule applies to a psychotherapist's *entire operation*, not just to information in electronic form. The privacy rule does not allow for a psychotherapist to segregate that part of his or her practice to which HIPAA standards apply.

Plaintiff attorneys clearly intend to make full compliance into a national standard of care which will be applied to you in the event of ethical or administrative complaint or malpractice litigation. Don't be a fool and try to avoid HIPAA compliance.

Psychotherapists must obtain a patient's consent prior to using PHI to carry out "treatment," "payment," and "health care operations," **TPO**. A generalized consent form will be necessary when dealing with third parties and, as a practical matter, should be secured at the outset of treatment rather than waiting until the information is shared. *This form differs from and is not a substitute for the "informed consent" that is also typically obtained prior to the initiation of treatment.* (A sample form is on the CD-ROM.)

Providers can secure both forms of consent at the same time; however, **the generalized consent form must be visually and organizationally separate from other legal permissions and must be separately signed and dated.** The consent form must indicate that the individual has the right to revoke consent in writing. Any actions the psychotherapist may have taken before receiving notice that the consent has been revoked would not be covered by the revocation.

Special Authorization for Release of Psychotherapy Notes

The Privacy Rule contains a definition of Psychotherapy Notes similar to what we in the profession have historically referred to as "process notes." Authorizations are forms that psychotherapists typically refer to as releases and they meet certain requirements specified by the privacy rule. Briefly stated, an authorization for release of psychotherapy notes *must* contain the following:

- A specific definition of the information to be used or disclosed
- To whom the information is going to be disclosed
- The purpose of the disclosure
- An expiration date
- The right to revoke
- The right not to authorize the disclosure. [A sample is on the CD-ROM.]

The privacy rule states that <u>a general consent alone</u> is insufficient when a third party requests Psychotherapy Notes; it requires psychotherapists to obtain specific patient authorization for the use and disclosure of such notes. Psychotherapists will have to ensure that any entity requesting Psychotherapy Notes has provided a valid authorization before releasing those notes. Or, alternatively, psychotherapists will have to secure authorization from the patient before providing information contained within the Psychotherapy Notes in response to requests. Additionally, when seeking consultation from another provider for treatment purposes, patient authorization must be obtained in order to disclose information in Psychotherapy Notes. Simply because a client requests release of Psychotherapy Notes does not mean the practitioner must comply since the notes are "for the exclusive use of the therapist who created them. "

Minimum necessary disclosure.   When PHI is disclosed or used, the privacy rule requires psychotherapists to share the *minimum* amount of information necessary to conduct the activity. The privacy rule also applies to PHI available internally to employees so they can do their jobs (e.g., a billing clerk may have access to the minimum amount of information needed to perform the billing role that would not include clinical information). In a treatment context, the minimum necessary provision does not apply.

Therefore, psychotherapists are free, as permitted by state law, to share information they wish with another provider for the purpose of providing treatment, as permitted by authorization. Minimum necessary disclosure does not apply to requests for information that require authorization above and beyond the general consent, such as with Psychotherapy Notes. This is because the information to be disclosed is specifically described by the authorization itself.

Use and disclosure.   There are a number of circumstances in which the privacy rule permits psychotherapists to make certain disclosures without consent or authorization. These may include providing information to or related to:

- A public health authority
- A health oversight agency
- A coroner or medical examiner
- The military, Veterans Affairs, or another entity for national security purposes [e.g., per the PATRIOT Act]
- A hospital or other type of facility for its facility directory
- Workers' Compensation Laws
- Victims of abuse, neglect and domestic violence
- Other situations as required by law—consult your attorney!

Patients: Their rights and records.   Under HIPAA, patients in many states will now have greater access to their records and greater knowledge of how their records will be used than ever before. They will also benefit from the enhanced protection of Psychotherapy Notes.

Patients have the right to:
1. Consent to use and disclosure of their PHI
2. Receive notice of use and disclosure of their PHI
3. Access their PHI for inspection and amendment
4. To request amendments to their PHI
5. To have an accounting of how their PHI was used and shared

1. Right of notice.   Under the HIPAA privacy rule, patients have the right of notice. This means ***the obligation is on the psychotherapist*** to inform patients about potential uses and disclosures of their PHI and their right to limit those uses and disclosures. *Provision of health care services may be conditioned on the patient's willingness to provide consent to disclose.*

2. Patient requests for restrictions.   As part of the consent process, psychotherapists must inform patients that they have the right to request restrictions on the use and disclosure of PHI for treatment, payment, and health care operations (TPO) purposes. The consent also must state that the psychotherapist is not required to agree to an individual's request. However, the psychotherapist must agree to "reasonable requests" for restrictions such as a request that information not be sent to specific individuals or a request that information be sent to a particular location. If the psychotherapist does agree to a particular restriction, that agreement is binding. Psychotherapists are not required to accept disclosure restrictions that could compromise their professional judgment or conclusions.

3. *Patient access to PHI records.* With limited exception, a patient is allowed to inspect and obtain a copy of the PHI record. The privacy rule defines a "designated record set" as the medical and billing records maintained by the provider and used to make decisions about the patient. Psychotherapists can require that the request be made in writing. The request must be fulfilled within thirty days (five days in California).

Patients *do not* have the right to:

- Inspect or obtain a copy of Psychotherapy Notes
- Inspect information compiled in "reasonable anticipation" of, or for use in, a civil, criminal or administrative action
- Access information systems that are used for quality control or peer-review analysis

In states that have laws guaranteeing patient access to all the psychotherapist's records, including Psychotherapy Notes, state laws will probably apply since they enhance a patient's right of access to information.

4. *Patient amendment of records.* "Right of amendment" refers to patients' right to request a change in their PHI if they feel the PHI is incorrect. A psychotherapist can deny requests for Record amendments if he or she is not the originator of the information or if the information recorded is accurate and complete.

5. *Accounting for disclosures.* "Right of Accounting" refers to the individual's right to receive a listing of all disclosures of any PHI for the previous six years in which the information has been maintained. (A sample Disclosure Log Sheet is on the CD-ROM.)

"Business Associate"—a new category of person or agency (not defined by HIPAA as a covered health service entity) is created by HIPAA defined as a person or organization other than a member of the therapist's work force who receives PHI from the therapist to provide services to, or on behalf of, the therapists. Business associates include bookkeepers, lawyers, collection agencies, clearinghouses, shredding services, computer repair service, transcription agencies, accountants, off-site storage, paging services, and voice mail services (see footnote at beginning of this chapter). PHI may only be disclosed to business associates after the therapist has obtained a written contract that the business associate will appropriately safeguard the information under HIPAA compliance information. Operationally, this should minimally include a compliance contract with your Notice of Privacy Policy attached. You might include a clause that you have personally reviewed your policies and that your contractor has had an opportunity to ask questions and discuss your policies with you. Also include a clause that any subcontractors be held to the same policies and that sanctions are provided for breaches. Review periodically, and in case of breach document the steps you have taken to repair the breach including canceling the contract if necessary. Professional Web sites have sample Business Associate contracts. HIPAA allows disclosure of PHI to your malpractice carrier for purposes of obtaining or maintaining coverage, or for purposes of obtaining benefits or reporting claims or threats of claims.

2. The Security Rule

Overview: The security rule is about the protection of confidential Protected Health Information (PHI) that is maintained, transmitted, and/or stored electronically (EPHI). The security rule seeks to assure the confidentiality, integrity, and availability of EPHI. Since the security rule applies to entities as small as the solo practitioner and also to large mega-corporations, each health provider is required to address a series of security risks and then to document that assessment and how those risks are being addressed and periodically updated.

This means that you must conduct and document a full risk analysis of potential security breaches in your office, computers, and storage locations such as break-ins, computer viruses, fires, floods, and internet hackers. You must also document how you are addressing each security concern and how you will periodically re-assess your security issues.[6] Keep your assessment and your security plan in your new "HIPAA Compliance" file folder. What follows is a brief overview of what you must do.

The three HIPAA Security Rule standards: In conducting and documenting your risk assessment there are three categories of Security Rule standards that must be addressed as well as a series of "required" and "addressable" Implementation Specifications (not optional) that accompany each set of three standards.[7]

1. **Administrative Standards** address the implementation of office policies and procedures, staff training, and other measures designed to carry out security requirements. The Administrative Standards are:

- Assigned Security Responsibility: You must appoint a HIPAA Security Officer (yourself?) who is responsible for developing and implementing security protocols and who can answer client questions.
- Security Management Process: The HIPAA Security Officer must create and implement practices designed to prevent, detect, contain, and correct HIPAA violations.
- Workforce Security: The Security Officer must create a system that insures and limits appropriate employee access to EPHI.
- Information Access Management: You must create a system of passwords to guarantee that only authorized people have access to each type of client information.
- Security Awareness and Training: You must implement and document training of all people who have access to any EPHI.
- Security Incident Procedures: You must implement procedures to detect, correct, and discipline any breaches in EPI security.
- Contingency Plan: You must establish emergency procedures for responding to threats of security such as vandalism, fire system failures, and natural disasters.
- Evaluation: You must document the ways you regularly review and update your security standards.
- Business Associate Contracts: You must insure that all business associates (answering services, billing services, shredders, etc.) are trained properly and in compliance with HIPAA security rules.

2. **Physical Standards** relate to limiting access to the physical area in which electronic information are housed.
   - Facility Access Controls: You must control physical access to all locations where EPHI is stored to assure only appropriate people have access to or can remove EPHI.
   - Workstation Use: You must assure that each workstation that can access EPHI can only be used by authorized personnel.
   - Workstation Security: All devices must be secure so they cannot be moved or observed by non-authorized personnel.
   - Device and Media Control: You must insure that any devices or media (discs, etc.) are secure when changing locations or discarding.

3. **Technical Standards** concern authentication, transmission and other issues that may arise when authorized personnel access EPHI via computer or any other electronic devices.
   - Access Controls: You must ensure only appropriate access to EPHI by authorized users.
   - Audit Controls: You must create procedures that monitor for EPHI security breaches.

- Integrity: You must create safeguards to protect from improper alteration or destruction of EPHI.
- Person or Entity Authentication: You must implement procedures that ensure that the person attempting to access EPHI is in fact that person.
- Transmission Security: You must implement procedures that guard against unauthorized access to EPHI that is being transmitted over an electronic transmissions network.

3. The Transaction Rule

The transaction rule requires standard formatting of electronic transactions and Electronic Data Interchange standards including the Internet, leased lines, dial-up lines, or the physical movement of magnetic tapes, diskettes or compact discs to new locations. **ICD-9-CM will be the code set for diagnoses and CPT-4 and HCPCS codes for outpatient procedures.** We have yet to hear a legal rejoinder from the American Psychiatric Association on switching from DSM IV to ICD-9-CM, so prudence says try to use both codes for the present. See earlier footnote on the DSM.

MISCELLANEOUS ISSUES

Federal Substance Abuse Confidentiality Requirement: The federal confidentiality of substance abuse patient records statute establishes confidentiality requirements for patient records that are maintained in connection with the performance of any federally assisted specialized alcohol or drug abuse program. According to an analysis conducted by HHS of the interaction of this law (and regulations) with HIPAA, in most cases a conflict will not exist and health care professionals covered by both will be able to comply with both sets of requirements.

Joint Consents may be obtained by a group of providers who also provide a *joint* Notice of Privacy Practices. All covered individuals must be identified on both forms. Note that if a client revokes a joint consent then the therapist is under an obligation to inform in writing all individuals named on the joint consent of the revocation.

Combined Consents: HIPAA allows you to combine a consent for disclosure of PHI with other informed consents so long as it is spatially and visually separate and separately signed and dated. However, **authorizations for disclosure of Psychotherapy Notes must be a separate form**.

HIPAA National Provider Identification Rule: By March 23, 2007 all HIPAA covered entities must have obtained an identification number to further aid HIPAA goals or increased standardization and security. Watch your newsletters or organization Web sites on how to obtain your new provider number.

BASIC FORMS YOU MUST HAVE IN PLACE NOW

1. **Notice of Privacy Practices** that explains to clients, employees, and contractors your HIPAA compliance policies. Copies must be readily available at the office or sent upon request. YOUR NOTICE OF PRIVACE PRACTICES MUST BE POSTED IN A CONSPICUOUS PLACE IN YOUR OFFICE WHERE PATIENTS CAN READ IT. Should there be a phone intake or an emergency situation the NPP and Informed Consent must be sent and or provided for signature as soon as possible. IF YOU HAVE A WEB SITE POST BOTH ON IT FOR INFORMATION AS WELL AS DOWNLOADING.

2. Your **Informed Consent for Treatment** that you have always used explaining therapy, limits of confidentiality, cancellation policies, financial responsibility for legal fees, and the like—the consent for use of disguised client information for the purposes of research, consultation, and training may be included here. Should you be using any of this information for marketing products be certain to include that release as well. The suggestion now is that you either fax or email the short Informed Consent for Assessment Consultation or have it available in your waiting room prior to the first personal contact (sample form on the CD-ROM). You could then easily accompany it with your Notice of Privacy Practices and ask for both to be filled out and signed ahead of time—simply explain that the federal government now requires it.

3. General **Consent for Release of Information** to use or disclose information for TPO purposes (Treatment, Payment, and health care Operations).

4. **Authorization to Disclose Psychotherapy Notes** including: *what* you have provided, *to whom* and *when* you provided it, and *the purpose* for which it was provided. This form *may not be combined with any other form.*

5. **Request for Amendment of Personal Health Information**

6. A **HIPAA Compliance Checklist** signed, dated, and periodically updated to document your compliance.

7. **Business Associate contracts.**

TAKE HIPAA SERIOUSLY AS YOUR WAY OF CONTRIBUTING TO PRIVACY IN A SOCIETY WHERE PERSONAL PRIVACY IS GRAVELY THREATENED. PUT SOME WORK INTO IT IN GOOD FAITH WITH THE AWARENESS THAT WE MUST ALL DO OUR PART TO ENSURE OUR INDIVIDUAL PRIVACY!

Disclaimer: Impact of HIPAA on the forms available with this book. Changes in the federal law known as the *Health Insurance Portability and Accountability Act (HIPAA— 45 CFR 160 et seq.)* have begun to impact the ways in which health care information is obtained, stored, used, and disclosed. Due to HIPAA's "preemption clause," which bars HIPAA from preempting state laws that offer as much or more protection for patient privacy than HIPAA itself, various state offices have been set up to clarify practitioner obligations. The forms associated with this book may not be sufficient for where you practice so check with your local professional organizations and offices of state government.

How *HIPAA* applies to the forms with this updated edition: The reader is advised to make sure to provide copies of the Notice of Privacy Policies (available for the professions at the society Web sites below) in conjunction with use of the following documents provided with this updated edition:

1. Informed Consent for Psychotherapy Assessment Consultation
2. Informed Consent for Dynamic Psychotherapy or Psychotherapeutic Consultation (Individual, Couple, Group, and Family)
3. Informed Consent for Infant Relationship-Based Therapy
4. Informed Consent for Work with Children and Adolescents
5. Permission to photograph, audio tape and/or videotape
6. Psychotherapy Client Questionnaire

In addition, the reader is advised to provide the following information along with the Notice of Privacy Policies:

"Federal law requires me to provide you with the Notice of Privacy Policies for safeguarding your personal and protected health information. However, because the federal law is not as yet fully implemented in California, I will follow California state law where it is as protective or more protective of your privacy than *HIPAA*, and where *HIPAA* allows me to use California state law."

The main sources of information consulted for this document are the American Psychological Association Insurance Trust (APAIT.org), the California Association of Marriage and Family Therapists (camft.org), and the American Association of Marriage and Family Therapists (aamft.org). Dr. Ofer Zur's HIPAA Compliance Kit (www.drzur.com) and the American Psychological Association's compliance kit were also consulted. Required forms and basic guidelines are on all of these Web sites.

NOTES

1. The main sources of information consulted for this chapter are the American Psychological Association Insurance Trust [APAIT.org], the California Association of Marriage and Family Therapists [camft.org], and the American Association of Marriage and Family Therapists [aamft.org]. Dr. Ofer Zur's HIPAA Compliance Kit (www.drzur.com) and the American Psychological Association's compliance kit were also consulted. Required forms and basic guidelines are on all of these Web sites.

2. HIPAA was passed in 1996 guaranteeing the sanctity of our psychotherapy notes. The same year the Redmond Supreme Court Case (see main book text for summary) also guaranteed the absolute privacy of psychotherapy notes. At this point should you receive any type of demands whatsoever for your notes—from insurance companies, public agencies, attorneys, or private parties—explain that you cannot comply with the demand due to Federal HIPAA laws and the Redmond Supreme Court Decision. If pressed, ask to speak with their attorney so you can explain, or speak with your own attorney so that you do not respond inappropriately. Additionally, not only does HIPAA prohibit any coercion of your clients for their psychotherapy records or notes, but even with the special HIPAA client Release of Psychotherapy Notes form (on the CD-ROM) the psychotherapy notes by law belong to you for *your exclusive* use so that *you alone* may choose to release only a summary, only selected portions, or nothing at all. Note that some state laws may conflict with HIPAA so check with an attorney if in doubt.

3. Because disability or death could happen to us at any time, or because we might leave the setting in which records were created, throughout this document I suggest that all folders have a clear label on front so that later anyone, ourselves included, encountering the folder later can at a glance see its HIPAA status. Three pages of sample labels are provided on the CD-ROM to assist you. Each folder should have a dated termination summary (sample provided) in clear view for the same reason—i.e., so that we or a custodian of our records can later tell at a glance how long the record should be kept. And so that when the file folder is purged and shredded the termination summary can be easily removed for permanent storage as a record that we did see the client.

4. **Disclaimer:** This is only a rough sketch of definitions and basic HIPAA compliance information for psychotherapists in solo practice. The HIPAA legislation would

fill a twenty-foot shelf and the state-by-state analyses of how this federal legislation dovetails with state legislation would fill another sixty feet of shelf space, so this is the bare minimum to get started. Think of HIPAA compliance as an ongoing project and plan to update as regulations change and as the state-by-state analyses become available and expand. Check your professional publications and Web sites for more information and be prepared to consult an attorney on questions. *Do not think you can escape HIPAA*, there are too many loopholes and plaintiff attorneys clearly plan to turn compliance into a national standard of care. Use the ideas and forms herein at your own risk.—L. E. Hedges

5. It seems highly unlikely to me that the American Psychiatric Association will tolerate for long the federal government scrapping the DSM that it has spent decades and millions of dollars developing, but so far the rule is ICD-9 diagnoses. Most clinicians continue to use DSM until some clerical worker at an insurance company rejects the diagnosis. Try to educate the worker about the DSM and its importance. Then ask to speak with a supervisor and if the call for ICD-9 persists have them fax you a copy of the possible mental health diagnoses—there are only a few and they are badly developed. I would not recommend ordering the very expensive AMA code books, they include all medical diagnoses and only have a few pages for us. Make the insurance company send you the few pages or copy them from your doctor's office if necessary.

6. All of our national mental health associations maintain on their Web sites (see footnote 1, page 241) information on how to comply with the security rule. A particularly useful guide is "The HIPAA Security Rule Primer" available at www. apaprac-tice. org. Also available at the same site is a workbook that can take you systematically through all of the relevant concerns and suggest ways of addressing them.

7. The Implementation Specifications can also be found in the Security Rule itself located at: www.cms.hhs.gov/HIPAA/HIPAA2/regulations/security/default.asp.

14

Practicing Defensively

Facing the challenge of liability in psychotherapy means learning how to practice defensively. And that means carefully examining our practices to be certain that we remain mindful of our own safety as well as our obligations to our clients and to our profession.

Practicing defensively begins with acknowledging to ourselves that we are operating a business that is governed by the ethical considerations of our profession and regulated and policed by the state or province in which we practice. As such, psychotherapy is essentially a public rather than a private affair. Our awareness that therapy works only when it exists in an atmosphere of privacy and confidentiality has lulled us into forgetting that all aspects of the therapeutic process are at all times potentially open to public scrutiny and that we must be prepared to be accountable for our procedures, policies, decisions, actions, and inactions.

We know that our personalities and our spontaneity are the only real tools we have in the relatedness work of psychotherapy. So we dislike the idea that our every move is subject to being questioned in an adversarial setting. We resist the idea that we must practice with an ethics committee, a licensing board, and a judge and jury sitting on our shoulders while we engage in the intimacies of the psychotherapeutic relationship. But being angry and indignant at the public powers that may intervene to question us doesn't change our essential situation—we are licensed to be servants of the common weal and are therefore ultimately accountable to the people whether we like it or not. The adulation and the sense of personal power that often accompany our work can easily lead us into feelings of omniscience and omnipotence that can prove detrimental to ourselves, our clients, and the psychotherapeutic process. Staying grounded in solid, humble, and responsible practices that prepare us to be publicly accountable for our work is the only safe way to go.

Practicing defensively means that we examine carefully our motivations for being psychotherapists. Most of us entered the profession hoping in one way or another to be helpful by studying how the human mind works. This makes it easy for us to become trapped in either aspect of our motivation—the helpful aspect or the study and learning aspect. We can easily lose ourselves in being helpful and practicing therapeutic dedication to a fault while endangering ourselves in the process. Or we can become so involved in our theories about how therapy works or in maintaining our personal ideas and standards of practice that we lose track entirely of the fundamental and dynamic human relatedness dimension inherent in our work.

Practicing psychotherapy defensively means that we do not foolishly assume that we understand for one minute the subtleties of the laws and ethics that govern our profession. Ethical principles and the huge and complex network of existing legal precedents have many implications for our daily activities and we need to be prepared to seek peer and expert opinion any day on the ethical and legal aspects of actions and inactions we are considering. As a precautionary measure we need to seek consultation on our cases on a regular basis to ensure our therapeutic objectivity as well as to create documented trails of responsibility for ourselves.

Practicing defensively means that we create records that demonstrate professional thought and responsibility every step of the way—in full awareness that the confidentiality of the treatment process can be compromised in many ways and that the seal of our records can be broken quite easily. At the outset we set up informed consent contracts with risk and benefit considerations and a full disclosure of how we work. We make an initial assessment of problems and issues along with developing a general plan of how we intend to proceed and we document the assessment discussions, consultations, and therapeutic processes. We maintain notes on each and every professional contact that is appropriate to the nature of our work. We seek out and document periodic consultations. We do periodic reviews, including reassessments and updated informed consents at every juncture of the therapeutic process. We terminate the process carefully and thoughtfully, documenting by way of brief review the treatment process and outcome.

Practicing defensively means being ultra-sensitive to the dimension of interpersonal boundaries and to how idiosyncratic each person's sense of boundedness is, based upon her or his individual relationship history. Ever assuming that we or anyone else has a firm or clear sense of what constitutes good or appropriate boundaries is an error because boundaries are always personal and are always being interpersonally negotiated. A therapeutic position that might constitute adequate respect of boundaries for one client may be grossly invasive or quite neglectful for another. The way that boundaries are considered, discussed, negotiated, and documented is unique with each client and needs to be carefully considered at all times, especially with an eye to how various third parties might potentially view the developing definitions, since third parties can exert influence over the relationship and intrude into the process in confusing and sometimes dangerous ways.

While it is now clear that multiple roles and dual relationships are only unethical to the extent that they are exploitative and damaging, what is not clear is how third parties might come to view multiple roles and dual relationships during or after the fact. Since third parties can interfere with and interrupt therapeutic processes in a variety of ways, whatever roles and relationships we do engage in with our clients must at all times be considered in the light of how others might view them. While many therapists object to this kind of consideration as intruding into the intimacy of the therapeutic relationship, experience teaches us that dual and multiple roles that can be questioned in any way by third parties—uninformed as they may be—are potentially destructive to the therapeutic process as well as dangerous to the therapist. Keeping multiple roles in the public eye, seeking frequent consultations, and documenting the process and discussion with the client along with the transferences and countertransferences stirred up are useful safeguards but are not fail-safe.

Taking the *person* in psychotherapy seriously at all times while never taking any memories, relationships, or facts presented in the therapeutic process concretely or literally goes a long way toward preventing the resistance to transference remembering from being acted out either inside or outside of the therapeutic relationship. Remembering that most of what many of our clients have to tell us cannot be communicated in simple words, pictures, or narratives keeps us forever searching the subtleties of the relating process itself for clues about the deep emotional patterns that people want help in understanding. Our job—however we may choose to pursue it—is to invite relatedness and then to help people come to understand how they approach, engage, and retreat from that relatedness based on deeply ingrained emotional patterns. Believing or not believing, validating or not validating, and reassuring or not reassuring have no consistently useful place in psychotherapy because our goal is the understanding and transformation of emotional relatedness patterns, not simply calming or placating distressed clients.

Practicing defensively means that our modes of working are clearly delineated in the records we keep on each client. Whether we are utilizing or prefer a cognitive, intellectual, or insight-oriented mode of working; or a mode based more on responding to developmental deficits; or a mode based on interpersonal relationship development (Stark 1999); it is incumbent on us to make our ways of working clear to our clients, to seek out adequate consultation, and to document clearly our philosophies and ways of working.

Practicing defensively means living with the ongoing realization that neglect, trauma, and emotional injury from childhood are universal to a greater or lesser degree, and that these injuries are associated in the client's mind with early relationships that were experienced as neglectful or traumatic. People seek out professional therapy to help them understand and transform the current effects of traumas they experienced much earlier in life. The farther down the developmental ladder the injury occurred, the more pervasive and/or significant the effects are likely to be in later personality development and relationships. When very early relational injuries are involved and emotional dependency develops in the therapeutic relationship, the terrors of connecting become transferred from early traumatic situations into here-and-now relatedness with the therapist, and various forms of accusations are an integral part of the expectable process.

Clients are highly motivated toward resisting the re-experiencing of emotional traumas from the distant past in present relationships. But psychotherapeutic transformation necessarily entails the re-experiencing and working through of previously established emotional relationship patterns in the present with the actual person of the therapist and in the real time and space of the current therapeutic relationship. Achieving optimal responsiveness with early developmental trauma regularly entails: (1) two people living through a long prodromal period of safety development; (2) two people cooperating in a mutual study of the ways they approach each other to achieve contact and then how a diminishment of intensity or a rupture of connection regularly occurs; (3) two people noticing how at or near the moment of interpersonal contact transference-based terrors appear that are expressed as panic and somatopsychic agony that interrupt connections and threaten to destroy the relating, and (4) two people working through mutually defined aspects of the terrors that regularly accompany interpersonal emotional connections by studying how two at first tend to limit and then later learn to expand their mutual seductions, emotional surrenders, and personal transformations (Maroda 1999).

The truly exciting and wonderful interpersonal work of spontaneous loving and relating in psychotherapy can only occur in a therapeutic environment in which both people experience safety and transformation. Practicing psychotherapy defensively entails making all aspects of the professional and personal relationship as free as possible from potential harm to either party.

Disclaimer and List of Attorneys

This book and the CD-ROM accompanying it are designed to provide continuing education information to mental health professionals. However, since no one (including the instructor) can possibly stay abreast of the ever-changing ethical and legal dilemmas, you must be prepared to seek out expert professional consultation and ethical-legal counsel on all questionable matters that come up in your practice. The forms provided are the ones I have developed that cover the needs of my practice. You can adapt these forms to your needs.

The following attorneys practice in this specialty. They may be able to assist you with legal and ethical issues that arise in your practice or to refer you to someone in your area.

John Fleer, Esq.
1333 Broadway Ave. #600
Oakland, CA 94612
(510) 465-3922

A. Steven Frankel, Esq., Ph.D.
3527 Mount Diablo Blvd., #269
Lafayette, CA 94549
(925) 283-4800

O. Brandt Caudill Jr., Esq.
Callhan, McCune & Willis LLP
111 Fashion Lane
Tustin, CA 92780
(714) 730-5700

Robert Cowley, Esq.
717 Murphy Road
Medford, OR 97504
(541) 245-7320

Richard Leslie, Esq.
P.O. Box 90400
San Diego, CA 92169-0400
(858) 456-0695

Michelle H. Licht, Esq.
2029 Century Park East #300
Hidden Hills, CA 91302
(818) 348-2394

Kerry L. McBride, Esq.
4590 Allstate Dr.
Riverside, CA 92501
(951) 320-1444

James Rogers, Esq.
125 South Highway 101, Suite 101
Solana Beach, CA 92075
(858) 792-9900

Robert Sullivan, Esq.
915 L Street, Suite 1000
Sacramento, CA 95814
(916) 442-8888

Pamela Ann Thatcher, Esq.
28 E. Grand Ave.
2nd Floor
Corona, CA 91714
(909) 270-0124

Bryant L. Welch, Esq.
P.O. Box 90400
Potomac, MD 20854
(301) 983-4344

Chris Zoppati, Esq.
Callhan, McCune & Willis LLP
111 Fashion Lane
Tustin, CA 92780
(714) 730-5700

References

Abidin, R. R. (1995). *Parenting Stress Index* (3rd ed.). Odessa, FL: Psychological Assessment Resources.

Ackerman, M. (1995). *Clinician's Guide to Child Custody Evaluations*. New York: Wiley & Sons.

Ackerman, M. J., and M. C. Ackerman. (1997). Child custody evaluation practices: A survey of experienced professionals (revisited). *Professional Psychology: Research and Practice* 28, 137–45.

Ackerman, M. J., and K. Schoendorf. (1992). *The Ackerman-Schoendorf Scales for Parent Evaluation of Custody (ASPECT)*. Los Angeles: Western Psychological Services.

Ainsworth, M. D. S. (1979). Infant-mother attachment. *American Psychologist* 34, 932–37.

Alexander, F. (1961). *The Scope of Psychoanalysis*. New York: Basic Books.

Amato, P. R., and J. G. Gilbreth. (1999). Nonresident father's and children's well being: a meta-analysis. *Journal of Marriage & the Family* 61, 557–73.

American Psychological Association. (1987). *General Guidelines for Providers of Psychological Services*. Washington, D.C.: American Psychological Association.

———. (1991). Specialty Guidelines for Forensic Psychologists. *Law and Human Behavior* 15, 655–65.

———. (1992). *Ethical Principles of Psychologists and Code of Conduct*. Washington, D.C.: American Psychological Association.

———. (1993). Record Keeping Guidelines. *American Psychologist* 48, 308–310.

———. (1994). Guidelines for Child Custody Evaluations in Divorce Proceedings. *American Psychologist* 49(7), 677–80.

———. (1999). *Standards for Educational and Psychological Testing*. Washington, D.C.: Author.

———. (2002). Ethical Principles of Psychologists and Code of Conduct. *American Psychologist* 57, 1060–73.

American Psychological Association Ethics Committee (1998). Report of the Ethics Committee, 1997. *American Psychologist* 53, 969–80.

———. (1999). Report of the Ethics Committee, 1998. *American Psychologist* 54, 701–10.

———. (2000). Report of the Ethics Committee, 1999. *American Psychologist* 55, 938–45.

———. (2002). Report of the Ethics Committee, 2001. *American Psychologist* 57, 646–53.

Audrey, R. (1966). *The Territorial Imperative*. New York: Kodansha International.

Baer, R. A., and J. Miller. (2002). Underreporting of psychopathology on the MMPI-2: a meta-analytic review. *Psychological Assessment* 14(1), 16–26.

Bathurst, K., A. Gottfried, and A. Gottfried. (1997). Normative data on the MMPI-2 in child custody litigation. *Psychological Assessment* 9, 205–11.

Bollas, C. (1979). The transformational object. *International Journal of Psycho-Analysis* 59, 97–107.

Bricklin, B. (1984). *Bricklin Perceptual Scales*. Furlong, PA: Village Publishing.

———. (1990). *Perception of Relationship Tests (PORT)*. Furlong, PA: Village Publishing.

Brodzinsky, D. (1993). The use and misuse of psychological testing in child custody evaluations. *Professional Psychology: Research and Practice* 24, 213–18.

Butcher, J. N., J. R. Graham, Y.S. Ben-Porath, A. Tellegen, W. G. Dahlstrom, and B. Kaemmer. (2001). *MMPI-2: Minnesota Multiphasic Personality Inventory-2: Manual for Administration, Scoring, and Interpretation* (revised edition). Minneapolis: University of Minnesota Press.

Butcher, J. N., J. N. Perry, and M. M. Atlis. (2000). Validity and utility of computer-based test interpretation. *Psychological Assessment* 12(1), 6–18.

Caldwell, A. B. (2002). *Guide for Understanding, Presenting, and Defending the Custody Report*. Los Angeles: Caldwell Report.

Canter, M. B., B. E. Bennett, S. E. Jones, and T. F. Nagy. (1994). *Ethics for Psychologists: A Commentary on the APA Ethics Code*. Washington, D.C.: American Psychological Association.

Committee on Ethical Guidelines for Forensic Psychologists. (1991). *Law and Human Behavior* 6, 655–65.

Craig, R. J. (1999). *Interpreting Personality Tests: A Clinical Manual for the MMPI-2, MCMI-III, CPI-R, and 16PF*. New York: Wiley & Sons.

Eissler, K. R. (1953). The effect of the structure of the ego on psychoanalytic technique. *Journal of the American Psychoanalytic Association* 1, 104–43.

Ferenczi, S. (1952). *First Contributions to Psycho-Analysis*, compiled by J. Rickman. New York: Brunner/Mazel.

———. (1955). *Final Contributions to the Problems and Methods of Psycho-Analysis*. New York: Brunner/Mazel.

———. (1962). *Further Contributions to the Theory and Technique of Psycho-Analysis*. New York: Brunner/Mazel.

Fingarette, H. (1969). *Self-Deception*. New York: Routledge & Kegan Paul.

Fraiberg, H. (1982). Pathological defenses in infancy. *Psychoanalytic Quarterly* 51, 612–34.

Folberg, J., and A. Taylor. (1984). *Mediation: A Comprehensive Guide to Resolving Conflicts without Litigation*. San Francisco: Jossey-Bass.

Freud, S. (1895). Project for a scientific psychology. *Standard Edition* 1, 283–388.

———. (1912). Papers on technique: the dynamics of transference. *Standard Edition* 12, 92–108.

———. (1914). Recollecting, repeating, and working through (further recommendations on the techniques of Psychoanalysis II). *Standard Edition* 12, 145–56.

———. (1915). Observations on transference love (further recommendations on the technique of Psychoanalysis III). *Standard Edition* 12, 159–71.

Gerard, A. (1994). *Parent-Child Relationship Inventory*. Los Angeles, CA: Western Psychological Services.

Gootee v. Lightner, 274 Cal. Rptr. 697 (Ct. App. 1990).

Gould, J. W. (1998). *Conducting Scientifically Crafted Child Custody Evaluations*. Thousand Oaks, CA: Sage.

Graham, J. R., Y. S. Ben-Porath, and J. L. McNulty. (1999). *MMPI-2 Correlates for Outpatient Community Mental Health Settings*. Minneapolis: University of Minnesota Press.

Greene, R. L. (2000). *The MMPI-2: An Interpretive Manual* (2nd ed). Needham Heights, MA: Allyn & Bacon.

Greenberg, L., and J. Gould. (2001). The treating expert: a hybrid role with firm boundaries. *Professional Psychology: Research and Practice* 32, 469–78.

Greenberg, S. A., and D. W. Shuman. (1997). Irreconcilable conflict between therapeutic and forensic roles. *Professional Psychology: Research & Practice* 28, 50–57.

Greenson, R. (1965). The working alliance and the transference neurosis. In *Explorations in Psychoanalysis*, pp. 199–225. New York: International Universities Press, 1978.

Grotstein, J. (1994). Foreword. In *Working the Organizing Experience*, ed. L. E. Hedges, pp. 17–33. Northvale, NJ: Jason Aronson.

Hedges, L. E. (1983). *Listening Perspectives in Psychotherapy*. Northvale, NJ: Jason Aronson.

———. (1992). *Interpreting the Countertransference*. Northvale, NJ: Jason Aronson.

———. (1993). In praise of the dual relationship. *The California Therapist* May/June, 46–50; July/August, 42–46; September/October, 36–41. (Reprinted in Hedges 2000b.)

———. (1994a). *In Search of the Lost Mother of Infancy*. Northvale, NJ: Jason Aronson.

———. (1994b). *Remembering, Repeating, and Working Through Childhood Trauma*. Northvale, NJ: Jason Aronson.

———. (1994c). *Working the Organizing Experience: Transformation of Psychotic, Schizoid, and Autistic States*. Northvale, NJ: Jason Aronson.

———. (1994d). Taking recovered memories seriously. *Issues in Child Abuse Accusation* 6(1), 1–30. Northfield, MN: Institute for Psychological Therapies. (Reprinted in Hedges 2000b.)

———. (1995). False accusations against therapists. *The California Therapist* March/April, 35–45.

———. (1996). *Strategic Emotional Involvement*. Northvale, NJ: Jason Aronson.

———. (1997). Prevention of false accusations against psychotherapists. *The California Therapist* July/August, 48–50. (Reprinted in *The Forensic Examiner*, September/October, 1998, 18–20 and in Hedges 2000b)

———. (1998). *Achieving Optimal Responsiveness with Early Developmental Trauma*. Paper presented at the 21st Annual International Conference on the Psychology of the Self, San Diego, CA, October. (Reprinted in Hedges 2000b).

———. (2000a). *False accusations: genesis and prevention*. Paper presented at a Division 31 panel, "In Defense of the Therapist: The False Accusation Argument," at the American Psychological Association Convention in Boston, August, 1999.

———. (2000b). *Terrifying Transferences: Aftershocks of Childhood Trauma*. North-vale, NJ: Jason Aronson.

———. (2000c). The California continuing education gold rush fiasco. Unpublished manuscript available on the Internet at lhedges@pacbell.net.

Hedges, L., R. Hilton, V. W. Hilton, and O. B. Caudill. (1997). *Therapists at Risk*. Northvale, NJ: Jason Aronson.

Heilbrun, K. (1992). The role of psychological testing in forensic assessment. *Law and Human Behavior* 16, 257–72.

Heinze, M. C., and T. Grisso. (1996). Review of instruments assessing parenting competencies used in child custody evaluations. *Behavioral Sciences & the Law* 14(3), 293–313.

Hilton, V. W. (1993). When we are accused. *Journal for Bioenergetic Analysis* 5(2), 45–51.

Howard v. Drapkin, 222 Cal. App. 4th 459, 462 (1990).

Johnson, S. (1991). *Symbiotic Character*. New York: Norton.

Johnston, J., M. Kline, and J. Tschann. (1989). Ongoing postdivorce conflict: effects on children of joint custody and frequent access. *Journal of Orthopsychiatry* 59, 576–92.

Kafka, F. (1926). *The Castle*. New York: Schocken.

———. (1937). *The Trial*. New York: Vintage.

———. (1979). *The Basic Kafka*. New York: Pocket Books.

Kanaya, T., M. H. Scullin, and S. Ceci. (2003). The Flynn effect and U.S. policies: the impact of rising IQ scores on American society via mental retardation diagnoses. *American Psychologist* 58, 778–790.

Keith-Spiegel, P., and G. P. Koocher. (1995). *Ethics in Psychology: Professional Standards and Cases*. New York: Random House.

Khan, M. (1963). The concept of cumulative trauma. *Psychoanalytic Study of the Child* 18, 286–306. New York: International Universities Press.

Kirkland, K. B., and K. L. Kirkland. (2001). Frequency of child custody evaluation complaints and related disciplinary action: A survey of the Association of State and Provincial Psychology Boards. *Professional Psychology: Research and Practice* 32(2), 171–74.

Kitchener, R (1988). Dual relationships: What makes them so problematic? *journal of Counseling and Development* 67, 217–21.

Kohut, H. (1971). *The Analysis of the Self*. New York: International Universities Press.

———. (1977). *The Restoration of the Self*. New York: International Universities Press.

Laborde v. Aronson, 92 Cal. App. 4th 459, 462 (2001).

Lamb, M. E., and J. B. Kelly. (2001). Using the empirical literature to guide the development of parenting plans for young children: a rejoinder to Solomon and Biringen. *Family Court Review* 39(4), 365–71.

Lazarus, A. A., and O. Zur. (2002). *Dual Relationships and Psychotherapy*. New York: Springer.

Little, M. (1981). *Transference Neurosis: Transference Psychosis*. Northvale, NJ: Jason Aronson.

———. (1990). *Psychotic Anxieties and Containment: A Personal Record of an Analysis with Winnicott*. Northvale, NJ: Jason Aronson.

Lorenz, Y, (1952). *King Solomon's Ring*. New York: Crowell.

Maccoby, E. E., and R. H. Mnookin. (1992). *Dividing the Child.* Cambridge, MA: Harvard University Press.

Maroda, K (1999). *Seduction, Surrender, and Transformation.* Hillsdale, NJ: Analytic Press.

Maturana, H., and F. Varela. (1987). *The Tree of Knowledge.* Boston: New Science Library.

Melton, G. B., J. Petrila, N. G. Polythress, and C. Slobogin. (1987). *Psychological Eevaluations for the Courts: A Handbook for Mental Health Professionals and Lawyers.* New York: Guilford Press.

Millon, T. (1987). *Manual for the MCMI-II* (2nd ed.). Minneapolis: National Computer Systems.

———. (1994). *Manual for the MCMI-III.* Minneapolis: National Computer Systems.

———. (1997a). *Millon Clinical Multiaxial Inventory-III manual* (2nd ed.). Minneapolis, MN: National Computer Systems.

Morey, L. C. (1991). *The Personality Assessment Inventory Professional Manual.* Odessa, FL: Psychological Assessment Resources.

Natterson, J. (1991). *Beyond Countertransference. The Therapist's Subjectivity in the Therapeutic Process.* Northvale, NJ: Jason Aronson.

Peterson, J. L., and N. Zill. (1986). Marital disruption, parent-child relationships, and behavior problems in children. *Journal of Marriage and the Family* 48, 295–307.

Pope, K., and J. Vasquez. (1991). *Ethics in Psychotherapy and Counseling: A Practical Guide for Psychologists.* San Francisco, CA: Jossey-Bass.

Saposnek, D. T. (1983). *Mediating Child Custody Disputes.* San Francisco: Jossey-Bass.

Schwaber, E. (1979). *Narcissism, Self Psychology and the Listening Perspective.* Prepresentation reading for lecture given at the University of California, Los Angeles on the Psychology of the Self-Narcissism, October.

———. (1983). Psychoanalytic listening and psychic reality. *International Journal of Psycho-Analysis* 10, 379–91.

Shuman, D. W., S. Greenberg, K. Heilbrun, and W. E. Foote. (1998). An immodest proposal: Should treating mental health professionals be barred from testifying about their patients? *Behavioral Sciences and the Law* 16, 509–23.

Silberg v. Anderson, 50 Cal. 3d 205, 21 (1990).

Solomon, J., and C. George. (1999). The development of attachment in separated and divorced families: effects of overnight visitation, parent and couple variables. *Attachment and Human Development* 1(1), 2–33.

Stark, M. (1999). *Modes of Therapeutic Action.* Northvale, NJ: Jason Aronson.

Stern, D. N. (1985). *The Interpersonal World of the Infant.* New York: Basic Books.

Strachey, J. (1934). The nature of the therapeutic action of psychoanalysis. *International Journal of Psycho-Analysis* 15, 117–26.

Tomm, Y, (1991). The ethics of dual relationships. *The Calgary Participator. A Family Therapy Newsletter* 1:3. (Reprinted in *The California Therapist*, January/February 1993.)

Tronick, E., and J. Cohn. (1988). Infant-mother face-to-face communicative interaction: age and gender differences in coordination and the occurrence of miscoordination. *Child Development* 60, 85–92.

Tustin, F. (1986). *Autistic Barriers in Neurotic Patients.* New Haven, CT: Yale University Press.

Welch, B. L. (2000). *Reducing Your Suicide Liability. Insight: Safeguarding Psychologists against Liability Risks*. Amityville, NY: American Professional Agency.

Wendling, T. (1999). When psychologists cross the line. *Cleveland Plain Dealer*, a three-part series, December 5–7.

Winnicott, D. W. (1949). Hate in the countertransference. *International Journal of Psycho-Analysis* 30, 69–75.

———. (1958, revised 1975). *Through Paediatrics to Psycho-Analysis*. New York: Basic Books.

———. (1965). Birth memories, birth trauma, and anxiety. In *Through Paediatrics to Psycho-Analysis*, 243–54. New York: Basic Books.

———. (1971). *Playing and Reality*. London: Tavistock.

———. (1974). Fear of breakdown. *International Review of Psycho-Analysis* 1, 103–7.

Index

About the Contributors

Steven Frankel, Ph.D., J.D., is an ABPP certified clinical psychologist (PSY3354) and an attorney at law (SBN 192014). He received his Ph.D. in clinical psychology from Indiana University and completed an internship at Columbia University's Psychiatric Institute. Dr. Frankel has been on the faculty of the University of Southern California for over thirty-five years and is currently a clinical professor of psychology. He served as an adjunct professor of law at Loyola Law School (Los Angeles) and is now an adjunct professor at Golden Gate University School of Law. He has taught courses on healthcare policy, regulation of healthcare practice, and mental disorder and the law. He has authored over fifty articles and book chapters. He has won the USC Award for Teaching Excellence early in his academic career and is nationally recognized for his expertise, sense of humor, and ability to bring his course material to life.

Ira Gorman, Ph.D., ABPP, was a psychologist and court-evaluator in Orange County, California, for twenty-five years before his death in 2005. He trained many mental health professionals in the art of child custody evaluations. He wrote a chapter for this book only weeks before his advanced cancer was diagnosed. His wife, his family, and a whole community of colleagues and loved ones mourn his loss.

Lawrence E. Hedges, Ph.D., ABPP, is the leader of a thirty-five-year clinical research project into the origins of human relationships at the Listening Perspectives Study Center in Orange, California. Dr. Hedges travels widely, lecturing and consulting with psychotherapists on their most difficult-to-treat clients. His work on how early childhood trauma impacts the psychotherapeutic relationship has led him to a keen awareness of how the growing consumer complaint and litigational processes that surround the practice of psychotherapy today are threatening to undermine it and destroy its effectiveness. Dr. Hedges is the author of many articles and ten clinical texts on the practice of dynamic relational psychotherapy and psychoanalysis including, *Listening Perspectives in Psychotherapy*, *Interpreting the Countertransference*, and *Terrifying Transferences: Aftershocks of Childhood Trauma*.

David G. Jensen, J.D., is an attorney in California; currently, Mr. Jensen is employed by the California Association of Marriage and Family Therapists in San Diego, California, as a staff attorney. Mr. Jensen is a frequent lecturer and author of articles on legal and ethical issues. He resides in Chula Vista, California, with his wife, Jodi, and his two sons, Matt and Trevor.

Pamela Ann Thatcher, Commissioner, hears matters as a judge pro tem for the Riverside Superior Court, including family law, misdemeanor and felony arraignments, child support hearings, traffic, small claims, and limited civil matters. Prior to taking a position on the bench, Commissioner Thatcher focused her private practice of law in the defense of mental health professionals. For twenty-two years, she defended psychologists and marriage family therapists in civil and licensing matters. She is a graduate of the University of LaVerne (Bachelor of Arts, double major in history and political science–magna cum laude, 1980) and Loyola Law School (Juris Doctorate, 1983).

All contributors to this book are active in teaching continuing education courses to mental health professionals. Other contributions of these authors can be located on the following Web sites: ListeningPerspectives.com, sfrankelgroup.com, camft.org, and ContinuingEducationCentral.com.